London School of Economics Industrial Relations Series
General Editor: Professor B. C. Roberts

WORKERS' PARTICIPATION IN MANAGEMENT IN BRITAIN

In the same series

Reluctant Militants: a study of industrial technicians
B. C. Roberts, Ray Loveridge, and John Gennard

Workers' Participation in Management in Britain

R. O. CLARKE
D. J. FATCHETT
and
B. C. ROBERTS

HEINEMANN EDUCATIONAL BOOKS
LONDON

Heinemann Educational Books Ltd

LONDON   EDINBURGH   MELBOURNE
TORONTO   AUCKLAND   JOHANNESBURG   HONG KONG
SINGAPORE   IBADAN   NAIROBI   NEW DELHI
KUALA LUMPUR

ISBN 0 435 85210 8

First published 1972

Published by Heinemann Educational Books Ltd
48 Charles Street, London W1X 8AH
Printed in Great Britain by Willmer Brothers Limited, Birkenhead

Foreword

This study of workers' participation in management has been carried out in the Department of Industrial Relations at the London School of Economics, with the generous support of the Department of Employment, as an independent inquiry. It has also been made in association with the International Institute for Labour Studies as part of an international programme of studies of workers' participation in management. The aim of the International Institute for Labour Studies has been to encourage research into workers' participation in management within the context of a common analytical framework, in a range of countries with differing systems of industrial relations.

The British report has focused mainly on an analysis of the concepts of participation, on the evolution of ideas and policies on participation, and on the extent to which participation can be said to exist within the contemporary pattern of management in private industry.

The investigation was carried out by R. O. Clarke and D. J. Fatchett, under the direction of B. C. Roberts, who has edited the final report. A large number of people have helped in the making of this report, including especially the considerable number of firms that completed the questionnaire. Great help was received from the Department of Employment Statistics Division in the selection of the sample. Special thanks are due to Sheila Rothwell, who compiled much of the bibliography and did the tedious job of checking references and the preparation of the manuscript.

Mr Clarke is now with the OECD, Paris, and it should be pointed out that that Organisation has no responsibility for any views expressed, or statements made, in this book.

B. C. ROBERTS

Contents

Task-Based Participation
Autonomous Work-Groups
Consultative and Decision-Making Councils
Current Views

List of Tables

Table
Number

Introduction

The Pattern of Workers' Participation

There runs through the history of industrial development the continuous thread of opposition to the exercise by management of an unrestricted power to treat a worker as either a commodity or a servant whose duty is to do neither more nor less than carry out his master's bidding. As spontaneous protest gave way to the organized process of collective bargaining the balance of advantage which favoured the employer in a *laissez-faire* labour market was made less one-sided. Protection against the vicissitudes of unemployment, sickness, injury and low wages which strong trade unionism offered brought a degree of security to workers. Through their control over entry and the way they did their work those who were in skilled trades were able to temper the authority of management. For the rest, the best that they could do was to exercise such bargaining powers as they possessed when the labour market was favourable. Even when their bargaining position was strong trade unionism did not entirely satisfy those workers who believed that the arbitrary exercise of power by the employer was no more justified in industry than it was by an authoritiarian government in the state. Long before parliamentary democracy had been fully achieved and the right to vote extended to workers, voices were raised in support of the right of workers to participate directly in the management of the enterprises in which they worked.

Despite the long interest in the concept of industrial democracy, the idea is still surrounded by confusion and acute differences of opinion as to its meaning and its desirability. Professor Walker has distinguished four main types of industrial democracy:[1]

1. Democratization of ownership

[1] K. Walker, Industrial Democracy, The Times Management Lecture, 1970.

2. Democratization of the government of the enterprise
3. Democratization of the terms of employment
4. Democratization of the process of management

Each of these types has attracted its protagonists and its opponents. Although each of these concepts will be discussed in the course of this study, it is not the intention of the authors to determine what is the true nature of industrial democracy. The principal concern of this study is to enquire into the various ways and to what extent workers participate in the process of management.

As a matter of practical significance, it has been through the process of belonging to representative organizations, which have exercised pressure on their behalf, that workers in Britain have mainly sought to influence and where possible control the process of management decision-making. Workers' participation has generally been thought of as an alternative method to collective bargaining—a method which gave workers the opportunity to voice their opinions and in the extreme case determine company policies and operational decisions, through a structure of councils and procedures which owed nothing to trade union organization. The distinction has been sharpened by the fact that underlying the concepts of collective bargaining and workers' participation has been the notion that collective bargaining was inevitably predicated on the existence of two sides, whereas the direct participation of workers in management assumed a unitary frame of reference.

That participation in the management process may be achieved through a variety of institutional forms and occurs at different levels of decision-making in the enterprise is clearly a fact. The analytical approach adopted in this study is designed to enable discussion to be focused on the extent to which participation is at present taking place in the context of the existing structure of the enterprise and pattern of industrial relations at the level of the enterprise. The contemporary situation is examined against the background of the historical evolution of the idea of workers' participation in management and changing notions of the role and functions of workers and managers in modern society.

In recent years, 'participation' has been the subject of a vast amount of discussion which has ranged so extensively as to include not only the present topic of workers' participation in management, but also participation of students in the government of institutions of higher education and public administration.

The purpose of this study is not, however, to become involved in a general discussion of participation in society, but rather to discuss, review and analyse workers' participation in management within the enterprise. In order to do this satisfactorily, it is important at the outset to define and discuss the framework of analysis that will be used. Each of the terms associated with participation poses problems of definition and concept; it is therefore necessary to make clear how the basic elements in the practice of workers' participation in management decision-making are understood by the authors of this study.

(1) *Workers*

The concept of workers' participation in management implies a clear-cut distinction between the roles and functions of workers and managers. The distinction is in a fundamental respect quite clear, but operationally there are areas where roles overlap and functions are not sharply divided. There is a certain element of ambiguity in the term 'worker' since a manager clearly works, and many workers exercise some managerial responsibility. However in the context of this study 'worker' will be understood as describing an employee, male or female, adult or juvenile, whatever his or her occupational category, who does not have executive authority in the specific organizational context (managers themselves, in relation to their superiors, are potential participants).

A further element of ambiguity arises from the fact that a worker is not only someone who occupies a particular work-role that is subordinate to management, he may also be a member of a trade union or another type of vocational organization. The activities of trade unions and vocational associations necessarily involve a degree of workers' participation, but this is not the only way in which workers can participate in management decision-making. They may participate as individuals and collectively through a variety of forms of organization as well as through trade unions or other bodies. The extent to which workers are trade unionists and the role of the unions in the making of managerial decisions have long been issues of major importance.

It is necessary to distinguish clearly between representation of workers by a professional trade-union representative and representation of workers directly by one of themselves. In the one case the representative may be an outside expert; in the other he will be an inside 'amateur' exercising the role of manager. Each type of representative has its advantages and drawbacks; much of the argument about workers' participation turns on the pattern of representation and conflict of roles and responsibilities that arise.

In discussing in concrete terms any specific scheme of workers' participation in management it is necessary to make clear which groups of workers are involved, which method of representation is used and in which level of managerial decisions the workers concerned wish to have the right to participate.

(2) *Management*

If the definition of worker gives rise to difficulties in terms of role and authority, so too does the concept of management. Difficulty arises from the fact that management is at the same time a decision-making activity, a system of authority and an elite group with particular social attributes.[1]

In this study, management is regarded primarily as a decision-making process through which the aims of the enterprise and the methods of achieving their attainment are decided. The emphasis is on the function of management rather than on its role as a social class, though this aspect will not be ignored.

The hierarchical authority aspects of management are of importance when considering workers' participation in management. Many decisions, for instance, can be made only at higher levels within the hierarchy, thereby affecting the pattern of any system of workers' participation.

Authority is significant in other ways too. Desire for participation in management signifies desire to have a voice in decisions which directly affect personal as well as social interests. Or to put the matter another way round, it implies an unwillingness to accept the exercise of arbitrary authority. In this respect authority is bound up with considerations of legitimacy. Authority which is not accepted as legitimate rests upon power,

[1] F. Harbison and C. A. Myers in *Management in the Industrial World* (McGraw-Hill, New York 1959), viewed management as an economic resource, an authority system and as an elite social grouping.

which may be countervailed by other power. Where power is in balance the legitimacy of authority must rest upon function and the participation of those over whom authority must be functionally exercised in the decision-making process.[1]

Clearly, a knowledge of the structure of an enterprise, and where power, in terms of decision-making, lies within it, is essential when it comes to considering schemes for participation. Formal participative structures might be of limited value if they did not have regard to the important decision-making points in the enterprise. Consequently, workers' participation at any level will be limited in effectiveness to the extent to which decision-making power is dependent upon other levels of authority within the managerial hierarchy.

The decisions made by management vary greatly; some are far-reaching, others trivial. Some affect workers immediately, others only very indirectly. The content of managerial decisions also differs; whereas some relate to wages and working conditions, others are financial or commercial, or relate to production or to discipline. Although the data presented in Chapter 4 illustrate the extent of workers' formal participation in decision-making as seen by the firm in all of these areas, it is necessary to classify decisions into various categories. Managerial decisions concerning wages, organization of work and discipline are seen as of immediate crucial importance to workers; while decisions relating to the raising of capital and the basic distribution of the firm's earnings have generally been seen by management as fundamental to the long-term existence of the firm. Traditionally, workers have been, through their unions, basically concerned about levels of pay and security of employment, and management has long recognized that collective bargaining on wages and working conditions is a legitimate constraint on its freedom of decision-making. In other areas, such as changes in working methods and discipline, consultation has been of some importance. It has not been usual for firms to either consult or bargain with their employees on such questions as the raising of capital or the distribution of dividends, though some advocates of industrial democracy have seen wider participation in these areas as almost an acid test of a genuine sharing of

[1] For an examination of authority and its legitimacy in relation to industrial organization see A. Fox, *A Sociology of Work in Industry* (Collier-Macmillan, London 1971).

managerial authority. Since these decisions are of fundamental significance to management it was of some importance to discover from managers the extent to which workers' participation in these matters might be said to occur. To obtain this information a questionnaire was sent to a sample of 1,562 private firms and the nationalized industries. This enquiry is described in Chapter 3.

(3) *Participation*

The concern of this study is to investigate the concept of participation as a process through which workers share in decision-making that extends from and beyond the decisions that are implicit in the specific content of the jobs they do. Participation is seen as including any process whereby workers, whether as individuals or through a union or other organization, have a share in the reaching of managerial decisions in enterprises.[1] This share may be achieved through such different methods and levels of participation as collective bargaining, the appointment of worker-directors, consultation, autonomous workgroups, and particular styles of management.

Although it would be possible to define participation in terms of specific processes that exclude collective bargaining, to do so would be to eliminate one of the most important methods of participation in management decision-making. Moreover, in practice it is often difficult to draw sharp dividing lines between one type of participation and another.

Participation in management has often been seen as involving a different process from collective bargaining. In collective bargaining there are two sides, unions and employers, facing each other as adversaries, but ultimately seeking an agreement. In the 'participation' process the opportunity is given either to individual workers or to trade union organizations to be represented on management decision-making bodies. It is generally assumed when workers or unions have a direct voice in the making of managerial decisions that the 'two sides' attitude will, at least to some degree, give way to a common frame of reference. How-

---

[1] Compare R. Likert, *New Patterns of Management* (McGraw Hill, New York 1961), p. 242. He considers that 'participation' should not be thought of as a single process or activity, but rather as a whole range of processes and activities.

ever, although the collective bargaining process differs from direct participation the end result may not be entirely dissimilar. The object in collective bargaining is to achieve a jointly agreed rule to regulate the issue in dispute so as to permit the enterprise to continue satisfactorily; in the participation process the end is a managerial decision that is more acceptable to the workers and thereby more effective and efficient than a decision made unilaterally by management.

The participative processes whereby workers become involved in decision-making at more than one level of the managerial hierarchy, such as collective bargaining and joint consultation or as worker-directors, are all generally indirect,[1] in the sense that workers normally participate through representatives rather than in person. In the case of collective bargaining, participation may be through the shop steward, the branch officer or the paid union official.

A major characteristic of representative participation is that the range of decisions with which it is concerned generally involves collective policy issues, and it may extend to processes which help to set or shape the overall goals of the enterprise and are 'governmental' in nature.

These characteristics are much less important in the form of participation that primarily involves decisions relating to the immediate task or environment of the workers concerned; this type of participative decision is generally task-based, and much more likely to be 'direct' than 'indirect', thereby excluding the need for representation. Restrictive practices and forms of job-enrichment and job-enlargement can be seen as major methods of task-based participation.

These two main approaches to participation may be characterized as power-centred and task-centred. Participation that is power-centred aims at extending the bargaining power of the workers within the enterprise and at making managerial decision-makers more accountable either to the unions or directly to the workers. The ultimate objective of some supporters of power-centred participation is to change the fundamental authority-relationship in industry as a means of changing the character of society

---

[1] See C. J. Lammers, 'Power and Participation in Decision-making in Formal Organisations', *American Journal of Sociology*, Vol. 73, No. 2 (September 1967), p. 205.

The task-centred approach emphasizes participation as a device likely to increase job satisfaction, and with it productivity, and also to improve industrial relations, thereby facilitating the attainment of managerially set goals for the enterprise. Arguing along these lines an increasing body of management literature has been concerned with the creation of an organizational pattern in which workers are permitted to exercise a greater degree of control over their work environment and performance. The opportunities for participation in decisions relating to tasks which are available to workers at present are examined in the course of this study.

(4) *Enterprise*

It is necessary to emphasize that the present work does not deal with such matters as participation by trade unions in the broad management of the nation's affairs. It is concerned with workers' participation in management in the enterprise, and for this purpose 'enterprise' is defined as 'an organization in which individuals are gainfully employed'.

This definition excludes purely social organizations and organizations to which services are contributed voluntarily, on an unpaid basis. It *includes* not just manufacturing firms or joint-stock companies, but organizations such as government departments, schools, hospitals, farms and fishing vessels; and the nationalized section of industry as well as the private sector.[1] However, in this study the focus is upon private and public industrial organizations.

Having defined 'enterprise' in this broad way it is hardly necessary to stress that organizations differ greatly and that the extent to which they provide an opportunity for their workers to participate varies widely. Much will depend upon the structure of the organization and the means by which the compliance of members with the necessary performance of their tasks is secured. Etzioni has drawn attention to three common types of organization—coercive, normative and utilitarian.[2] In organizations

[1] F. E. Emery, *Characteristics of Socio-Technical Systems* (Tavistock Doc. No. 572, January 1959), p. 1.
[2] A. Etzioni, *A Comparative Analysis of Complex Organisations* (The Free Press, New York 1961). For other typologies, see Peter M. Blau and W. Richard Scott, *Formal Organisations* (Chandler, San Francisco 1962) and Talcott

where compliance is secured by coercion, members are generally obedient, but the lower ranks tend to develop a sense of alienation from the organization, as in the Army. It is interesting to note in this respect that the Army has sought to overcome this problem by an improvement in communications and concern for the welfare of the individual. In normative organizations, such as voluntary associations, members tend to develop a more positive and intense involvement in the actions necessary to achieve their goals. In utilitarian organizations, such as firms, workers have an instrumental role and tend to have a low level of interest in the achievement of the goals of the organization, which are decided at the top of the structure.

In addition to the factors and relationships focused upon by Etzioni, other elements in the situation also have a significant influence on the extent to which workers have an opportunity to participate in managerial decisions. Such factors, for example, as size, technology, pattern of ownership, and the degree of specialization, centralization and formalization of the organizational processes associated with these basic elements that determine the shape and structure of firms inevitably influence the extent and quality of participation.[1]

(5) *Arguments for Greater Participation*

Consideration can now be given to the arguments advanced as to why there should be greater participation. Broadly, four arguments are used.[2] Greater participation as such is desirable:

(1) as a means of promoting the satisfaction and personal development of the individual worker;

(2) on the ground that workers should have a greater say in decision-making at work, as a means of extending democracy from the political to the industrial sphere;

Parsons, 'Suggestions for a Sociological Approach to the Theory of Organisations', *Administrative Science Quarterly* (1956).

[1] D. S. Pugh, D. J. Hickson, C. R. Hinings, K. M. Macdonald, C. Turner, and T. Lupton, 'A Conceptual Scheme for Organisational Analysis', *Administrative Science Quarterly*, Vol. 8, No. 3 (December 1963).

[2] The arguments set out in the following pages are reported since they form the basis of so much discussion about participation. It must be said that such discussion rarely makes clear what form of participation is envisaged, in what type of decision, and at what level. The arguments should be read with this in mind.

(3) as a means of improving industrial relations;

(4) as a means of increasing efficiency.

(a) *The Promotion of Satisfaction and Personal Development of the Worker.* The argument about happiness and personal development rests on the belief that most work can and should be satisfying to the worker, both as to the task itself and as to the physical and social environment in which it is performed; that wherever possible work should afford the worker a means of developing his personality; and that participation can assist to these ends. The belief has been well expressed in the Papal Encyclical 'Mater et Magistra', 1962.

> We... are convinced that employees are justified in wishing to participate in the activity of the industrial concern for which they work.... We are in no two minds as to the need for giving workers an active share in the business of the company for which they work —be it a private or a public one. Every effort must be made to ensure that there is indeed a community of persons concerned about the needs, the activities and the standing of each of its members.[1]

Basing itself on the importance of human dignity, the Encyclical goes on to say: 'All this implies that the workers have their say in, and make their own contribution to, the efficient running and development of the enterprise.'[2]

Satisfaction and personal development are, of course, hard to measure, but there is some evidence, mostly from American sources, to support the view that participation can be both satisfying and challenging. Blumberg's summing-up of a number of studies notes that 'far up on the list of factors making for satisfaction in work is the desire, among all groups, for autonomy, responsibility, control, and decision-making power on the job'.[3] Another authority states that 'the greater the degree of control that a worker has (either in a single dimension or as a total composite), the greater his job satisfaction'.[4]

It has been suggested by Tannenbaum that a 'participative

[1] The wording used is from the translation by the Rev. H. E. Winstone, *New Light on Social Problems* (Catholic Truth Society, London 1963), para. 91.

[2] *New Light on Social Problems*, op. cit., para. 92.

[3] P. Blumberg, *Industrial Democracy: The Sociology of Participation* (Constable, London 1968), p. 119.

[4] R. Blauner, 'Work Satisfaction and Industrial Trends in Modern Society', in W. Galenson and S. M. Lipset (eds.), *Labor and Trade Unionism* (John Wiley, New York 1960), p. 346.

approach may be particularly effective in creating a work environment that is more rewarding [than the traditional system]
psychologically to organization members. Furthermore, it is possible that the positive effects on organizational performance of
this approach may be more apparent in the long run than in the
short.'[1] Again, 'a larger role for workers in the decision-making
processes within their organizations could lead to improved per-
formances in some situations'. 'In general,' says Tannenbaum,
'organization members *want* to exercise control, and they therefore find in participation an important source of gratification'.[2]
He finds three satisfactions emerging from participation. First, it
satisfies the need for independence. Secondly, it brings material
rewards since the decisions arrived at are likely to be more con-
sonant with self-interest, and the control exercised seen as less
arbitrary. Thirdly, participation reduces frustration and is in-
trinsically satisfying and challenging.

Writing on the principles of good management, Wight Bakke
has argued that productive work is the main source of personal
development and satisfaction and that the organization must
give the maximum possible opportunity for significant participation and self-expression to the individual.[3] Having designated
self-realization as a determinant of motivation Bakke says that
in our culture self-realization 'is intimately bound up with the
degree to which people are able to participate, under intelligent
and rational leadership, and the degree to which they have an
effective voice in determining the rules and conditions under
which, and the plans according to which, they live and work'.[4]

(b) *The Extension of Democracy.* The argument for greater
industrial democracy is based on the ground that though,
through the electoral system, the worker as a citizen enjoys a
voice in the government of the society in which he lives, he has
no such opportunity at his place of work. There he is an
'employee', party to a contractual relationship rather than a citizen
of an industrial community. He may be protected by law and

[3] A. S. Tannenbaum, *Social Psychology of the Work Organisation* (Tavistock
Publications, London 1966), p. 94.
[2] A. S. Tannenbaum, 1966, op. cit., p. 98.
[3] E. Wight Bakke, 'The Function of Management' in E. M. Hugh-Jones (ed.),
Human Relations and Modern Management (North Holland Publishing Co.,
Amsterdam 1958), p. 223.
[4] Op. cit., p. 241.

by collective agreements; he may be able through his union to exercise a countervailing power against managerial decisions. But he is subject to managerial orders and management is not accountable to him. His livelihood may disappear if it is in the interests of shareholders that an uneconomic unit should close down. It has been argued that when the great majority of individuals are denied the opportunity to take an effective part in reaching the decisions which vitally affect their lives, they are not only being deprived of a right they ought to enjoy but political democracy is itself being diminished.[1]

The argument for industrial democracy which is based upon the analogy with political democracy raises a number of difficulties.[2] The main task of industry is to produce goods and services that will satisfy the economic and social demands of the community. To achieve this goal industry must be efficiently managed: this means that decisions relating to what will be produced, where and when, are subject to constraints in time and cost that are different from the constraints that are involved when political parties ask the electorate to choose between them at a general election. In the process of political democracy we choose our representatives and who is to govern for a period of time. The process of parliamentary democracy relates to the making of law and the approval of the government's stewardship. It would in theory be possible to establish a similar procedure to control industrial enterprises, and it is on this analogy that the Germans have established their *Aufsichtsräte* and the Yugoslavs their workers' councils. Each of these systems of political control entails, once the managers have been chosen, that they should, subject to rendering an account, have a high degree of freedom to govern. Any notion that industry can effectively be administered by continuous committees, general assemblies or referenda is certain to end in organizational chaos and economic disaster, since for technological and economic reasons many decisions

---

[1] T. B. Bottomore, *Elites and Society* (Penguin Books, Harmondsworth 1966), p. 122. See also E. Fromm: ... the vast majority sell their physical, or an exceedingly small part of their intellectual capacity to an employer to be used for purposes of profit in which they have no share, for things in which they have no interest, with the only purpose of making a living, and for some chance to satisfy their consumers' greed'. *The Sane Society* (Routledge and Kegan Paul, London 1956), p. 295.

[2] For a full discussion of the relation of industrial democracy to political democracy see C. Pateman, *Participation and Democratic Theory* (Cambridge University Press, London 1970).

in industry must be taken swiftly and be carried out expeditiously.

In arguing for industrial democracy drawing on the parliamentary model of political democracy, Clegg emphasized the significance of the role of opposition as the essential condition.[1] In his opinion this could only be found in the role of the trade union and the process of collective bargaining. In this conclusion he joined with the Webbs in seeing industrial democracy, not as a process of direct participation in the making of managerial decisions, but of circumscribing their effect through the establishment of rules regulating the range of managerial action that might be taken without securing the agreement of the union, or its representatives concerned. The right to oppose is clearly an essential element in any democratic system; however, it is a necessary, but not in itself a sufficient condition.

(c) *Participation as a Means of Improving Industrial Relations.* As a means of improving industrial relations, participation has had its advocates for a considerable time. As long ago as 1917 the first Whitley Report said:

> A permanent improvement in the relations between employers and employed must be founded upon something other than a cash basis. What is wanted is that workpeople should have a greater opportunity of participating in the discussion about and adjustment of those parts of industry by which they are most affected.[2]

It is argued that at the present time many decisions affecting workers are taken without their being involved, or even consulted about them beforehand, and sometimes without their being told about them till long after. As a result the 'we' and 'they' aspect of industrial relations is emphasized. Workers do not feel involved in the decisions that are taken and do not associate themselves with management's need to overcome problems. Nor, for that matter, do they associate themselves with the goals of the enterprise as a whole.

It is further argued that workers have become alienated from the purposes and organization of industry because they are denied

---

[1] H. A. Clegg, *Industrial Democracy and Nationalisation: A Study prepared for the Fabian Society* (Blackwell, Oxford 1951).

[2] Reconstruction Committee: Sub-committee on Relations between Employers and Employees and Employed, *Interim Report on Joint Standing Industrial Councils*, Cmnd 8606 (H.M.S.O., London 1917), para. 24.

an opportunity to participate in the control of their immediate work processes.[1] Without this degree of participation in the decisions which are of immediate importance to them workers are unable to develop a sense of loyalty and attachment to the organization, its function and purposes.[2] When workers feel a sense of alienation they often respond to their situation by adopting an aggressive and hostile attitude to the exercise of managerial authority. Industrial relations tend, therefore, to be adversely affected by the failure of management to understand the need to integrate workers into the structure of decision-making at those levels which to them are significant.

There is, unfortunately, no satisfactory means of objectively measuring good industrial relations. Moreover, there is some difference of opinion between managers and trade unionists as to the extent that participation may be a factor of importance in improving industrial relations. When both groups were asked by Allen what they thought of workers' participation in management as a means of improving labour relations, 53 per cent of trade unionists thought that it was either helpful or very helpful, but the corresponding figure for management was only 29 per cent.[3] Nevertheless, there is evidence to suggest that the more a worker is enabled to exercise control over his task, and to relate his efforts to those of his fellows, the more likely he is to adopt a co-operative attitude and a positive commitment to achieving the goals of the enterprise without conflict and the breakdown of the normative pattern of relations between management and workers.[4] It has, however, been suggested that the advocates of participation have put a great deal of weight on rather slender factual foundations.[5]

(d) *Participation as a Means of Increasing Efficiency.* Participation is also advocated as being conducive to higher efficiency. The involvement of workers, it is argued, taps their very considerable knowledge of their work and their often under-used abilities.

[1] R. Blauner, *Alienation and Freedom, The Factory Worker and his Industry* (University of Chicago Press, 1964).

[2] Cf. F. E. Emery and E. Thorsrud, *Form and Content in Industrial Democracy* (Tavistock Publications, London 1969).

[3] A. J. Allen, *Management and Men. A Study in Industrial Relations* (Hallam Press, London 1967), p. 38.

[4] Ibid.

[5] G. Strauss, 'Participative Management: a Critique', *International Labour Research*, Vol. XII, No. 2, Ithaca, New York (November 1966).

The more they are informed and involved, the readier they will
be to accept technological change, even unpalatable change. By
helping management to be better informed of workers' views,
participation improves the quality of the decisions made. The
involvement of workers spurs managers on to greater efficiency,
and the satisfaction of workers' needs and moral rights makes
for a contented and efficient labour force. Finally, participation,
it is argued, increases efficiency by its contribution to industrial
peace. It must also be added that proof of these propositions is
hard to establish.

The earliest work on the relationship between participation and
efficiency was probably that carried out by Lewin and his
associates.[1] The basis was an experiment using groups of boys in
the United States in the late 1930s. The boys were divided,
under adult leaders, into an authoritarian group, a democratic
group and a *laissez-faire* group. Superficially, the authoritarian
group proved the more productive, but its production fell when
the supervisor was not present, whereas production in the democratic group did not. Quality and satisfaction were higher in the
democratic group. The *laissez-faire* group fared worst on all
counts.

Members of the Tavistock Institute have been responsible
for important experiments which have endeavoured to give
workers greater control over their tasks, by establishing autonomous working groups, integrated into the enterprise as a whole.
Miller and Rice suggest that such techniques have procured
'significant improvements in both human satisfaction and in
productivity'.[2]

An early summary of work by Viteles concluded that:
'employee participation in decision-making in a democratic
atmosphere created by "permissive" leadership facilitates the
development of "internal" motivation and serves to raise the
levels of the employee production and morale'.[3] Tannenbaum,
reviewing the research, is less definite: 'Although the evidence
available is by no means conclusive, a larger role for workers in

---

[1] The results of a series of experiments are summarized in R. K. White and
R. Lippitt, *Autocracy and Democracy* (Harper and Row, New York 1960).
[2] E. G. Miller and A. K. Rice, *Systems of Organisation* (Tavistock Publications, London 1967), p. xii.
[3] M. S. Viteles, *Motivation and Morale in Industry* (Norton, New York
1953), p. 164.

the decision-making processes within their organizations could lead to improved performance in some situations'.[1] A sceptical, even jaundiced view has been taken by Strauss, who suggests that the research reports available concern such special cases that it would be wrong to generalize from them. Are participative techniques of management the cause of high production, or are they merely associated with other aspects of management which are the real cause? Is not participation sometimes expensive? 'The case for participation in my opinion', Strauss concludes, 'is not as strong as some have proposed'.[2]

The survey by Allen, already reported, asked managers and trade unionists for their views on workers' participation in management as a means of improving productivity. Eighteen per cent of the trade unionists thought it would be very helpful and 36 per cent helpful. For managers the corresponding figures were 6 per cent and 28 per cent.[3]

Finally, there is a reminder by Brayfield and Crockett that: 'satisfaction with one's position in a network of relationships need not imply strong motivation to outstanding performance within that system', and that 'productivity may be only peripherally related to many of the goals towards which the industrial worker is striving'.[4]

Thus the broad arguments for greater participation have been reviewed, some weaknesses have been pointed out, and some assessments of them cited. But it will be recalled that attention was drawn earlier to such factors as difference in type and level of decision and the differences between workers' needs, to which might be added the great variety of organizational structure and differences in the technology employed where people work. Unfortunately, it is not possible within the scope of this book to investigate systematically the relation between organizational and technological factors, though it is recognized that these might be critical variables in determining the need for and extent of participation in managerial decision-making.

---

[1] A. S. Tannenbaum, *Social Psychology of the Work Organisation* (Tavistock Publications, London 1966), p. 94.

[2] G. Strauss, 'Human Relations—1968 Style', *Industrial Relations*, Vol. 7, No. 3 (May 1968), p. 6.

[3] Allen, op. cit. (1967), p. 43.

[4] A. H. Brayfield and W. H. Crockett, 'Employee Attitudes and Employee Performance', *Psychological Bulletin*, Vol. 52, No. 5 (1955).

(6) *Workers' Propensity to Participate*

Another question that needs to be clarified at this stage is whether workers wish to participate in managerial decisions (of some kind or at some level). There is limited direct evidence as to the overall desire for participation. Yet based upon what is known about attendance figures for trade union meetings, the desire might not be strong. Roberts,[1] for instance, in the early 1950s, estimated that in British industry generally, the level of attendance among branch memberships was usually between 3 per cent and 15 per cent, with a heavy concentration between 4 per cent and 7 per cent. The figures for craftsmen were appreciably higher. In their sample of workers, Goldthorpe *et al.*[2] found a similar low level of involvement in trade-union activities. Only seven out of the 101 interviewed attended trade-union branch meetings on a 'regular basis'.[3]

The low level of active participation in trade-union affairs indicated by these figures provides some evidence for doubting that there is a high degree of interest in participation in management. Further evidence is to be found in the experience of the degree of active readiness to participate shown by workers employed in some of the firms that have experimented in industrial democracy.[4]

In evaluating the desire for participation, it is necessary to distinguish between groups of workers and types of decisions; it is probable that the level of interest will vary according to type of worker, and the nature of decision under discussion. It has already been noted that the skilled worker has a greater participation rate in trade-union affairs. Also, with reference to political activities, it has been found that, although there was a certain consistency in political participation rates in the white-collar and

[1] B. C. Roberts, *Trade Union Government and Administration in Great Britain* (Bell, London 1956), p. 95. See also R. J. Alexander, 'Membership in a Printing Union', *Sociological Review*, New Series, Vol. 2 (1954).

[2] J. H. Goldthorpe, D. Lockwood, F. Bechhofer, and J. Platt, *The Affluent Worker: Industrial Attitudes and Behaviour* (Cambridge University Press, London 1968).

[3] Ibid., p. 99.

[4] Cf. W. A. Robson, *Nationalised Industry and Public Ownership* (Allen and Unwin, London 1960), p. 357. See also A. Flanders *et al.*, *Experiment in Industrial Democracy: A Study of the John Lewis Partnership* (Faber, London 1968), p. 85. Less than 23 per cent of the men and 22 per cent of the women in their sample had been actively involved, by being candidates, in one of the John Lewis Partnership's participative institutions.

skilled manual groups, a marked difference becomes apparent with the unskilled worker, who exhibits a limited propensity to participate.[1] More specifically, Goldthorpe *et al.* asked their respondents whether they agreed more with the view that 'unions should just be concerned with getting higher pay and better conditions', or that 'unions should also try to get workers a say in management'.[2] Of the interviewed craftsmen 61 per cent agreed more with the latter view, in contrast to 22 per cent of process workers, and 28 per cent of the assembly workers,[3] thus suggesting that the desire for participation was related to the type of worker involved. In turning to the type of decision, the economic calculative commitment to the firm that Goldthorpe *et al.* found in their sample of workers largely determined the type of decision in which they were interested. Their predisposition for what Clark Kerr has called the 'limited-function' firm[4] leads in turn to their favouring also the 'limited-function' trade union, the union, that is, which concentrates its activities almost exclusively on their economic protection and advancement.[5] Similarly, a Norwegian study by Holter[6] also indicated a limited commitment by workers to certain areas of decision-making. She found that, although there was a widespread, but perhaps vague and diffusive desire for more participation in decisions about the firm, at the same time, relatively few felt, under the existing conditions, a need to expand customary fields of activity to include decisions at top management level. Yet Holter did find a desire for participation, a desire that concerned the workers' own jobs and immediate work environment. While recognizing the inherent difficulties of inter-cultural comparisons the evidence does seem quite strong, and indeed Holter's conclusions are supported in an unpublished study of steel-workers in this country.[7]

To sum up, the present state of knowledge does not give a

[1] T. Cauter and J. Downham, *The Communication of Ideas* (Chatto and Windus, London 1954).

[2] It is probably possible to argue that, rather than being opposed, these two views are complementary.

[3] J. Goldthorpe *et al.*, op. cit. (1968), p. 109, Table 47.

[4] Clark Kerr, 'What became of the Independent Spirit', *Fortune* (June 1953).

[5] Clark Kerr, op. cit. (1953), p. 109.

[6] H. Holter, 'Attitudes towards Employee Participation in Company Decision-making Processes', *Human Relations*, Vol. 18, No. 4 (1965).

[7] An unpublished pilot study (1969) by G. Hespe, P. Little and A. J. Watt of the Medical Research Centre Social and Applied Psychology Unit, University of Sheffield, conducted at a steel works, would seem to support the findings

definitive answer to the fundamental question of to what extent workers want to participate. Nevertheless, discussions of the desire to participate direct attention to the basic fact that workers are not a single-minded, homogeneous group, nor can decisions be taken for granted as having a uniform importance and interest.

The extent to which workers are prepared to accept responsibility for such decisions as what to produce, for whom and in what quantities, how to design the product, what machinery to buy; how to organize the flow of work, and how to sell the product when made, will depend upon many factors. The number of non-managerial workers who are able and ready to participate in management decisions, other than those that directly affect their immediate jobs and work-loads, would in fact appear to be limited. This is not to say that the mass of workers would not support a demand from their unions to participate in such decisions, or even to support those individual workers who show the necessary degree of interest in the making of such decisions and press their right to have their views considered.

No reference has so far been made to profit-sharing and co-ownership schemes; such schemes have often been seen as an important means whereby workers may be given a stake in their employing enterprise, and an incentive to pursue its goals. However, evidence suggests that the great majority of existing schemes do not fulfil the aims of their more ambitious protagonists as effective forms of participation. Rewards have generally been too remote from individual effort to give much incentive, and too small to create by themselves a sense of identification with the enterprise. This is borne out by the extent to which workers receiving shares under share distribution schemes in some companies sell them rather than leave them to appreciate.[1]

of Holter. The present authors thank G. Hespe *et al.* for permitting this reference to their manuscripts. See also R. Blauner, op. cit. (1964), p. 18, where he says: 'The average worker does not want the responsibility for such decisions as what, for whom, and how much to produce; how to design the product; what machinery to buy; how to distribute jobs; or how to organise the flow of work. It is only when these decisions directly affect his immediate job and work load that he expects labour organisation to influence policy on his behalf . . .'

[1] In the case of I.C.I., whose share distribution scheme, started in 1964, has yielded £26m. of shares, only about 40 per cent are still retained by workers. It should be added that the firm regard the scheme as having met with a 'measure of success'. (Letter from I.C.I. Ltd dated 31 July 1969.)

The principles and administrative provisions of such schemes are usually entirely in the hands of management, and accordingly workers are unlikely to feel themselves bound up with them. Indeed, one investigator comments, in relation to a study of employee shareholding schemes: 'with one exception companies do not appear to have thought it worthwhile to consult trade unions, though in some cases they informed them as a matter of courtesy'.[1]

But most important, in relation to participation in decision-making, few profit-sharing or co-partnership schemes include provisions for such participation. Even where the whole of the ownership of an enterprise is vested in the workers, as in the John Lewis Partnership, there may be 'very little sharing of power . . . as between management and rank and file'.[2]

As a result of his study of participation, Sawtell reached a similar conclusion. 'There does not seem to be any correlation between the level of participation and profit-sharing as it is usually understood,' he says, adding that 'The ownership of a few shares does not cause an employee to identify with the company's objectives.'[3]

In the light of these findings, it cannot be assumed that profit-sharing and co-partnership schemes will in themselves ensure active workers' participation in management. Nevertheless, they need to be taken into account since they may reflect relevant ideological characteristics of the management of a particular enterprise, or their existence may affect factors such as the propensity to participate. Moreover, there is evidence of a European-wide trend in favour of national schemes of profit-sharing.[4] In the survey made for this study questions were therefore asked about the existence of such schemes, and an attempt has been made to assess their influence on management decision-making.

[1] Acton Society Trust and G. Naylor, *Sharing the Profits* (Garnstone Press, London 1968), p. 108.

[2] A. Flanders *et al.*, op. cit., p. 192.

[3] R. Sawtell, *Sharing Our Industrial Future* (Industrial Society, London 1968), p. 27.

[4] Increasingly such schemes are taking new forms involving sharing of growth or capital formation. The scheme promulgated by law in France is referred to in Chapter 8: a number of European schemes are described in *Workers' Negotiated Savings Plans for Capital Formation* (O.E.C.D., Paris 1968 and 1970).

I The Worker in the Enterprise: Changing Concepts

The Early Days

Up to the industrial revolution the conditions under which ordinary people did their work changed slowly, when they changed at all, over the centuries. The mass of people worked on the land, some worked as craftsmen and tradesmen and some as servants and soldiers. Most people lived close to a subsistence standard—sometimes mere survival was as much as could be expected. But the organization of society gave some protection to the peasants and craftsmen, masters looked after their retainers and in local communities people helped each other. Since most people worked on the land or as apprentices and servants, employment was more secure than it was to become, and where contracts of employment existed, lengthy periods of notice of termination were commonly required. Working hours may have been long but the man working on his own account had a place in a social order which gave him a measure of security and recognized status.

As the industrial revolution spread, conditions of work changed. Either squeezed off the land or attracted by the expanding urban communities workers found their conditions of employment determined by the vagaries of a labour market. Increasingly workers were brought together in factories. The cost of machinery necessitated its intensive utilization. Motive power and integrated production demanded a labour force that worked by the clock and was subject to an imposed discipline. Though there were numerous exceptions, the typical employer felt little responsibility for those who worked for him: he merely bought their labour by the hour. Workers were regarded simply as a factor of production, their status and security a matter of economic circumstances rather than social obligation.

As industry and its human problems grew, the industrial order of things came to be increasingly challenged. Prominent in the working-class ferment of the 1820s and 1830s were Robert Owen and his followers, who were concerned with replacing existing industrial society with a society based on co-operative production. One notably ambitious project of those years was the Grand National Guild of Builders, which was intended to place the whole of the building industry on a co-operative basis. Another was the Equitable Labour Exchange, opened in 1832, at which products were classified according to the time spent on their production and the appropriate rate of wages of the producer, the producer depositing his products and taking away other products of equivalent value, or a promissory note. Both projects were poorly organized. The Builders' Union was subject to a determined attack by employers and collapsed with the Grand National Consolidated Trade Union in 1834. The Labour Exchanges encountered internal discord, proved uneconomic, and likewise disappeared.[1]

But interest in different forms of industrial order continued. The growth of the self-governing workshops in France around 1850, associated with Louis Blanc, influenced the Christian Socialists F. D. Maurice, J. M. Ludlow, Charles Kingsley, Tom Hughes and Edward Vansittart Neale, to work for the establishment of similar works in Britain, for which purpose they formed the Society for Promoting Working Men's Associations. At the same time the most important union of the day, the Amalgamated Society of Engineers, radically reviewing its policies after its heavy defeat by the engineering employers in a major dispute in 1851–52, and influenced by the Christian Socialists, also turned its attention to a new industrial order. On 22 April 1852 its Executive Council resolved that: 'hostile resistance of labour against capital is not calculated to enhance the condition of the labourer. We therefore advise that all future operations should be directed in promoting the system of self-employment in associative workshops, as the best means of effectively regulating the conditions of labour'. Several workshops were established as a result of this surge of interest; but their early demise occurred with monotonous regularity. The first and final report of the Society for Promoting Working Men's Associations re-

[1] See G. D. H. Cole, *The Life of Robert Owen* (Macmillan, London 1930).

corded that 'Each one of these associations had quarrelled with and turned out its original manager within six months'.

Despite the unfortunate experience of the 1850s efforts continued to be made to build productive societies that would match the success of the co-operative consumer societies. A notable example was the Ouseburn Cooperative Engine Company. founded in the north-east in 1871 on the strength of loans and share deposits by workers and directed by the charismatic James Rutherford, clergyman and doctor of medicine. By the end of September 1871 it already employed more than 300 people. Again the failure was dismal. The company suffered strike action, made bad debts, encountered legal problems, experienced excessive overtime, restrictive practices, and lack of discipline. In liquidation it paid 1s. 3¼d. in the pound.[1]

Not all productive societies failed. Cole calculated that between 1862 and 1880 some 163 of them were registered under the Industrial and Provident Societies Act, 1852, promoted by Ludlow and Neale. In 1882 the Cooperative Productive Federation was formed to strengthen the twenty or so societies that were operative at the time and to propagate co-operative co-partnership.[2] In 1884 a separate organization, the Labour Association, was founded to promote co-partnership and profit-sharing; its members, in its early days, were required to adopt the principles that workers had a right to share in the profits, to become shareholders and to participate in management.[3] The Royal Commission on Labour of 1891 traced 126 co-operative producers, and Cole noted 206 in 1903.[4] The mortality rate continued to be high, however, and it was noteworthy that the

---

[1] For the story of the self-governing workshops see Benjamin Jones, *Cooperative Production* (Oxford 1894); B. Potter (later Webb), *The Co-operative Movement in Great Britain* (Allen and Unwin, London 1930), Ch. 5 (first published 1891); G. D. H. Cole, *A Century of Cooperation* (Allen and Unwin, London 1944), Chapter XI; S. and B. Webb, 'Cooperative Production and Profit Sharing', *New Statesman* (Special Supplements, 1914–15).

[2] J. Leonard, *Cooperative Co-Partnership Production Societies* (Co-operative Production Federation Ltd, Leicester 1965). The Federation is still in existence. In 1966, according to Coates and Topham, 1968, it had 23 affiliated societies, the largest employing 1,595 people. Sawtell records the membership as 18 (Sawtell, op. cit., 1968; p. 32).

[3] The Labour Association is today the Industrial Co-Partnership Association, a body dedicated to extending co-partnership and improving industrial relationships.

[4] G. D. H. Cole, *A Century of Cooperation* (Allen and Unwin, London 1944).

B

societies included few of size and few from the basic industries:
the boot and shoe, clothing and printing industries tended to
predominate.

Writing of these nineteenth-century experiences the Webbs
were

> ... driven to conclude, on the evidence, that the relative ill-success
> of Associations of Producers—their almost invariable experience of
> finding themselves thwarted, their high hopes disappointed, and their
> very continuance a perpetual struggle—is due to something in them-
> selves, to be sought for in that which is common to them all, whatever
> their trades and whatever their countries . . . it is the very form itself
> that is ill-adapted to survive.[1]

What the experiences had in common, as the Webbs pointed
out, were poor workshop discipline, inadequate knowledge of the
market, and slow response to technical change. Enterprises with
such failings had little hope of surviving in a competitive
economy.[2]

Failure was the result of most forms of attempt to give the
worker a voice in determining his working life that seemed to
be denied him under capitalism as generally practised; the
romantic attempt of the 1830s to replace the industrial order of
the time, and the idealistic attempts to build new forms of
enterprise within the existing order. The first briefly attracted
mass support, then vanished like snow in heat: the second never
gained widespread or lasting support amongst the pragmatic men
who formed the active core of the trade-union movement.
Capitalist employers were hardly likely to warm to either of these
attempts to make their role redundant. But not all employers were
content with the existing order of things. Some, notably those
who were of the Quaker faith, felt a strong sense of obligation
to those who worked for them.[3] Other employers were concerned about the undesirability of strife between capital and

---

[1] S. and B. Webb, op. cit. (1914–15). See also S. and B. Webb, *A Constitution
for the Socialist Commonwealth of Great Britain* (Longmans, London 1920),
pp. 154–61.

[2] S. and B. Webb, op. cit. (1914–15).

[3] For an interesting early statement see David Power, *On the Responsibilities
of Employers* (London 1849). For an early review of profit-sharing see N. P.
Gilman, *Profit Sharing between Employer and Employee* (Houghton Mifflin,
Cambridge, Mass., 1889). See also D. F. Schloss, *Methods of Industrial
Remuneration*, 3rd ed. (London 1898), pp. 239–419. The results of official
enquiries concerning profit-sharing are given in Cmnd 7458, 1894; Cmnd
8748, 1895; and Cmnd 6496, 1912.

labour and sought ways to ensure industrial peace. Often their search sprang from a sense of common interest, though in some instances the motivating force was a desire to keep out the trade unions. In almost none of these cases, however, was there any suggestion that workers should have any say in management; the common approach of such firms, apart from trying to give good wages and conditions, was simply to share their profits.

The Webbs have recorded[1] the first British profit-sharing scheme as starting in 1829, but suggest that it was not until 1865 that interest in profit-sharing became significant. Again the schemes tended to be short-lived, and rarely provided for any real transfer of authority.[2] An experience that attracted much attention was that of the Yorkshire colliery of Henry Briggs, Son and Co., who, in 1865, converted their business into a joint-stock company, induced their workers to take up shares and made provision for profit-sharing and, from 1869, for a worker-shareholder to be elected as a director. The scheme was not, however, a success, and was discontinued in 1875 following a strike.[3] A later and much more durable experience was in the gas industry.[4] In 1889 the General Manager of the South Metropolitan Gas Company, Mr. (later Sir) George Livesey, introduced a profit-sharing and share distribution scheme. In 1896 the South Metropolitan Gas Act provided for the worker shareholders to elect 'a director or directors to take part in the management of the affairs of the Company'. Similar schemes operated in the Commercial Gas Company and the South Suburban Gas Company, and all three operated smoothly until they were discontinued when the industry passed into public ownership in 1948.

Benevolent, thoughtful and even opportunist employers may have looked to profit-sharing as a bridge spanning the conflicts and combining the interests of capital and labour, but workers and their unions showed little enthusiasm for it. For them the rewards of profit-sharing seemed too far from their control, too unpredictable and often too meagre to mean

---

[1] S. and B. Webb, op. cit. (1914–15).

[2] The Webbs (ibid.) found four cases where the enterprise had been given to workers and nine where workers were allowed to sit on the board.

[3] Gilman, op. cit. Schloss, op. cit. (1898), p. 357, adds: '... at no time do the workmen appear to have been able to exercise any sort of control in the management of the company, in whose affairs they had practically no voice'.

[4] See also chapter 6, p. 139.

much. For the unions particularly, too many schemes seemed intended to attract the worker's loyalty away from his union to his employer.

So, like the other two forms of workers' participation described, profit-sharing failed to satisfy workers' aspirations for a greater say in their working lives. In fact the weight of trade-union activity had come to be directed in quite another way from those described so far.

Though the unions' social insurance functions and the struggles to achieve statutory protection for union activity had long been important, the weight of union work had usually lain in preserving or improving wages and working conditions and in seeking to control the job. It was in these ways that unions sought participation within the enterprise. In relation to wages and conditions they laid the foundation for collective bargaining, which was to become the principal form of participation in Britain. In relation to job security and working practices their efforts encouraged job control by the working group, or the district committee. Collective bargaining brought them a measure of joint regulation with the employers, of wages and conditions: job control led to restrictive practices, often accepted by employers as 'the custom of the trade',[1] and to struggles with employers over managerial prerogatives.

What restrictive practices are about has been described, with exceptional understanding and clarity, by Sidney Webb:

> ... a complicated network of usages and regulations, differing from district to district, and often from establishment to establishment. ... These customs and rules had been built up during several generations, with the more or less explicit acquiescence of the employers. ... To their own particular network of rules and customs each set of workmen attached enormous importance. ... These conditions, as the workmen held, formed an essential part of their individual contracts for service. What the employer paid for was their labour exercised under these conditions. Invidious as some of them might appear to persons without the wage-earner's knowledge, they had been found by experience, so it seemed to the men, to be indispensable safeguards of the customary rate of wages—necessary defences against a progressive degradation of their standard of life. ... Nor was the existence of such a network of usages altogether

---

[1] It should not be overlooked that the discussion of trade unions in the nineteenth century deals mainly with craft unions, many with practices established over a century or more.

detrimental or distasteful to the employer doing a steady-going business in quiet times. ... Just as the weight of the atmosphere is not felt as pressure, the long-continued customs of establishment that sought no change sometimes failed even to reach the employer's consciousness. He was often unaware of their existence.[1]

But equally the employer was often very much aware of their existence, and working practices were not only maintained in the reasonable and defensive manner Sydney Webb described but aggressively. Thus the Webbs refer to a letter of the 1830s from the Builders' Union: '... as you have not treated our rules with that deference you ought to have done, we consider you highly culpable and deserving of being severely chastised'.[2] Nassau Senior spoke of trade-union committees prohibiting the employer from 'using machinery, or materials which they think may enable him to do with less human labour'. The combined labour on the canals, he said, 'will not allow any one to be discharged for idleness, or for drunkenness or even for theft'.[3] The engineer Nasmyth complained to the Royal Commission on Trade Unions, 1867, that before an employer 'can introduce even some of the most obvious improvements he will have to consider: "Will my men like this; will they turn out?" '[4] Control was exercised over new starters, and that great engineer Sir William Fairbairn described how as a young man he tried to obtain engineering work in London but was unable to get work because he could not obtain membership of the Millwrights' Society.[5] Much later, in April 1897, the Monthly Journal of the Amalgamated Engineers carried a report of a case where the union's committee framed a code of rules: 'One of the employers objected to our dictation, and offered us counter-proposals which we rejected. After some straight talking, and an application of our machinery for one day, he wrote me accepting our proposals, and that it was a case of the strong having no regard for the weak'.[6]

---

[1] S. Webb, The Restoration of Trade Union Conditions (Nisbet, London 1917), pp. 8–12. See also E. H. Phelps Brown, The Growth of British Industrial Relations (Macmillan, London 1959), pp. 286–90.

[2] S. and B. Webb, History of Trade Unionism (Longmans, London 1920), p. 129. (See also ibid. p. 75, for an employers' protest.)

[3] Nassau Senior, Industrial Efficiency and Social Economy (Henry Holt and Co., New York 1920). Senior was writing in the 1850s.

[4] Parliamentary Papers, 1867–8, Q.219222.

[5] W. Pole (ed.), The Life of Sir William Fairbairn, Bart. (Longmans, London 1877), p. 92.

[6] A lengthy list of alleged 'Trade Union Restriction and Interference' is

The Webbs have said of the time: 'It seems to have been habitually taken for granted that the workman had not merely to fulfil his contract of service, but to yield implicit obedience in the details of his working life to the will of his master'.[1] Certainly management was much more autocratic than it is today, but the examples quoted above show clearly that it was far from exercising an absolute autocracy, particularly where skilled labour was concerned. Occasionally friction about job practices led to major and widespread disputes. Two such disputes in the engineering industry are of particular interest. At the end of 1851 the engineering employers of London and Manchester banded together in an attempt to establish, against militant opposition, their right to operate piece-work, to require overtime to be worked as they saw fit, and to employ other than skilled workers on the increasing number of specialized machine tools, requiring little skill in operation, then coming into use. The employers were overwhelmingly victorious in the dispute but their success did not prevent recurrence of the issue in conflict. In the far wider seven months' engineering dispute of 1897–8,[2] (ostensibly about working hours but basically about managerial prerogatives) piece-work, overtime working and classification of operators were again at issue. The Terms of Settlement of the dispute began with the words:

> The Federated Employers, while disavowing any intention of inter-fering with the proper functions of Trade Unions, will admit no interference with the management of their business, and reserve to themselves the right to introduce into any federated workshop, at the option of the Employer concerned, any condition of labour under which any members of the Trade Unions here represented were working at the commencement of the dispute in any of the workshops of the Federated Employers....[3]

Again the employers' victory was overwhelming, but whatever else they gained they did not actually secure the sweeping rights to determine working practices that they achieved on paper.

contained in a collection of papers prepared for the Federated Engineering Employers in respect of the engineering dispute of 1897–8 (London, November 1897).

[1] S. and B. Webb, op. cit. (1920), p. 167.

[2] See R. O. Clarke, 'The Dispute in the British Engineering Industry, 1897–8', Economica (London, May 1957).

[3] The Federated Engineering Employers, Conditions of Management (London, January 1898).

Logically there was no reason why workers should not have said to the employer, when industrial usages were becoming established in the nineteenth century, 'these are the conditions on which I will agree to work for you'.[1] Though there were other reasons the determining factor was, of course, that in most industries, in most places and at most times, the employer was in a much stronger bargaining position than the worker: within fairly wide limits he could dictate his terms. He did so with a clear conscience, taking his stand on the right of ownership of the means of production, his managerial expertise and on the social conventions of the day.

By the end of the nineteenth century, then, the position of the worker in employment was clearly established. Basically his relationship with the employer was a contractual one. He had nothing to do with the commercial and financial decisions made in the enterprise; he and his fellows might exercise a measure of control over job practices, but fundamentally the employer laid down the ways in which work was done. However, the worker had developed, through his trade union, a means of resistance to those managerial decisions that affected him adversely, and the ground had been prepared for the future growth of collective bargaining.

What had been the role of the State in respect of the status of workers during the industrial development in the nineteenth century? There had been protective measures such as the Factories Acts and Truck Acts, the Acts establishing the legality of trade unions and Acts relating to conciliation. But it is interesting to reflect on why Parliament, active in regulating the functions of shareholders and directors and in establishing a code for safety, health and welfare, did not attempt to provide a constitution for the company,[2] did nothing to define the status of the worker in his job; did nothing to provide for his participation in decisions that affected his working life. This can only be due to the prevailing belief of the time that the State should intervene as little as possible: there were few signs that workers or employers wished it otherwise.

---

[1] See W. Milne-Bailey, *Trade Unions and the State* (Allen and Unwin, London 1934), p. 339. Milne-Bailey cites an idea of Lord Milner's of capital being hired by labour at a fixed rate.

[2] See E. H. Phelps Brown, *The Growth of British Industrial Relations* (Macmillan, London 1959), p. 209.

The Years of Ferment, 1910–22

After a period in which standards of life had been improving steadily, if slowly, the early years of the twentieth century saw a check, and in some cases a decline, in real wages. Among workers there was mounting discontent, culminating in the wave of industrial action that hit Britain in 1910–11. In this atmosphere men again started to question the fundamental beliefs of industrial society.

The challenge of the 1830s has already been noted. But, although the weight of activity in respect of participation passed to collective bargaining and job control, men did not lose all thought of achieving an industrial order in which control of the enterprise and industry itself rested with the workers. From the time of the First International in 1864 there was a rising tide of interest in achieving a new industrial order through socialism, though numerically it had little support, at least until the 1890s. None the less, the idea of fundamental changes in society had never enjoyed a sustained popularity: the Webbs pointed out, in the great mass of evidence produced for the Royal Commission on Labour, 1891–94, 'we find from beginning to end absolutely no claim, and even no suggestion, that the trade union should participate in the direction of industry, otherwise than arranging with the employers the conditions of the wage-earner's working life'.[1]

In the changed situation that prevailed around 1910 one school of thought adopted the syndicalist ideas then prevalent in France. Industrial action, it argued, should be taken by trade unions reconstructed on an industrial basis, culminating in a general strike which would secure political power. This accomplished, the new society would be based on a flexible federation of autonomous associations, collectively managed by 'workers by hand and brain' whose relations would be self-adjusting. Though syndicalism was not without influence[2] it was too alien to take deep roots in Britain, and by the outbreak of war in 1914 was of little importance. But its appearance was important in at least one respect. Previously, workers' approaches

[1] S. and B. Webb, *History of Trade Unionism* (Longmans, London 1920), p. 650.

[2] For example, it strongly influenced the celebrated pamphlet published by the Reform Committee of the South Wales Miners, entitled *The Miners' Next Step* (1912).

to control or greater participation had, broadly, looked to a change in the industrial order to be achieved by political means; sought new forms of enterprise within the existing framework; or, again accepting the existing framework, sought to advance workers' influence by industrial action. Now a change in the industrial order was sought through industrial action.

A different approach, native to Britain and influenced by the British outlook, was that of the Guild Socialists, primarily a group of intellectuals associated with, but outside, the trade-union movement. Particularly from about 1912 they advocated that the workers should take all opportunities to encroach on managerial control of industry. When control had been secured, workers—professional, technical, clerical and manual—would run their industries through the guilds they would set up. Non-industrial interests would have their own forms of government and national economic policy would be the responsibility of a special body, which would, however, leave the maximum autonomy to the guilds.[1]

The theory of Guild Socialism was developed mainly by three men, A. J. Penty, S. G. Hobson and G. D. H. Cole. Penty, an architect influenced by William Morris, deplored the way in which industry had developed and harked back to the medieval practice whereby guilds of masters and craftsmen regulated production. The new guilds, Penty thought, could be developed from existing trade unions, with masters included. The main unit of production would be the small workshop, with the guild taking responsibility for quality of output. Distribution would be through co-operative societies, and national government would be by a lower house elected on a territorial basis and an upper house elected by the guilds.[2]

Hobson considered that the wages system, which he saw as treating labour as a commodity, had been the prime creator of the undesirable character of modern industrial society. He proposed that each industry should be run by a national guild, chartered by the State and comprising all workers in its industry. Managers would be elected. Land, buildings and machinery used by the guilds would be leased from the community. A Guilds Council would co-ordinate guild activities

[1] For a recent review of Guild Socialism see S. T. Glass, *The Responsible Society: the Ideas of the English Guild Socialist* (Longmans, London 1966).
[2] A. J. Penty, *The Restoration of the Guild System* (Swan, London 1906).

and deal with demarcation problems. Conventional State machinery would deal with matters outside the scope of the guilds. Trade unions should prepare for the new order by reorganizing on an industrial basis, by admitting all those working in their industry and by adopting industrial policies aimed at achieving control. Industrial democracy did not imply inefficiency, but if a choice had to be made between the ends of democracy and efficiency Hobson would choose democracy.[1]

Cole shared Hobson's views to a considerable extent. More than Hobson, however, he stressed the need for research and preparatory planning and for practical steps to be taken to prove the value of the guild socialist system by example. He also envisaged the possibility of a transitional period of nationalization preceding full democratization. His ideal was self-government, which he defined as 'the conscious and continuous exercise of the art of citizenship'. Another contribution with which Cole was much concerned was the policy of encroachment on managerial control already mentioned—encroachment not by seeking to share power with management but by securing exclusive control over such functions as workers could exercise unaided, such as appointing supervisors and setting works rules. Subsequently the unions should seek, wherever possible, to enter into a collective contract to cover the whole output of the shop.

Cole also worked out means whereby the interests of the consumer and the community generally could be protected in relation to the guilds, and a system of local and regional communes, as the basic social units, heading up to a national commune. Industrially, Cole envisaged elected shop and works committees, district committees, and, at the head of each guild, an executive committee, with formal authority in the hands of a delegate meeting. Guild officials would be appointed by the relevant committees, factory officials would be elected by works committees, foremen by the workers in the shop, and works managers by the works as a whole.[2]

Cole's hope of practical experience was realized, at least briefly and partially, when a movement among building workers led to the formation, in 1920, of Guild Committees in Manchester and

---

[1] See particularly S. G. Hobson, *National Guilds, an Inquiry into the Wage System and the Way Out* (Bell, London 1919).

[2] See G. D. H. Cole, *Self-Government in Industry* (Bell, London 1917) and *Guild Socialism Restated* (London 1920).

London. By the end of the year progress was sufficient to justify the establishment of a National Building Guild, of which Hobson became General Secretary. The venture was facilitated by the post-war building boom. There was much building to be done and the financial arrangements for subsidizing building by local authorities, including a cost-plus basis of payment, were such that building operations could be carried on even where capital was short.

For a time the Building Guild flourished, though opinions about its effectiveness have differed.[1] Efforts were made to set up guilds in other industries, but there was difficulty in obtaining financial support and they came to nothing. Meanwhile the Government cut back its housing programme and changed from cost-plus to fixed-sum accounting, and by 1922 the Building Guild had disintegrated. According to those involved in the Guild its demise was due to the general economic slump, the unhelpfulness of the Ministry of Health and the opposition of building employers: others spoke of disciplinary problems, over-manning, inexpert management and buying, hiring of unqualified labour, and acceptance of unprofitable jobs. The critics seem to have the better case. As Cole said, more than twenty years later: 'The verdict is, I think, final against attempts to transform the economic system by voluntary association of producers in competition with better equipped capitalist rivals'.[2] The Guild Socialist movement did not long outlive the fall of the Building Guild, many of its supporters turning towards the Communist Party.

While guild socialism was attracting support amongst intellectual critics of the industrial order a movement with much more powerful support was forming on the shop floor.

As already mentioned, from about 1906 industrial discontent had been growing, chiefly for economic reasons. After the outbreak of war in 1914, while the general mood was intensely patriotic there was ample cause for unrest in the workshops. The

[1] For a recent review of the Building Guild see Glass, op. cit. (1966), and for earlier accounts see M. B. Reckitt and C. E. Bechhofer, *The Meaning of National Guilds* (Palmer, London 1920); R. Postgate, *The Builders' History* (N.F.B.T.O., London 1923); S. G. Hobson, *Pilgrim to the Left, Memoirs of a Modern Revolutionist* (London 1938); G. D. H. Cole, *Self-government in Industry* (Bell, London 1917), and G. D. H. Cole, *A Century of Cooperation* (Allen and Unwin, London 1944), pp. 284–92.

[2] Ibid., 1944 p. 292.

changeover from peacetime to wartime production, the exodus of
male workers to the armed forces and the influx of women, the
rapid rise in prices, the unprecedented problems of wages as rates
of pay soared for some workers while others were confined by
wages agreements (including some long-term agreements) were
all disturbing factors. Britain was not used to industrial change
of this speed and order, and there was little provision, at least
to start with, for co-operation between Government and Industry, for national joint consultative or advisory machinery.
Often there was little understanding between them either. In
the workshops many inexperienced production workers on piece-
work were earning more than skilled maintenance fitters or
machine-tool setters on time-work. Piece-work, with its associated
problems of fixing prices or times, was spreading as long production runs became more common. Rapid changes in production
were making craftsmen increasingly anxious about job practices;
particularly they were anxious about dilution—the introduction
of less skilled workers to do work hitherto done by skilled men.

Trade-union leaders were naturally anxious to preserve the
established customs of their members' trades, but they were
under tremendous pressure from the Government and the employers to relax such customs as might hinder production. At the
Treasury Conference of 1915 the unions agreed, subject to
some guarantees, to a series of demands for relaxation. But the
agreement was made over the heads of the men on the shop
floor, and many of them were disturbed by the pressures on
them and apprehensive about giving up cherished protective practices. Their officials, they felt, were committed to allowing the
employers to have their way, so far as the practices were concerned. The unions had done little to build formal works-based
organization and the men therefore sought unofficial leaders and
found them in the shop stewards, workers who had hitherto had
few union functions other than collecting members' subscrip-
tions.

From 1915 on (the catalyst being a wages dispute on the
Clyde) militant unofficial workers' organizations—shop stewards'
committees, workshop committees and works committees—developed rapidly, and on a considerable scale, in the industrial
areas.[1] With the growth of works committees came a growth

[1] For the growth of the shop stewards' movement see B. Pribicevic, *The
Shop Stewards' Movement and Workers Control*, 1910–22 (Blackwell, Oxford

of interest in workers' control. For a short time, in 1915, unions were represented on local Armaments Committees and in the management of new National Shell Factories.[1] These arrangements were short-lived, but the brief experience of workers' representation in management had given some popularity to ideas of workers' control.

In respect of the Clyde, Cole has written:

> But, whatever the immediate claims put forward by the leaders of the Clyde shop stewards may have been, there is no doubt that, in a remoter sense, they were aiming at a complete transformation of the industrial system, and at the substitution for the capitalist control of industry of a system based on communal control and involving full participation in management by the organized workers.[2]

The Russian Revolution, and the part played in it by workers' councils before they were subordinated to the State, strengthened the convictions of those who saw the British Works Committee as a vehicle for transforming the industrial system.

But in planning for post-war reconstruction radical ideas were not confined to the left. The Whitley Committee,[3] for instance, proposed a structure of Joint Standing Industrial Councils to discuss matters of common concern to their industries, their joint membership satisfying the workers' claim to a share in the control of industry. Under the National Councils, District Councils and Joint Works Committees were proposed, all of which would operate within the national framework. Only trade unionists would sit on the workers' side of the committee.

In fact, though numerous Joint Standing Industrial Councils were set up following the Whitley Reports, most of the big industries preferred to retain their own established machinery. Even where National Councils were established, little was done to stimulate the formation of District Councils or Works Com-

---

1959); G. D. H. Cole, *Workshop Organisation* (Clarendon Press, Oxford 1923); J. T. Murphy, *Preparing for Power* (Cape, London 1934); and W. Hannington, *Industrial History in Wartime* (Lawrence and Wishart, London 1940).

[1] Cole, op. cit. (1923), pp. 89–90.

[2] Cole, op. cit. (1923), pp. 91–92.

[3] Ministry of Reconstruction Committee on the Relations between Employers and Employees. The Committee issued a series of Reports in 1917–18. For a review of the Whitley proposals and subsequent experience see H. Clay, *The Problem of Industrial Relations* (Macmillan, London 1929), pp. 449–71; a contemporary outside view is given in National Industrial Conference Board, *Problems of Labor and Industry in Great Britain, France and Italy* (N.I.C.B., Boston, Mass., 1919).

mittees, and in few cases was an articulated structure of national, local and works committees set up as envisaged. The main success of the Whitley proposals was in the field of public employment. In private industry they met opposition from employers, who saw them as likely to infringe managerial prerogatives, and sometimes from trade unions, who preferred the ways to which they were used to the form of organization proposed.[1]

The employers, if not convinced by the Whitley proposals, were not unaffected by the mood of post-war reconstruction. A statement by the Federation of British Industries in 1919 quoted with some approval (though carefully excluding the commercial aspects of management) Gosling's Presidential address to the T.U.C.:

> ... in the daily management of the employment in which we spend our working lives, in the atmosphere and under the conditions in which we have to work, in the hours of beginning and ending work, in the conditions of remuneration and even in the manners and practices of the foremen with whom we have to be in contact, in all these matters we feel that we, as workmen, have a right to a voice—even to an equal voice—with the management itself. Believe me, we shall never get any lasting peace except on the lines of democracy.[2]

We are strongly of the opinion (the Federation said) that the workers in every industry should be given the fullest possible voice in the determination of the conditions under which they are employed.

The employers' interest was not roused solely by the spirit of the times. In part if came from concern about the activities of the shop-stewards' movement and the ideas propagated by the guild socialists. But it also owed much to the growing demand for nationalization.

Nationalization was not a new idea. It had been discussed by the T.U.C. as long ago as the 1880s and 1890s, and in 1908 the Port of London Act had set a pattern for a nationalized industry, establishing a Board with eighteen members elected by users and ten appointed by public authorities. The concept of

---

[1] Cole, op. cit. (1923), p. 120.
[2] Federation of British Industries, *The Control of Industry, Nationalisation and Kindred Problems* (F.B.I., London 1919).

nationalization was political as much as industrial. By 1918[1] it enjoyed wide support in the labour movement, from intellectuals to hard-headed union leaders—who saw in it a practical way in which power could be achieved, whereas they found guild socialism too woolly and impractical, and the 'workers' control' of the militant Left too radical and dogmatic. The primary objects of nationalization were to transfer ownership from shareholders to the public, and to operate industry as a public service rather than for profit[2]—workers' control was at most a secondary goal—but guild socialists and militant shop stewards could support it as a step on the road to achieving their own ends.

In the flush of enthusiasm for post-war reconstruction several ambitious nationalization plans were mooted. Miners, railwaymen and post-office workers were particularly active supporters of such plans. Nationalization of the mines received weighty support from the Report of the Sankey Commission in 1919.

But what came of it all? In retrospect many of the ideas of workers' participation or control put forward in these years of ferment, between 1910 and 1922, seem strangely unrealistic. They left little permanent mark on the face of British industrial relations. Syndicalism and guild socialism faded into long-term aspirations for public ownership. Whitley-type committees became a permanent feature in public employment but had limited success in private industry. Shop stewards had come to stay. In some cases, as in engineering, they were fitted into negotiating procedures within the firm and placed formally under union control. Numerically they declined rapidly after 1920 when, as unemployment mounted, active shop stewards tended to find themselves amongst the unemployed and militancy noticeably diminished.

Ideas of industrial reform had flourished in the atmosphere created by the end of the war and the changeover to peacetime production, with its seemingly insatiable sellers' market. With the slump of 1921, an orthodox Conservative government and growing unemployment, with employers concerned about cutting costs, including labour costs, to the bone, workers' control had become unpropitious. The energies of the trade unions, them-

[1] In 1918 the Labour Party adopted its famous Clause 4, calling for common ownership of the means of production, and the best obtainable system of popular administration and control of each industry and service.

[2] It was hoped that nationalized industry would give a more efficient service than private industry and at the same time set an example with the good wages and conditions it would afford its members.

selves greatly weakened by declining membership and bargaining power, were bent on preserving their members' jobs, pay and
conditions rather than changing the industrial order. Finally,
such impetus as the movement for reform had retained was to
disappear with the unsuccessful General Strike of 1926.

Politically, however, the Labour Party's formal commitment to
public ownership remained, and it was in this area that the next
sign of interest was to come.

The Nationalization Debate

The main public boards created in the 1920s—the Central Electricity Board and the British Broadcasting Corporation—were
of no interest from the point of view of participation. Controversy
arose, however, when the Labour Government of 1929 promoted
the London Passenger Transport Bill.[1] The Minister of Transport responsible, Herbert Morrison, believed that appointments to
Boards should be made solely on the grounds of the contribution the individual director could make to the enterprise and
not on the ground of representation of interests. Morrison's
view[2] was hotly contested within the labour movement, particularly by the Transport and General Workers' Union, in a debate
that continued through the 1930s.

Morrison wanted workers to serve on the boards of nationalized industries, but only as individuals possessing the necessary
capacity. His opponents sought direct workers' representation, up
to a 50 per cent representation within the board. So far as the
T.U.C. and the Labour Party were concerned the controversy
was settled by a joint decision of 1935 that the right of workers'
organizations to representation on the governing boards of
socialized industries and services should be secured by Statute.[3]
What form or extent of representation was not specified.

The next major contribution to achieving workers' participation in the public sector came in 1944, when the General Council

---

[1] This measure did not, in fact, reach the Statute book and it fell to the
incoming national Government of 1931 to enact the London Passenger
Transport Act, 1933. One part-time director of the Board created by that
Act was a trade-union official, and he resigned union office on taking up his
appointment.

[2] See H. S. Morrison, *Socialisation and Transport: the Organisation of
Socialised Industries with particular reference to the London Passenger Transport
Bill* (Constable, London 1933).

[3] *Labour Party Annual Conference Report* (1935), p. 18.

of the T.U.C. issued its Interim Report on Post-War Reconstruction.[1] It was proposed that trade unions should continue to exercise their negotiating functions at the workshop level, but that consultative machinery should be established to deal with all other internal matters. Board members would continue to be professional, and selected on grounds of competence. The Board would be accountable to the public through a Minister responsible to Parliament. Though the Board would be selected on the ground of its 'competence efficiently to administer the industry' the Report considered that experience gained in the collective organization of labour was a strong qualification for board membership because of the managerial competence it engendered. It was important, the Report added, to appoint people with such experience to the boards, thereby, without making the individual directors accountable to any but the public interest, ensuring 'that the views of the industry's workers on its management receive full consideration'. An appropriate method of selection might be for the T.U.C., after consulting the appropriate unions, to present a list of candidates from whom the Minister would make his selection. Members so appointed 'should surrender any position held in, or any formal responsibility to, the trade union'.[2]

The nationalization Acts passed by the Labour Government that came to power in 1945 followed closely on the proposals of the T.U.C.'s Report. They required the industries to establish consultative machinery at all levels, and stipulated experience in the organization of workers as one of the criteria for the selection of board members. In practice the board members appointed on this basis were very much in the minority on the boards. Their union experience usually lay outside the industries which they joined, and they were expected to give up union office on appointment. There was no suggestion in the Acts that the workers should share in the control of the industries. The pattern

[1] Participation in the enterprise in the private sector was not proposed. It is interesting that the Report listed the objectives of the trade-union movement as relating firstly to wages and conditions, secondly to maintaining full employment, and only thirdly as 'to extend the influence of workpeople over the policies and purposes of industry and to arrange for their participation in its management'.

[2] The quotations are from T.U.C., *Interim Report on Post-War Reconstruction* (London 1944).

of the nationalization Acts was not to change until the re-nationalization of steel in 1966.

Joint Consultation

The emphasis placed by the nationalization Acts on consultative machinery was a reflection of the value then being placed on joint consultation.

Formal joint consultation had been practised in Britain before the first world war, though by relatively few firms. As has been shown, many joint committees were set up during the war and shortly after, but such committees did not, for the most part, survive the cold climate of the 1920s. With the onset of the second world war, however, conditions were again favourable to the establishment of joint consultative committees. There was a general feeling that workers' knowledge and abilities were not being fully utilized in support of the war effort; the hectic rate of change in wartime production, and the massive movement of labour, were other factors demanding effective means of communication between management and labour. Furthermore, with the changed balance of power between management and workers, management had good reason to take note of workers' views—whether in negotiation or through consultation. Lastly, the main likely source of dissidence, the Communists, from 1941 on put their weight behind co-operation for efficient production.

Not only was joint consultation highly successful during the war, but its virtues continued to be extolled for some years after.[1] This may be partly accounted for by the continuation of full employment and a sense of common national interest in the economically difficult days that followed the war. Partly it was, as Clegg has said, 'a feeling that labour deserved a more important share in the running of the nation's affairs than it had been accorded before the war'.[2] The value placed on joint consultation at the time is well evidenced by a debate in the House of Commons on a motion urging the Government to

[1] British joint production committees were the subject of two studies by the International Labour Office (I.L.O., 1943 and 1944) and influenced the form of joint enterprise committees set up in several European countries, by statute or by national agreement, after the war.

[2] H. A. Clegg, *A New Approach to Industrial Democracy* (Blackwell, Oxford 1960). Clegg was speaking more particularly of national affairs, but his remarks also applied to the enterprise.

continue its efforts to encourage joint consultation and joint consultative machinery. Speakers of widely varying political shades of opinion vied with each other in praising consultation, and there was virtually no discordant note. The Minister of Labour, in the same debate, reported that a Special Supplement to the Ministry's Industrial Relations Handbook, dealing with Joint Consultation, had sold 4,500 copies within six weeks of publication.[1]

In the nationalized industries the setting up of statutory consultative machinery after nationalization created a new interest which of itself probably generated some success, particularly where the machinery was promoted enthusiastically from the top, as in the Electricity Supply Industry.[2]

Both in private industry and in the public sector the value placed on joint consultation—at least on consultation through formal machinery within the enterprise—fell during the 1950s. Some committees fell into disuse. Lack of enthusiasm by management or workers led to many committees dealing with trivia, which in turn caused loss of interest. But the main reason for the decline in activity of the committees was, as indicated in Chapter 2, the growth of work-place bargaining.

The Growth of Work-Place Bargaining[3]

Between the wars, more or less realistic rates of pay and working conditions had been negotiated nationally in many industries.

[1] *Hansard*, 5 April 1950.

[2] See R. D. V. Roberts and H. Sallis, 'Joint Consultation in the Electricity Supply Industry, 1949–59', *Public Administration*, Vol. 37 (Summer 1959); and H. Sallis, 'Joint Consultation and Meetings of Primary Working Groups in Power Stations', *British Journal of Industrial Relations*, Vol. III, No. 3 (November 1965).

[3] For analyses of the growth of work-place bargaining see A. I. Marsh, *Managers and Shop Stewards* (Institute of Personnel Management, London 1963) and A. Flanders, *Industrial Relations: What is wrong with the system?* (Institute of Personnel Management, London 1965). Assuming a correlation between work-place activity and number of shop stewards, a measure of the increase in activity in a major industry is given by A. I. Marsh and E. E. Coker, 'Shop Steward Organisation in the Engineering Industry', *British Journal of Industrial Relations* (June 1963), p. 177, who report a 72 per cent increase in A.E.U. shop-stewards in federated establishments between May 1947 and December 1961. Other figures exemplifying the trend, for the same industry, are those for the total number of conferences held under the industry's procedure agreements, showing an increase from 2,145 in 1954–5 to 7,499 in 1966 (249.6 per cent). (Source: *Annual Reports* of the Engineering Employers' Federation.)

From 1939 on, however, though the main working conditions, such as the length of the working week, continued to be reasonably effectively regulated by national negotiation, labour shortage and the inflationary environment made the nationally agreed rates increasingly unrealistic. A tendency developed for workers to receive either supplementary rates or simply higher rates than those agreed nationally.

More and more, work-place conditions came to be regulated by bargaining in the work-place, where the increased power given to the work group by full employment could be deployed to good effect. The field of bargaining broadened, to include matters which had previously been regarded as matters for consultation rather than negotiation.[1] Finally, the variant of productivity bargaining opened up greater access to information and participation in a still wider variety of decisions that had previously been regarded purely as matters for management.

The extent of payment by results in British industry, with its recurrent opportunities for bargaining on job prices or times, was another stimulant to work-place bargaining.

Clearly the growth of work-place bargaining, while perhaps decreasing the extent of workers' participation through formal joint consultation, increased participation through negotiation. As Lerner remarked: 'Works bargaining has given the rank-and-file union member a greater voice in determining the actual conditions of his work and the size of his pay packet'.[2]

Summary

On the whole the workers of the nineteenth century accepted the prevailing industrial order, though there were times, particularly in the early part of the century, when they tried to change it. They had to accept it: low educational standards, the social climate of the age, the extent of unemployment and the weak bargaining position of most workers saw to that. Furthermore, experiments with other forms of industrial organization such as the self-governing workshops proved unsuccessful. In the circum-

[1] See, as quoted in Chapter 2, W. E. J. McCarthy, *The Role of Shop Stewards in British Industrial Relations*, Royal Commission on Trade Unions and Employers' Associations, Research Papers I (H.M.S.O., London 1966).
[2] S. W. Lerner, 'Factory Agreements and National Bargaining in the British Engineering Industry', *International Labour Review* (I.L.O., Geneva, January 1964).

stances the unions came to see their industrial role as being to build up a countervailing power to that of the employer, by seeking control of the job on the shop floor and by bargaining to maintain or improve wages and conditions. The growth of collective bargaining machinery towards the end of the century signified the unions' willingness to deal with the employer as they found him, rather than to try to take over the enterprise. Politically, the unions could see little future in seeking radical structural changes in industry; such strength as they could muster they used mainly to obtain protective legislation as regards their members' safety at work and their own uncertain legal position.

As for the employers, though there were always some who were paternalistic and who felt ties of social obligation towards their employees, many regarded the contract of employment as constituting little more than the purchase of labour. Nearly all employers took it for granted that ownership and technical expertise gave them the right to run their establishments as they wished and that that right must be upheld. Many resented the activities and even the existence of trade unions.

Between 1910 and 1922 the surge of militancy associated with syndicalism, guild socialism and the shop stewards' movement, aimed at establishing a new form of industrial society, or at least obtaining shop-floor control of certain types of decision-making within the enterprise. Then, after militancy had been defeated by economic forces, came a quiescent period lasting until the second world war, followed by a period in which workers placed confidence in a combination of negotiation and joint consultation. Later came the growth of work-place bargaining, which gave workers more say in decisions taken in the enterprise. Until at least the mid-1960s the growth of work-place bargaining not only absorbed a great deal of unions' energies, but by giving them a means of increasing workers' influence and improving their conditions in the work-place, deflected them from seeking influence through more formal, structural means of participation. Meanwhile, the unions' political interest in industrial structure had centred on public ownership, though they found the form adopted after the great debate of the 1930s to be relatively unsatisfying in practice.

Employers' attitudes changed significantly from the first world war. The lessons learned from industrial psychology during the war, followed by the work of Elton Mayo and his school, convinced many employers that good human relations was good business. The 'human relations' school encouraged the belief that bad industrial relations, low morale and low labour efficiency merely signified that management were failing to meet workers' needs for information about the enterprise and to be treated as human beings. Such beliefs fitted comfortably with the belief that management and workers ought to function as a single team and that it was wrong to think of there being 'two sides' to industry. The goodwill and 'know-how' of workers could be harnessed through joint consultation and efficient communications.

But these beliefs did not satisfy the needs of an industrial world in which there was full employment and workshop bargaining conducted by powerful work-groups, and as the 1960s wore on they started to give place to the view, built on the work of behavioural scientists such as Maslow, Argyris, Likert, Mac-Gregor, Sayles and Herzberg, that organizational behaviour was 'the product of a complex system of interaction between a wide variety of determinants'.[1] In particular, involvement in productivity bargaining signified management's recognition that the power of the working group was such that managers were not free to deploy labour in the most efficient manner without the agreement of the working group.

Over the years the extent of workers' participation in industry has varied with the ebb and flow of ideas and economic and political forces. In the early part of the nineteenth century perhaps only a few groups of craftsmen exercised any great control over their work and conditions. At times like the first world war many workers exercised a considerable influence on managerial decisions. In the last thirty years, participation both through negotiation and through processes of consultation has undoubtedly increased. Its present extent and form will be analysed in the chapters that follow.

On the whole the employers' policies throughout the period surveyed here have been influenced by changing economic circumstances, by advancing technology and the growth in the size of organizations. They have been concerned with the rising

---

[1] J. Child, *British Management Thought: A Critical Analysis* (Allen and Unwin, London 1969). Concepts of management based on the more sophisticated approach are discussed in Chapter 7.

demands of the trade unions and the extension of collective bargaining in area and in scope. When employers have felt a social obligation to share some responsibility for managing the enterprise, or more usually their profit, with workers, or where employers have seen some form of participation as good for efficiency or industrial relations, or both, they have introduced a variety of schemes, but these have had little effect on industrial relations.

For workers and their organizations two clearly distinguishable alternative approaches have been followed, the one concerned with replacing the whole order of industry, the other concerned with achieving greater control of the job within the existing system. Which approach was followed depended on the prevailing economic and social climate.

2 The Forms of Participation Within the Enterprise

Consultation

Consultation takes place on an informal basis in most industrial organizations every day. It is the method by which, for instance, the supervisor seeks the views of those he supervises on a wide range of topics. Important, for example, in such informal consultation will be discussions on the nature of a particular task in hand, and the way it should be performed, the final decision being left to management. The range of topics dealt with and the value of such discussions are extremely difficult to quantify.

Informal consultation is usually contrasted with the process by which workers' representatives are invited to sit on joint worker-management committees; however, the range of topics discussed at the formal level is different in important respects from the issues that are the subject of daily task-centred consultation. The subjects of formal consultation are generally broad policy matters considered by management to be of common interest, and could involve all questions relating to efficiency and social issues, although excluding traditional areas of negotiation. In a major study[1] of formal consultation, the National Institute of Industrial Psychology considered this particular form of participation as a natural development from deputation and negotiation. Others saw formal joint consultation as a way of making the worker a full partner in industry.[2]

Paradoxically, the two conditions that were insisted upon in the establishment of formal joint consultation—no encroachment upon managerial rights, and no discussion of those topics that were generally considered to be within the usual ambit of

---

[1] National Institute of Industrial Psychology, *Joint Consultation in British Industry* (Staples Press, London 1952), p. 29.

[2] G. S. Walpole, *Management and Men* (Cape, London 1944).

negotiation[1]—led to what has been accepted as a decline in joint consultative committees. However, the data obtained from the surveys set out in Chapter 3 would seem to indicate a continuing, though limited, importance for formal consultation. The position might well not be as negative as considered by McCarthy, who stated that 'formally constituted joint meetings between management and unions at plant level, had become largely ritualistic and unimportant gatherings where the two sides met simply in order to register some of the agreements and disagreements that they had previously decided informally beforehand'.[2] However, because of the insistence that consultative committees should be advisory, and equally because of a growth in the power of the working group, and the working-group representatives, a decline of interest in consultative committees has resulted. For instance, in a Political and Economic Planning study, a shop steward's views on formal consultation were recorded:

> We did originally have joint consultation after the war. It started off full of enthusiasm and ideas but, gradually, as we met, probably once a fortnight or once a month, the ideas that were brought forward gradually petered out and simply came down in the end to the quality of the tea in the canteen or something of that trivial nature.[3]

More and more, shop stewards became interested in the type of discussion that would lead to decision-making—i.e. they were more interested in negotiation than consultation. McCarthy has summed up the paradox in the following way:

> . . . the notion of joint consultation involves a paradox which stewards naturally find it difficult to accept. It presupposes that there are some areas of management activity . . . which are fit and proper subjects of joint determination by collective bargaining; on the other hand there are other areas . . . which must remain the *exclusive* prerogative of management, although they may be discussed with

[1] See G. S. Walpole, *Methods of Stimulating Interest in Production*, reprint of an address given to the Institute of Labour Management Annual Conference (October 1943), p. 8. 'We do not even discuss such things more than we can possibly help, because they contain a hint of antagonised viewpoints which is unpleasant'.

[2] W. E. J. McCarthy, *The Role of Shop Stewards in British Industrial Relations*, Research Papers 1, Royal Commission on Trade Unions and Employers' Associations (H.M.S.O., London 1966), p. 31.

[3] Political and Economic Planning, *Attitudes in British Management* (P.E.P., London 1965), p. 83.

workers' representatives. Yet it is also assumed that the main advantage of holding such discussions is that in matters of this kind the interests of the two sides converge rather than conflict.... Thus we come to the paradox: ... we reach a position in which it is suggested that agreements are only possible when the two sides are basically opposed; when they are really united there cannot be any question of an agreement.[1]

So it has been said that formal joint consultation in the strict sense

... cannot survive the development of effective shop floor organization. Either (the consultative committees) must change their character and become essentially negotiating committees carrying out functions which are indistinguishable from the formal process of shop floor bargaining, or they are boycotted by shop stewards and, as the influence of the latter grows, fall into disuse.[2]

This process is reflected in the decline in the number of consultative committees. In engineering, for instance, the number of joint production committees in federated establishments fell by a third between 1955 and 1961.[3]

Another possible reason for the relative lack of success of formal joint consultation could be a failure to understand its intended purpose. A report of a Ministry of Labour Working Party of officials[4] claimed this to be the case, and felt that some people had mistakenly seen formal joint consultation mainly as a method of creating a common purpose, or as a medium for disseminating management decisions. In this report, an attempt was made to state the aims of formal joint consultation—'What it can do, in its generally accepted form, is to enable management to explain proposals to representatives or workers, to hear their reactions and in the light of discussion to reach firm decisions which take workers' views into full account'.[5] Even this stated purpose of consultation would do little to satisfy the needs of those workers' representatives who want to be fully involved in decision-making. Such workers might well feel that full involve-

[1] McCarthy, op. cit., pp. 35–6.
[2] McCarthy, op. cit., p. 33.
[3] A. I. Marsh, and E. E. Coker, 'Shop Steward Organisation in the Engineering Industry', *British Journal of Industrial Relations* (London, June 1963), p. 183.
[4] Ministry of Labour, *Attitudes to Efficiency* (H.M.S.O., London 1966), p. 22.
[5] Ibid., p. 22.

ment in decision-making could only result from collective bargaining and might see joint consultation as an institutional obstacle to social progress.

Successful participation through joint consultation rests on the acceptance by managers and workers of certain common assumptions about their respective roles. Managers must be prepared to provide workers with an opportunity to be effectively consulted. This means that they must ensure that an adequate machinery for consultation exists. This may be achieved in a variety of ways, but whatever method is agreed upon management must clearly demonstrate that they have enabled the machinery to work effectively be ensuring an adequate flow of information and by the nature of their decisions. Workers for their part must be prepared to accept that the decisions arrived at by management fully take into account their stated interests and that these are given appropriate weight. The readiness of workers to enter into this type of compact with management will depend upon their perception of the nature of the enterprise and the role of management. This will in turn depend on a range of past experience, the value system prevailing in the firm and the influence of external factors such as statutory requirements, and the political and economic environment.

Workers and their representatives become involved in joint decision-making, as a result of bargaining.[1] As the focus in this study is upon participation within the enterprise, it is necessary to exclude those levels of collective bargaining that take place outside the enterprise, although it should be remembered that they are a form of indirect participation through which workers exercise influence over decisions concerning wages and working conditions.

Bargaining within the enterprise has, over the last two decades, largely been associated with the growth in importance of a particular representative participant, the shop steward. This does not mean that bargaining with individual workers does not exist

[1] Bargaining has been defined as 'the process by which the antithetical interests of supply, and demand, or buyer and seller, are finally adjusted' so as to end 'in the act of exchange'. R. M. MacIver and C. M. Page, *Society* (Macmillan, London 1953). See also N. W. Chamberlain, *Collective Bargaining* (McGraw-Hill, New York 1951), H. M. Levinson, *Determining Forces in Collective Bargaining* (Wiley, New York 1966), A. Flanders, 'Collective Bargaining: a Theoretical Analysis', *British Journal of Industrial Relations*, Vol. 6, No. 1 (March 1968), pp. 1–26.

—indeed it takes place every time an individual worker argues over a piece-work price or time—but that for the workers the major forms of bargaining are those conducted by the shop steward.

The growth in the number of shop stewards is indicative of the increasing appeal of this method of participation. The authors of Research Paper 10 for the Royal Commission made an estimate that there were about 175,000 shop stewards in British industry at the time of writing. 'This represents an increase of about 14 per cent over the last ten years'.[1] Other estimates have been made of the number of shop stewards, varying between 90,000[2] and 200,000.[3] The most recently published estimate has been made by Goodman and Whittingham,[4] who put the number at 125,000–130,000.

The most important characteristic of shop-steward bargaining has been its conduct of intra-plant relations on an informal and flexible basis, with substantive rules being reduced to a minimum. As Marsh has said, 'Workplace bargaining is evidently an area for understandings, *ad hoc* decisions with representatives at many levels of management, and of the application of custom and practice'.[5]

This type of *ad hoc* bargaining and joint decision-making has been fostered by management, both in a passive and an active way, as will be seen below. Also, some types of wage-payment systems seem passively to encourage this type of bargaining.

Managements have in many cases actively encouraged workshop bargaining because they recognize the desirability of speedy settlement of problems that could possibly lead to a disruption of production. This is partly a criticism of the formal grievance machinery that has developed in various industries. The length of time needed for disputes to go through certain grievance machinery was set out in the Royal Commission Research Papers

[1] W. E. J. McCarthy and S. R. Parker, *Shop Stewards and Workshop Relations*, Research Papers 10, Royal Commission on Trade Unions and Employers' Associations (H.M.S.O., London 1968), p. 15.

[2] H. A. Clegg, A. J. Killick and R. Adams, *Trade Union Officers* (Blackwell, Oxford 1961).

[3] T.U.C., *Annual Report* (1960).

[4] J. F. B. Goodman and T. E. Whittingham, *Shop Stewards in British Industry* (McGraw-Hill, London 1969).

[5] A. I. Marsh, *Managers and Shop Stewards* (Institute of Personnel Management, London 1963), p. 10.

2, Part 2.[1] It was estimated that for a grievance to be processed through the Engineering Procedure Agreement from works conference to central conference (if it went all the way) would take an average of thirteen weeks. Delays have been aggravated by the increase in numbers of disputes that are passing through procedure.[2] The evidence of Research Paper 2, Part 2, would seem to suggest, however, that engineering was slower than other industries in this respect. Nevertheless, any delay in dealing with issues arising is likely to be seen as acting in favour of management, as in the vast majority of cases issues are raised by workers. On the other hand, delaying tactics by management could result in a stiffened attitude on the part of workers' representatives, leading to increased militancy. Under conditions of full employment unofficial pressures have come to be a force to be reckoned with, and some managements have reacted by by-passing formal procedures when such pressures are applied. By-passing may take the form of instituting face-to-face confrontation between managers and the working group, incidentally creating further opportunities for participation.

Where the use of grievance procedures has increased it has imposed an additional strain upon the traditional system of industrial relations. Many local union officials are now unable to cope adequately with the increasing number of cases they are called on to deal with. Consequently, management has turned more and more towards the union representative within the enterprise, i.e. the shop-steward. By doing so, managements have accepted and fostered the bargaining role of the shop steward, by recognizing him as the most important representative of workers' opinions and, as such, a necessary participant in certain areas of decision-making. The research carried out for the Donovan Commission by the Government Social Survey indicates two ways by which managements have encouraged the activities of shop stewards.

72 per cent of stewards said they had 'unofficial' ways of approaching management, and almost all of them thought these were very important. Almost half who had a foreman said they could by-pass him if they needed, and a quarter claimed to be able to approach top

[1] A. I. Marsh and W. E. J. McCarthy, *Disputes Procedures in Britain*, Research Papers 2 (Part 2), Royal Commission on Trade Unions and Employers' Associations (H.M.S.O., London 1968), p. 22.
[2] Ibid., p. 28, Table 10.

management without going through the lower levels. More members usually approached the steward first with a union problem than the foreman.[1]

Secondly, managers were asked whether they would prefer to deal with shop-stewards or full-time union officials to solve a problem that might have arisen. The answer showed that 70 per cent of managers working in organizations that had shop-stewards preferred to deal with them, rather than with the appropriate full-time union official.[2]

The acceptance of the role of the shop-steward has not, however, led to a vast range of decisions being considered acceptable for collective bargaining. According to data published by the Royal Commission, the main areas of bargaining were wages and working conditions; 73 per cent of stewards claimed to be involved in dealing with working conditions and 56 per cent with wage issues, as standard practice.[3] These are areas of special importance to the steward's constituents, and it is not surprising, therefore, that stewards felt that an extension of their bargaining role in them was important. According to the same survey, 25 per cent of the shop-stewards wanted to extend their area of interest to financial policy and 23 per cent to discipline.[4] These new areas of interest have traditionally been considered to be within the ambit of unilateral management decision-making, and attempts to extend bargaining into new areas might often result in conflict before bargaining becomes the accepted practice.

During the last decade, a major innovation has occurred in collective bargaining practices with the advent of productivity bargaining, and this has undoubtedly resulted in a greater emphasis upon participation in the bargaining process, and in a wider range of decisions being made as a result of collective bargaining.

Apart from the main aim of enhancing efficiency, a growing number of enterprises have seen productivity bargaining as a means of achieving two goals—a rational wage structure related to productivity, and a means by which work-groups can participate actively in problem-solving. Indeed, productivity bargaining

[1] Government Social Survey, *Workplace Industrial Relations* (H.M.S.O., London 1968), p. 3.
[2] Ibid., p. 86 (para. 4.87).
[3] Research Papers 10, op. cit., p. 83 (Table 8).
[4] Government Social Survey, *Workplace Industrial Relations* (H.M.S.O., London 1968), p. 62.

has induced managements that have never before done so to invite workers to participate in making changes in working arrangements. It has also led to managements giving workers a great deal more information about the workings of the enterprise than has previously been the case. Though it is a by-product rather than the main aim, the stress often placed upon the participative role of the work-group and the individual is well illustrated by a statement made by E. W. Allsop (Employee Relations Manager, Mobil Oil Co.): 'Having identified his/our objective, we do not tell the employee how it must be achieved. We ask him whether he accepts the objective for himself. If so, we then invite him to work with us freely and equally to find ways and means by which the objective can be achieved—we call this participative management.'[1] The Confederation of British Industry has also stressed the need for involvement: 'It is important for the success of a productivity agreement that all levels of management and workpeople should be consulted at each stage of the negotiation and implementation of a productivity bargain in order that the implications of the proposed changes might be fully understood.'[2]

A further example of the greater extent of involvement resulting from productivity bargaining is given by the 'Midlands Shop Stewards Group' in their evidence to the Donovan Commission: 'Those of us involved ... found negotiations led to an involvement on a scale never experienced before on that site.'[3]

This need for consultation and involvement of workers seems to suggest that a management claim to manage regardless of views held by employees would be both ineffective when faced with restrictive practices, and inefficient in the use of labour. management is in no position to impose its will simply by claiming the right to manage.[4] This does not mean to say that

M

---

[1] From G. Llywelyn Jones, 'Guidelines in Productivity Bargaining', reprinted by *Personnel* (Business Publications, 1967).

[2] Confederation of British Industry, *Productivity Bargaining* (C.B.I., May 1968).

[3] Midland Shop Stewards Study Group, *Trade Unions at the Crossroads* (1966), p. 9.

[4] A. Flanders, *Fawley Productivity Agreements* (Faber, London 1964), p. 234. See Royal Commission Research Papers 4, p. 4, for the argument that, because of the shift in the balance of power, managements 'have to share with employees the right to reach decisions on matters on which previously they had been able to exercise the right unilaterally'. See also Engineering Employers' Federation, *Productivity Bargaining in the Engineering Industry* (E.E.F., London 1968), where

productivity bargaining is an abdication of managerial responsibilities—the success of most productivity agreements has depended upon managements being prepared to work out all the implications of the proposed changes and to put forward practical proposals. It is only after this stage, when management are fully able to discuss the implications of their proposals, that they can turn their attention to negotiating an agreement.

As was stated at the beginning of this discussion of productivity bargaining, there has been an extension of topics dealt with by collective bargaining, resulting from discussion of the relationship between the individual worker and productivity. This has meant that working practices, rules and customs, levels of overtime, and the use of machinery have been deemed bargainable, in an attempt by managements to remove impediments to increased productivity. It is at this point that a certain paradox becomes apparent. Workers' maintenance of impediments to efficient productivity has given them a bargaining position that has made it possible for them to exact a price for giving them up. Yet one of the managerial aims in initiating productivity agreements has been to gain control over the production process, and the payment system; thereby ostensibly eliminating the means by which workers had hitherto been able to influence managerial decisions. Despite the seemingly participative nature of productivity bargaining, implementation of productivity agreements might result in a decrease rather than an increase in future possibilities for participation, unless specific provision were made for the joint regulation of the agreement.

Worker Decision-Making

In the Introduction, reference was made to two types of situation in which workers might unilaterally make 'managerial' decisions: one such situation can be regarded as that of 'suggestions', in that workers are making decisions within parameters which are acceptable to management, since they facilitate the achievement of managerially designed goals for the enterprise; the other type, in contrast, carries constraint of management freedom to the point where the decisions which are designed to

---

it is suggested that productivity bargaining 'involves an acceptance not merely in intellectual but in emotional terms of the inescapability of shared responsibility with regard to efficient manpower utilisation and the effort–wage bargain' (p. 29).

achieve the goals of the workers are in direct conflict with those of management. In a given situation a particular pattern of work regulations imposed may contain both elements. In the newspaper printing industry, for example, unions unilaterally impose a range of restrictive practices which are tolerated by management, since even with them it has been possible to produce a newspaper profitably. It would be possible for management to refuse to accept the continuance of these practices as being in conflict with its economic goals, but the price of eliminating them might be so high that the cost would exceed the benefit.[1]

Unilaterally imposed worker practices may take the form of a long-established set of conventions and customs, which in many cases are either tacitly accepted or ignored by management. Where there is not willing acceptance, workers might be able to enforce traditional modes of behaviour through their collective strength. Custom and practice gives workers an opportunity to make a whole range of decisions relating to their task environment. For instance, decisions about the type of labour to be employed, the skill requirements for particular jobs, and the manning scales to be followed, are not infrequently unilaterally decided and enforced by the collective strength of the workers.

The restrictions imposed by workers on managerial freedom to make decisions constitute an important element in the power struggle between unions and employers. These accepted ways of working, the normative rules regulating the method of carrying out a task, acquire a value to workers that has been likened to a property right.[2] The significance of these 'restrictive practices' to management and to the collective bargaining process has been noted in the discussion of the development of productivity bargaining. Since the lifting of the restrictions imposed by workers is a necessary preliminary to the more efficient utilization of manpower, this step has been a major issue in the negotiation of most productivity agreements.

The removal of such practices has generally been secured at the cost of increased wages. The effect of giving up an established

[1] For a discussion of the economic and social aspects of restrictive practices, together with detailed examples, see Royal Commission on Trade Unions and Employers' Associations, Research Papers 4, *Restrictive Labour Practices*; see also *Report* of the Royal Commission on the Press, 1962.
[2] See R. Holmes, 'The Ownership of Work: A Psychological Approach', *British Journal of Industrial Relations*, Vol. V, No. 1 (March 1967).

restrictive practice is to weaken the bargaining power of the union, but it is generally compensated for by the development of a wider participative role through problem-solving and long-term arrangements.

The second function of restrictive practices, to secure a measure of job security, is fairly well documented in studies of workers' attitudes to technical change. For example, it has been said that, 'Opposition to technical change, where it exists, is almost solely a fear that it will cause unemployment';[1] or, as put another way, 'the most important factor in shaping the reactions to change, is the degree of economic security which the worker feels',[2] and finally a comment from a worker which was recorded in the P.E.P. report cited earlier, 'Naturally, if there's no orders in hand, a man says to himself, "If I work harder what's going to be the result? I'm going to work myself on to the Labour Exchange two months, maybe four months, sooner than I would if I could just carry on and work at the speed I'm doing".[3] Many restrictive practices have existed even through heavy unemployment (which may indeed have made it seem more than ever important to uphold them), but it has been suggested that some important practices are of comparatively recent origin.[4]

It is not the present purpose to examine whether restrictive practices as a form of worker decision-making achieve their dual purpose of increasing wages and job security, but to illustrate how through the effective application of restrictive practices decisions concerning manpower utilization may be determined in important respects unilaterally by the working group.

So far, consultation, bargaining and the imposition of restrictive practices have been examined separately; however, it must be emphasized that each method is part of the total system of industrial relations and does not exist completely independently. The process of decision-making can be influenced by a number of variables, some of which can be regarded as 'organizational' in that they are characteristics of the enterprise, and others as 'environmental' in that they can signify the influencing factors

[1] O. Banks, *The Attitudes of Steelworkers to Technical Change* (Liverpool University Press, 1960), p. 125.
[2] A. Touraine *et al.*, *Workers' Attitudes to Technical Change: an integrated survey of research* (O.E.C.D., Paris 1965), p. 8.
[3] op. cit., p. 76.
[4] Royal Commission Research Papers 4, op. cit., p. 4.

that result from viewing the enterprise as part of a wider social system.

It is necessary to remember that decisions themselves are of different types, and are of different orders of importance to workers. It would be exceptional if workers were as interested in a decision to appoint an overseas agent as they would be in a decision to close a production line. A managing director's decisions are likely to be more far-reaching than a foreman's. Desire to participate, ability to participate, and possible forms of participation will obviously vary according to these factors. The degree of interest taken by a worker will also be related to the personality of each worker concerned. More importantly, it will also be related to the role of the worker as an employee and as a union member or shop steward.

Organizational Variables

Four such variables—degree of unionization, size of enterprise, type of industry and form of ownership—have been assumed by the authors to be particularly important in relation to their possible impact upon opportunities for participative decision-making.

The degree of unionization is clearly a factor of major importance in determining the pattern of participation within an enterprise. From direct evidence it would seem to be not without significance that the best-known examples of constitutionally established industrial democracy, schemes of co-partnership and profit-sharing, have been established either in the absence of strong unionization or as an induced alternative to its development. However, the absence of unionization is not itself any guarantee that forms of participation alternative to collective bargaining and the development of systems of joint regulation will be established. Nevertheless some form of participation in the making of managerial decisions as they affect the carrying out of tasks will exist even in the most autocratically managed establishment, but these may be restricted to the minimum that is functionally necessary.

The more highly unionized a plant the more likely that a range of decisions will be decided through collective bargaining processes. Joint consultation may also exist, and, as will be shown, is of some supplementary importance.

The higher the degree of union organization, also, the more

likely it is that workers on the shop floor will have secured the power to make decisions unilaterally. Or, put another way, the more likely it is that management will have ceded, if only implicitly, its right to decide certain matters, thus accepting as a practical necessity the ability of shop stewards to impose certain restrictive practices.

It is possible that in the future participation through worker-directors nominated by unions, following the pattern which already exists in the steel industry, will be developed on a wider scale, in both the public and private sectors. This possibility and the issues to which it gives rise will be further discussed in Chapter 6.

The effect of size would seem to be of special importance since it is amply substantiated that in very small units of organization there are closer contacts between workers and managers, more mutual understanding and less institutionalized conflict. This is because it is easier to develop mutual confidence, communications are better and matters at issue can be more speedily resolved through close personal contact. In the very large concern employing many thousands close relations between higher management and workers are virtually impossible. Some evidence of the consequences of size will be discussed in Chapter 4.

In recent years great emphasis has been placed upon the relevance of technology to decision-making. While Woodward, for instance, has examined its importance in relation to organization structure,[1] others[2] have viewed technology as a major source of alienation, because of the limited job autonomy that is possible within some systems of technology, particularly those involved in mass production. The degree to which technology can determine role-content and role-means becomes important in relation to the discussion of those forms of horizontal participation[3] that attempt to widen the scope of task-based decision-making by workers.

---

[1] J. Woodward, *Industrial Organisation*: *Theory and Practice* (Oxford University Press, London 1965). Work done at the Tavistock Institute of Human Relations (see Chapter 6) has emphasized that the enterprise should be viewed as a socio-technical system.

[2] For example, R. Blauner, *Alienation and Freedom* (Chicago University Press 1964).

[3] One may distinguish between 'horizontal' participation, relating generally to decisions concerning the immediate task or environment of workers, and 'vertical' participation, generally involving collective policy issues and ex-

Despite the limited skill-content of some jobs within certain systems of technology, these same systems can be beneficial to particular groups of workers who hold strategic positions within the production process, and may thereby be enabled to exert considerable influence upon decision-making. The bargaining strength of particular groups of workers, employed, for example, on a car-assembly line, has often been discussed in this respect. As the cost of non-co-operation increases, the need for management to improve the extent of participation may seem a necessary alternative to costly stoppages.

Technology can also be important in determining the level of worker–management discussion, and the subject-matter discussed. In some cases the particular technology will remove the need for close supervision of shop-floor workers, and thereby reduce the extent of discussion between the worker and his supervisor. Then, too, the area of possible conflict over disciplinary matters is reduced.

Enterprises using advanced and complex technologies are likely to employ a labour force of an educationally higher level than those which use older and more simple technologies. It has been observed that more highly educated workers are more concerned about participation and more ready to accept a wider span of job responsibility than workers who are less well educated and trained. As the ratio of capital employed increases and the degree of integration of production processes extends, the significance of autonomous individual and work-group decisions grows.

These few examples show the importance that must be attached to technology as a characteristic of the enterprise in a discussion of participation. It was not practicable, unfortunately, to examine systematically the significance of technological factors within the sample of firms examined in this study.

It is often argued that certain types of ownership are more likely than others to increase workers' participation in management. If the capital of a firm is owned in whole or part by its workers, and managed therefore, in the interest of the workers, it is not unreasonable to expect the firm to be more participative than one in which the capital is owned by hundreds of outside shareholders, and run in their interests. Evidence relating to this

tending to processes which help to set or shape the overall goals of the enterprise.

assumption will be shown where the extent of participation in firms with profit-sharing is compared with that in respondent firms as a whole. It is also not unreasonable to expect that the ideology of profit-sharing, with its emphasis on the role of the worker, might be reflected in decision-making by the provision of formal structures for contact between management and worker. In the group responding to this enquiry there were 131 firms with profit-sharing schemes; it was therefore possible to examine them separately in this respect.[1]

Profit-sharing and co-partnership schemes as a means of identifying the worker with his firm have often been criticized by trade unions, mainly because the philosophy of such schemes often takes little account of competing interests. So, in their evidence to the Royal Commission, the Transport and General Workers' Union said:

> It is not our opinion that profit-sharing and co-partnership schemes have any appreciable effect on relations between management and employees, except in so far as the issue of special shares or the payment of a bonus upon profit is used, or is believed by the employees to be used, as a means of inhibiting freedom of action on their part.[2]

To varying extents, size, technology, unionization and ownership can be objectively measured; such a claim cannot be made as easily for another factor, management style, which might influence the opportunities for participation. Nevertheless, the adoption of a particular management style is extremely relevant in this respect.

Whereas one management might follow a style that laid stress upon collective bargaining, another might reject this concept of industrial relations in favour of a consultative system, or some combination of both styles. Whatever the general style of management, it would be incorrect to think of managers within a particular organization as homogeneous. One study of industrial leadership has noted four different styles among managers, which are described as 'tells', 'sells', 'consults' and 'joins'.[3]

[1] Of the 131 firms, 48 excluded manual workers, and 14 excluded administrative, clerical and technical staff from membership of schemes.

[2] Transport and General Workers' Union, *Written Evidence to Royal Commission on Trade Unions and Employers' Associations* (1966), p. 19.

[3] P. J. Sadler, *Leadership Style, Confidence in Management and Job Satisfaction* (Ashridge Management College, 1966).

Which of these styles is followed by a particular management or manager will clearly affect the opportunities for participation. The significance of a participative style of management is discussed further in Chapter 7.

Environmental Influences

The enterprise cannot simply be analyzed in terms of a closed system; decision-making behaviour will be influenced by external economic and social factors. In this context, it is possible to do no more than briefly discuss the influence of environment on attitudes towards participation as an important social variable.

The influence of the social environment on patterns of industrial relations has been emphasized in the models of industrial relations systems developed by John Dunlop,[1] and others. It is likely, though it was not possible to carry this investigation far enough to provide evidence for the view, that the great changes in the social environment—in the class structure, the education systems and attitudes to authority—are having an important effect on the relations between workers and managers. Since the expectations and perceptions of workers and managers are greatly influenced by their experiences in the wider society, these factors must be regarded as having a considerable bearing on the propensity to develop a participative behaviour pattern.

With the advance of technology, and rising affluence, workers have become more independent and more assertive of their perceived rights. Thus the immediate effects have been to stimulate conflict and to encourage aggressive collective bargaining. At the same time management has become more vulnerable to the economic pressure workers are capable of asserting, and more conscious of the social concern with democratic values. These changes in social attitudes have also greatly influenced the behaviour of political parties, which have inevitably responded to them by moving towards changes in the legal framework of industrial organization in both the public and private sectors.

The emphasis given by the Donovan Commission, followed by both the Labour Party's proposals and the 1971 Industrial Relations Act, has favoured the extension of participation through the development of the collective bargaining system at the level of

[1] J. Dunlop, *Industrial Relations Systems* (Henry Holt, New York, 1958).

company and establishment. The philosophy behind this trend has been a desire to strengthen the authority of central union organizations and to make union organizations at the enterprise level observe agreements and rules. This trend of development, though seen to be desirable in reducing the number of unofficial strikes, might be at the expense of restricting the degree of work-place participation through union sponsored activities.

The growth of schemes of employee participation in a number of European countries has clearly been stimulated by a belief that collective bargaining does not provide an adequate method of participation. Though to some degree participation through works councils and company supervisory boards has been seen as an alternative to collective bargaining, these developments have also been seen as a support to weak trade unions. However, even where trade unionism has been traditionally strong, such as in Norway and Sweden, interest in alternate forms of workers' participation has grown as collective bargaining has increasingly failed to satisfy critical employee and community needs.

Social attitudes and values are thus bound to influence the views, opinions and behaviour of management towards the process of decision-making and those areas which might be regarded as legitimate for workers' participation. Equally workers might consider greater involvement more desirable in the future than in the past and more necessary to achieve their economic and social aims.

There has been much discussion of the effect of increasing affluence on the attitudes and behaviour of workers. The argument whether wage earners are acquiring the attributes of the middle-class employee as they attain 'middle-class' levels of income and conditions of employment is by no means settled. Nor is the argument that 'white collar' workers, who are shedding their traditional attitudes to trade unions, collective bargaining and willingness to strike, are losing their middle-class social attributes.

Changes in the level of education will exert a growing influence on the behaviour of both workers and management in a variety of ways. As the labour force becomes increasingly composed of white-collar workers it is likely that they will become more widely concerned with issues of status and authority within the enterprise. It is possible that as the educational level of workers rises they will show an increasing concern to participate in the decisions which have an immediate effect on their status and economic well-being. On the other hand, an alternate consequence of these changes might be a level of militancy and aggressiveness which makes participation more difficult, but also a more necessary activity.

Changes in the labour market brought about by changes in the general economic climate, but more particularly by changes in the structure of industry, have a powerful effect on the desire and willingness to participate in management decision-making. The growth in the significance of the shop steward and the shift of collective bargaining to the work-place has been related to the maintenance of full employment. It would be manifestly more difficult for workers to participate in decisions to increase the efficiency of the enterprise in conditions of economic depression if this were at the expense of the jobs of some of their number. Nevertheless, it is precisely this kind of situation which presents the ultimate challenge to the concept of workers' participation, and it has to be met. There is, in fact, plenty of evidence that through the collective bargaining process, redundancy, regrading and other changes which involve decisions that have an adverse effect on some workers can be made and accepted. In the last resort neither workers nor management can resist the pressures on their behaviour which are generated by the environment in which the enterprise exists. Making the adjustments in organizational patterns required to accommodate behaviour that is being conditioned by the environment is, however, a task that is not always quickly or easily accomplished. It is particularly difficult when the interests concerned are deeply entrenched in organizational structures as firmly established as trade unions, business enterprises and governmental institutions.

3 The Extent of Participative Machinery

In the last chapter the main forms in which workers or their representatives are involved in managerial decision-making within the enterprise, namely consultation, bargaining and unilateral regulation of work and the factors that were most probably having an important influence upon them were discussed. In this chapter, these forms will be considered at greater length, in the light of their present extent and incidence and of recent experience. First, however, it is necessary to describe the method by which new information concerning participation in the enterprise was obtained for the present study.

The Survey

Examination of the information available concerning workers' participation in decision-making within the enterprise showed that there was a lack of factual detail. Surveys carried out for the Royal Commission on Trade Unions and Employers' Associations, for instance, contained much that was of interest but little that bore directly on some aspects of concern in this study. No detailed information was available about the extent or operation of collective bargaining machinery in the enterprise, nor about the extent to which other provisions are made through which workers might influence different types of managerial decisions. The last enquiry of any size about joint consultative machinery was conducted in 1948–50.[1]

In view of this lack of information it was decided to try to obtain a degree of factual information by a postal questionnaire to a representative sample of private firms and public enterprises.

[1] National Institute of Industrial Psychology, *Joint Consultation in British Industry* (Staples Press, London, 1952).

Since resources were limited it was necessary to confine the survey to employers. It was also necessary to limit the enquiry to as small a range of questions as possible in order to secure a reasonable response. It was hoped that even with these limitations the enquiry would provide a sufficient degree of information as to indicate the situation prevailing in Britain at the time the study was made.

The aim of the survey was to find out by what procedures, in which areas, and to how great an extent employees participated through the various means available. Factual information was therefore sought on trade union membership, on the existence of formal joint committees (both those meeting regularly for the purposes of negotiation and consultation, and those for dealing with specific topics); on profit sharing provisions and on suggestion schemes. Questions were asked about the degree to which employees would be able to influence twelve key areas of management decision-making. Information was also sought about the firms' recent experience of a strike or of restrictive practices. In order to obtain some impression both of the way in which the machinery was working and of managerial attitudes, separate questions were included about the effectiveness of the respective formal arrangements and about the methods used to communicate information to employees.

The questionnaire was devised in consultation with a number of firms and, in its final form, distributed by post in the autumn of 1968. For reasons of practicality it was decided to limit the main survey to the private sector of manufacturing, construction and transport.

The list of enterprises to be approached was that maintained by the then Ministry of Labour, which assisted in the drawing up of the sample. This was designed to give optimum coverage in relation to employing power while still reflecting adequately the characteristics of different sizes of firms. It included one in 20 of firms employing less than 100 workers; one in 16 of firms employing between 100 and 499; one in ten of firms employing between 500 and 999 and one in two of firms employing 2,000 or over.

The number of firms in the resultant sample was 1,562.

The initial response to the enquiry brought 513 replies (34 per cent) and this increased to 716 (46 per cent) following a first reminder and to 790 (just over 50 per cent) after a second reminder.

Of the final replies 649 (equivalent to a 41.5 per cent response rate) were usable. The 649 firms employed 845,024 employees; the industrial breakdown is given in Table 1.

Table 1   Industrial Coverage of Final Sample

Industrial Order		Number of Firms
III	Food, drink and tobacco	46
IV	Chemicals and allied industries	39
V	Metal manufacture	45
VI	Engineering and electrical goods	164
VII	Shipbuilding and marine engineering	13
VIII	Vehicles	28
IX	Metal goods not elsewhere specified	30
X & XI	Textiles and leather	52
XII	Clothing and footwear	53
XIII	Bricks, pottery, glass, etc.	15
XIV	Timber, furniture, etc.	15
XV	Paper, printing and publishing	45
XVI	Other manufacturing industries	24
XVII	Construction	52
XIX	Transport and communication	25
	Not classified	3
		649

Table 2 indicates the distribution of the final sample by size of firm.

Table 2   Size of Firms in Sample

Size of Firm	Number of Firms	Percentage of Total
Under 100	160	25
100 – 499	245	38
500 – 999	64	10
1,000 – 1,999	68	10
2,000 – and over	112	17

Responses proved to be heavily dependent on size of firm, ascending almost directly from 22 per cent for the firms employing under 100 workers to 96 per cent for firms employing 2,000 or over.

It was thought possible that the results might be distorted by many of the small firms being part of large organizations. This proved not to be the case: in fact it was found that the large firms were the more likely to be part of larger organizations (94 per cent of firms employing more than 2,000 compared with 38 per cent employing under 100). 69 per cent of all the respondent firms were part of larger organizations.

Since response to the questionnaire was based upon the perceptions of individual managers, whose assessments of the facts might be influenced by their own value judgements, it was necessary to make some check on the accuracy of the returns. Visits to 28 respondent firms, selected to give a rough cross section of the respondents as a whole, provided such a check. During these visits, every opportunity was taken to discuss replies with as many interested parties as possible. These visits provided sufficient information to suggest that the questionnaires had been completed with a substantial degree of accuracy.

It is a well known hazard of surveys that respondents tend to give undue weight to what they believe to be the most socially acceptable view when replying to questions. Although it was believed that there was a likelihood of this phenomenon affecting some of the replies to this survey, unfortunately it was not possible to obtain an accurate check on this source of bias. However the opinion was formed that it had not had any appreciable effect on the results.

To add to understanding of the position, limited enquiries were made of workers' experiences and attitudes in respect of participation in five establishments. The outcome of these enquiries also tended to confirm the general accuracy of the main survey results.

In view of the size and significance of nationalized industries and the development of thinking about participation linked with industrialization in Britain, it was decided also to extend the survey to the publicly owned industries. All of the major nationalized industries were covered, except the newly re-nationalized steel industry, which was omitted because at the time the enquiry was made the firms concerned had not been withdrawn from the private sector sample. Each of the nationalized industries which was approached co-operated and questionnaires of the form used in the main enquiry were completed in respect of establishments selected to represent a cross section of each industry's activities.

In the public sector, 22 manufacturing establishments in gas and electricity employing 27,617 were covered and 49 transport establishments employing 83,134. Four areas of the National

Coal Board, and 3 departments of the B.B.C. were also included, giving a total of 115,833 employees. Three of the establishments employed fewer than 100 workers; 36 employed between 100 and 499, 21 between 500 and 999; 11 between 1,000 and 1,999 and 7 employed 2,000 or over.

There were differences in the methods of sampling used for the private and public sector surveys. There are also differences between the private and public sectors in such relevant factors as the levels at which decisions are taken, as mentioned in Chapter 4. For these reasons the two surveys made are not wholly comparable and accordingly greater emphasis is given to the main survey, relating to the private sector. These differences should be borne in mind where comparisons are offered with the public sector.

Through the survey it was hoped to gain some idea of the extent to which a number of variables might be related to different types of participation. However, owing to the strictly limited nature of the survey it was recognized it would not be possible to do more than give a tentative indication of the importance of factors the authors believed might be of special significance. These were assumed to be the degree of unionization, the size of the firm, the type of industry, and the provision of opportunities by companies for their employees to share in the profits. More subtle, but perhaps equally important influences such as the attitudes and styles of management unfortunately could only be explored to a very limited extent within the scope of the postal survey.

The results of the survey will be discussed in this chapter and those that follow. In the present chapter attention is focused on the main forms of participation—consultation, bargaining and unilateral regulation by workers—and their extent.

Trade-Union Membership

Nationally the overall percentage of all employees who were in trade unions, excluding professional associations, in 1964, was 42.6 per cent. The distribution of this membership varies greatly between industries and between different grades of occupation.[1]

---

[1] See G. Bain, *Trade Union Growth and Recognition*, Research Papers 6, Royal Commission on Trade Unions and Employers' Associations; *The Growth of White-Collar Unionism* (Oxford University Press, 1970).

It also varies greatly between firms; unfortunately there are no national statistics that would show the density of union organization by enterprise or plant. In Table 3 the degree of trade union membership is given in general terms as it was returned by the firms in the private sector completing the questionnaire in this survey.

Each firm was asked to estimate the extent to which it was

Table 3   Estimated Extent of Trade-Union Membership in Firms

What is your estimate of the extent of trade union membership among your:	None		Small: up to $\frac{1}{3}$ of employees		Moderate: between $\frac{1}{3}$ and $\frac{2}{3}$ of employees		Substantial: above $\frac{2}{3}$ of employees		A condition of engagement	
	Number of firms	%	Number of firms	%	Number of firms	%	Number of firms	%	Number of firms	%
(i) Male manual workers	76	12	115	18	84	13	261	40	113	18
(ii) Female manual workers	204	34	88	15	72	12	153	26	77	13
(iii) Administrative and clerical staff	437	68	112	17	62	10	24	4	10	2
(iv) Technical staff	357	57	124	20	58	9	68	11	22	3
(v) Supervisors	361	56	137	21	53	8	60	9	28	4

To ascertain the variation of union membership with size of firm the proportions were calculated against size, for the most highly organized group —male manual workers—as shown in Table 4.

Table 4   Estimated Extent of Trade-Union Membership among Male Manual Workers, Related to Size of Firm

Size of firm	None		Small: up to $\frac{1}{3}$ of employees		Moderate: between $\frac{1}{3}$ and $\frac{2}{3}$ of employees		Substantial: above $\frac{2}{3}$ of employees		A condition of engagement	
	Number of firms	%	Number of firms	%	Number of firms	%	Number of firms	%	Number of firms	%
Under 100	48	30	46	29	15	9	29	18	22	14
100 – 499	26	11	52	21	43	18	78	32	46	19
500 – 999	1	1	13	20	8	13	36	55	6	11
1,000 – 1,999	1	1	3	2	8	12	38	56	18	27
2,000 and over	0	0	2	2	10	9	80	72	20	17

unionized. Unfortunately it was not possible to check the accuracy of these estimates. However, it is unlikely that inquiry of the unions themselves would have produced more reliable figures, since most unions do not have detailed membership figures by firms.

The picture that emerges suggests that trade-union organization was very weak in about one-third of the companies so far as male manual workers were concerned, and in about half of the companies employing female manual workers. However, when the size of the firms was taken into account the number of workers who would be affected by trade-union activity would be much greater than suggested by this table. This would be true of administrative, clerical, technical and supervisory grades, though the density of trade unionism in these firms, as is the case in the national picture, was apparently much lower than for manual workers. These categories are, however, joining trade unions in increasing numbers. It is possible, if union recognition becomes enforceable by law in the future, that within a very few years there will be a dramatic rise in the proportion of such staff organized.

While there was a close relation between the size of firms and the extent of union organization, it is interesting to note that union membership as a condition of employment was distributed rather evenly across the different size groups.

The numbers of trade unions that respondents believed had membership amongst their manual workers were:

Table 5   Numbers of Trade Unions in Firms

Number of trade unions	Private sector		Public sector	
	Numbers	%	Numbers	%
Under 6	426	77	55	73
6 – 10	111	17	17	22
11 – 15	21	3	1	2
Over 15	14	3	2	3

The main Nationalization Acts contained injunctions to the Boards and Corporations they set up to establish machinery for negotiation and consultation with bodies representative of organized workers. It was therefore not surprising to find from the survey that none of the establishments covered reported estimated union membership amongst male manual workers of less than two-thirds, and the remaining 18 per cent reported having a closed shop.

Formal Machinery

All firms who were members of employers' associations would be covered by the agreements negotiated for their industry, and would be direct or indirect participants in that industry's machinery. However, the survey sought to obtain an indication of the proportion of firms who had formally constituted their own joint bodies for either consultation or negotiation, or both.[1]

(1) *Any Formal Committees*

Of the 649 firms that replied to the questionnaire, 258 (39.4 per cent) apparently had no formal machinery of any character. The proportion without any committees either for negotiation and consultation, for consultation alone, or for negotiation alone, seems large in view of the growth of plant and company negotiations, but, as is well known, much plant and company bargaining takes place on an informal and continuing basis without formal procedures and without the signing of formal agreements.

The survey showed clearly that as firms grow larger they are more disposed to establish machinery for bargaining and/or consultation. Compared with 11 per cent of those firms employing more than 2,000, 45 per cent of those employing 100–500 and 68 per cent of those employing fewer than 100 had no formal machinery.

When the degree of unionization is examined, this, as might well be expected, turns out to be closely related to the establishment of formal machinery. Of the firms with fewer than one-third of their male manual workers unionized, 66 per cent had no formal bodies, compared with 25 per cent of those firms where unionization was greater than two-thirds. The main reason for the absence of any negotiating and or consultative committees

---

[1] Had it been possible to ask the unions to confirm the results, differences might have emerged, since there is reason to believe that management and unions do not always see eye to eye on whether a particular machinery exists or procedure is normally followed. These differences arise out of differences of perception and sometimes actual knowledge.

where there are low levels of unionization is probably lack of pressure from the union members and a reluctance on the part of management to encourage bargaining where it does not exist. It is necessary to emphasize that the absence of formal machinery is not evidence of an absence of participation, which may be taking place in other ways.

Inter-industry comparisons were also made to see whether certain industries were more likely than others to be lacking in formal machinery.[1] Reasons for the lack of formal machinery varied; in some industries, for example, small units predominate, and, as has been said, smaller firms are less likely to have formalized committees to deal with industrial-relations problems. In other industries, national negotiations might deal with many detailed problems, and thereby limit the scope for intra-firm negotiation. For these reasons no clear-cut pattern emerged.

(2) Consultative Committees

The major weaknesses of formal joint consultation have been outlined in some detail in Chapter 2: namely, that such bodies have limited or no executive power, and that workers' representatives tend to gravitate towards bodies or situations where decision-making can take place, and therefore often take relatively little interest in the working of consultative committees. The decline and eventual demise of consultative committees have been predicted; but the evidence set out below indicates that at the moment consultative committees have by no means disappeared. No attempt was made in this survey to estimate the viability or otherwise of consultative committees, by asking about the period of time a consultative committee had existed, or whether a previously existing committee had fallen into disuse.

In a survey conducted in the late 1940s, the National Institute of Industrial Psychology sent a questionnaire to all the 4,719 manufacturing establishments then employing more than 250 people. Of the 751 who replied, 545 (72.6 per cent) had some form of joint consultation.[2]

---

[1] Central Statistical Office, *Standard Industrial Classification* (H.M.S.O., London 1968). Use was made of the Industrial Orders for purposes of analysis.

[2] National Institute of Industrial Psychology, *Joint Consultation in British Industry* (Staples Press, London 1952), p. 21.

In the present study 207 firms (32 per cent) had a formally constituted body used solely for consultation, so it is clear that provisions for formal joint consultation have declined since the N.I.I.P. survey; though consultative bodies are still numerous. There may well, of course, be a considerable difference in the significance of consultation as a method of influencing managerial decisions. An examination of the provision for formal consultation against size of firm would seem to suggest that the extent to which employees generally are covered by some form of consultative machinery is rather greater than would be indicated merely by looking at the proportion of firms alone.[1]

Table 6   Consultative Committees Related to Size of Firm

Size of firm	Joint consultation Number of firms	%	No joint consultation Number of firms	%
0 – 99	19	12	141	88
100 – 499	54	22	191	78
500 – 999	30	47	34	53
1,000 – 1,999	35	52	33	48
2,000 and over	69	62	43	38

The figures show that size of firm is an important factor in determining the existence of a formal system of joint consultation. It does not follow that there is virtually no consultation in the smaller firm, since this may, and certainly does, take place on an informal basis.

The industry groups with the highest proportion of consultative committees were chemicals, shipbuilding, and food, drink and tobacco.

As there has been considerable criticism of joint consultation as a formal process, it was felt that some indications of the view the firms surveyed had of its effectiveness would be of interest. The results obtained as to the believed effectiveness of consulatation are inevitably impressionistic, since there are no standard criteria by which effectiveness may be evaluated. They may also be coloured by the fact that the individual member of management of the firms replying might have had no direct

[1] In another much smaller study by A. J. Allen, *Management and Men: a Study in Industrial Relations* (Hallam Press, London 1967), 52 out of 99 stated that there was some system of joint consultation at their work-place.

knowledge of the working of the consultative committee. Obviously it would have been of interest to ask other managers and employees' representatives in each firm to comment on the effectiveness of the same joint consultative body, but this was not possible within the limits of the present study.

From the survey it was found that joint consultative bodies were considered by management to be effective in 74 per cent of the 207 firms which had them, with 25 per cent considering them 'not very effective' and 1 per cent as 'useless'.

The meaning of 'effectiveness' may have differed considerably in the minds of different managers, though it is almost certain that all those who completed the questionnaire would have in mind effectiveness in terms of the achievement of managerial goals. It is, therefore, possible and even likely that the workers' representatives sitting on a joint consultative committee would not have been of exactly the same opinion. Moreover, had the survey been made of the rank-and-file workers on the one hand and the shop stewards on the other, further differences in the proportions holding views on the effectiveness of joint consultative committees would probably have emerged.

According to the thesis that workers' representatives gravitate to the centres of decision-making, it would seem likely that the effectiveness of joint consultative committees, which have little or no decision-making authority, would be lowest in those firms with a high degree of unionization. Derber,[1] for instance, found in his study of joint production committees that the consultative machinery was of prime importance where union organizations were weak and management was human-relations oriented.

An analysis was made of the survey of expressed effectiveness in relation to the extent of unionization. Although the number of respondents who replied to this question was only 32 per cent of the total, the distribution tended to confirm the hypothesis that consultation was likely to be perceived by employers as most effective where unions were non-existent or weak. However, the numbers of firms in the no-union or low-unionization categories were rather too small to give other than tentative support to the hypothesis.

Of the 54 consultative bodies which in managerial eyes were not very effective, or useless, 42 existed in establishments with

[1] M. Derber, *Labor-Management Relations at the Plant Level Under Industry-Wide Bargaining* (University of Illinois Press, Urbana 1955), p. 80.

unionization greater than two-thirds amongst the male manual workers. It could be that in these organizations, workers' representatives attached little value to consultation because of its limited decision-making powers. Nevertheless, other explanations might be possible; for instance that managers faced with high degrees of unionization give most of their attention to the area of collective bargaining, and that they themselves attach little importance to formalized consultation.

(3) Negotiating Committees

Negotiating bodies at plant level enable the workers' representatives to become involved in a joint decision-making process. By the establishment of procedural rules, unions participate in the determination of terms and conditions of employment. With the emphasis placed since the Donovan Report on formalization and on the strengthening and extension of collective bargaining, the domestic negotiating body seems likely to take on an increased importance.

In the survey questionnaire, a distinction was made between formally constituted bodies that were used solely for negotiation, and those bodies that, as well as having a negotiating function, also had a consultative role. It was found that a substantial proportion, 212 firms (32 per cent), had joint bodies with the dual function of negotiation and consultation, and 87 (13 per cent) had one that was used for negotiation only. It is clear that the line between negotiation and consultation is often difficult to draw, and it would appear that any division between them is far from rigidly observed in practice, whether the committees are separate or whether one committee combines the functions of negotiation and consultation. During the interviews with firms that were made to follow up the postal enquiry, managers often talked in terms of their consultative committees adopting functions of a similar nature to negotiation.

The figures show support for the belief that management–worker relations are tending to be increasingly conducted through a single committee for both negotiation and consultation. This development is in line with the tendency for negotiation to predominate over consultation, since in the nature of the situation it is likely that any issue raised as a consultative matter will become one of negotiation if the workers' representatives cannot obtain the satisfaction they seek. When the committee is composed of the same people this shift from consultation to negotiation becomes an easy transposition.

Altogether 299, nearly half, of the 649 firms had some form of negotiating machinery within the plant. Further analysis of the replies, given in Table 7, showed that it was the larger rather than the smaller firms that were more likely to have committees concerned with negotiation functions.

Table 7 Negotiation Machinery Related to Size of Firm

Size of firm	Negotiation machinery		No negotiation machinery	
	Number of firms	%	Number of firms	%
0 – 99	41	26	119	74
100 – 499	105	43	140	57
500 – 999	43	67	21	33
1,000 – 1,999	45	66	23	34
2,000 and over	65	58	47	42

An interesting fact emerged from the survey. Of firms employing fewer than 500, 73 said that they had separate consultative committees, whereas 146 had committees for negotiation or for negotiation and consultation combined. If formal joint bodies existed, then in those firms employing fewer than 500, they were more likely from these figures to be in the shape of committees partly or wholly for negotiating than solely for consultation.

In those firms without any formal committees, it appeared that the lack of unionization, as well as the size of the organization, was an important factor. It would not be unreasonable to expect the opposite to be true of the firms with negotiating bodies—the

Table 8 Negotiation Machinery Related to the Extent of Unionization

Extent of unionization	Negotiation machinery		No negotiation machinery	
	Number of firms	%	Number of firms	%
No unionization	14	18	63	82
Small (up to $\frac{1}{3}$)	32	28	84	72
Moderate ($\frac{1}{3}$–$\frac{2}{3}$)	33	39	51	61
Substantial (over $\frac{2}{3}$)	143	55	116	45
A condition of engagement	77	68	36	32

higher the level of unionization, the more likely it is that there will be a formalized negotiating function within the plant.

Nearly four-fifths of the firms which made union membership a condition of appointment had formalized negotiating procedures. It would seem that where unionization covered less than a third of the employees formalized machinery was not likely; with unionization between a third and two-thirds there seemed an equal possibility that there would either be no machinery or a negotiating body; but with unionization above two-thirds it was more likely that negotiating machinery would exist. The industry groups with the highest percentage of committees for negotiation only were shipbuilding and transport, but those with most committees used for both negotiation and consultation were metal goods, and engineering and electrical. Firms in construction had the lowest proportion of both types of committee.

Quite a high level of effectiveness was claimed by management for consultative committees, but a similar question relating to the effectiveness of negotiating committees showed that management had an even greater confidence in the negotiating bodies to which they were a party.

The degree of effectiveness of these bodies was regarded by management as very high indeed; only about 10 per cent of the 87 firms having negotiating bodies felt that they were not very effective.[1] A comparison with the figures for the effectiveness of consultative bodies shows quite an interesting difference: some 25 per cent of the 207 firms having separate consultative bodies—a much larger proportion—felt that in practice these bodies were less than effective.

The test of effectiveness, as in the case of consultative committees, is a subjective opinion given by management. It is possible that management would be reluctant to say that it was a party to inefficient machinery. Moreover workers' representatives on any one of the negotiating bodies involved, might well have a different point of view. Nevertheless the generally high opinion apparently held by management of the effectiveness of the joint negotiating committees is of particular importance, since it at least suggests that the prevalence of unofficial strikes has not led to a withdrawal of confidence by management in the joint negotiating arrangements at the company level. It would, how-

---

[1] Of the 212 firms which had joint negotiating and consultative committees just under 10 per cent thought that they were not very effective.

ever, be dangerous to draw the conclusion that management is satisfied with all aspects of the working of company negotiating machinery: or that on other tests the machinery would be as satisfactory as the response of management apparently suggests. Had more detailed investigation been possible it might well have revealed important qualifications to this general approval.

(4) *Negotiating and Consultative Machinery in the Public Sector*

As already mentioned, the nationalized industries are required by statute to establish machinery for negotiation and consultation with organizations representative of their workers. It is therefore not surprising that the survey made in the public sector showed a considerably greater extent of joint machinery than was reported from the private sector. Thus 60 per cent of the respondents in the public sector reported the existence of bodies used for both negotiation and consultation, compared with 33 per cent in the private sector. Negotiating bodies were reported by 35 per cent of the public sector respondents, compared with 13 per cent in the private sector, and the corresponding figures for consultative bodies were 49 per cent and 32 per cent. All public-sector respondents had some kind of formal joint machinery.

Enquiry was also made as to the respondents' views of the joint machinery, as shown, with comparative figures for the private sector in Table 9:

Table 9   View taken of Joint Machinery by Public and Private Sector Respondents

| | Firms with joint negotiating and consultative body | | Firms with negotiating body | | Firms with consultative body | |
| | Sector | | Sector | | Sector | |
	Public %	Private %	Public %	Private %	Public %	Private %
Extremely effective	11	14	6	16	11	8
Effective	83	78	94	74	64	66
Not very effective	6	9	0	10	25	25
Useless	0	0	0	0	0	1

The results suggest very slightly more satisfaction generally about joint machinery in the public than in the private sector.

(5) Strikes and Formal Machinery

The experience of a strike during the past two years might be taken as some indicator of employee participation or of the effectiveness of negotiating and/or consultative machinery. Although it is not known how far the firms which regarded their committees as 'effective' also experienced a strike it was found that there was some correspondence between the existence of formal machinery and strike incidence. For example, 45 per cent of firms with a joint negotiating and consultative committee had experienced a strike during the previous two years, compared with only 28 per cent of those without such a body. Similar results were found for negotiating machinery (46 per cent: 20 per cent) and also for consultative committees, though the difference was less marked (36 per cent: 28 per cent). Holding size constant the 'experience of a strike' became more likely as the ratio of unionization increased. Although too much weight cannot be attached to this result owing to statistical limitations, it does suggest that the view that a higher degree of unionization is equated with less conflict is open to question.

Specific Joint Decision-Making Arrangements

Negotiation can be seen as a process of joint regulation of specific areas of decision-making. In this respect it differs from consultation, which has no formal executive function. The outcome of deliberations in consultative bodies generally have no more than a purely persuasive force. In addition to these two main types of collective participation, other (hybrid) bodies exist: bodies which theoretically do not have a negotiating function, but whose decisions are binding upon those involved. In such bodies as these the worker has a quasi-managerial role. Bodies such as joint disciplinary committees that have the power to make binding disciplinary decisions fit into this hybrid category.

The disciplinary committees of the National Dock Labour Board are a case in point. These bodies have five members representing dock employers, and five representatives of the workers, and have power to deal with appeals involving discipline. The operation of such committees has been criticized—mainly because in difficult situations decisions are often avoided by a definite split between the management and union representatives.

From a union viewpoint, such bodies have been criticized because of the possible dangers of alienating members, who see the union as imposing discipline on their fellow-workers—a function that is easier to challenge when performed solely by management.[1]

Another type of body which falls into this category of specific committees is the safety committee, in which the workers' representatives may either have themselves, or may delegate to a fellow-worker, some executive responsibility for safety problems.

The results of the survey suggests that safety, redundancy and discipline offer the most likely areas for hybrid bodies. Of the firms that replied, 52 per cent had a joint safety committee; redundancy and discipline were dealt with by 25 per cent through formal joint procedures. It should be added that it is possible that some of the positive responses to the question about disciplinary committees could have been returned by firms which had formalized discipline procedure in which the workers' representatives were involved, not as envisaged, in a quasi-judicial function, but acting as counsel, with management still ultimately in the decisive judicial role.

Other possible specific joint arrangements covered in the questionnaire, dealing with such subjects as administration of sick pay, training, absenteeism and bad time-keeping, and control of scrap, were reported in relatively few establishments. However, one additional popular area of worker involvement in an administrative capacity seems to be provided by the existence of suggestion schemes. Out of a total of 262 firms with suggestion schemes, 144 (55 per cent), mostly the larger firms, involved workers' representatives in the administration of these schemes.[2]

An analysis of the replies according to industry showed that specific committees were most prevalent in the firms in the shipbuilding and metal industries, and least in those in the construction, and food, drink and tobacco groups.

In general, from the survey of private firms, specific committees were found to be more widespread where there were also committees for negotiation and consultation.

In the public sector the greater extent of formal machinery

---

[1] In Chapter 6 worker-directors are seen as being in a similar position to members of regulatory bodies in that they might suffer from criticism that they adopt managerial values.

[2] See Chapter 7, Table 26.

reported above does not, of course, necessarily signify that public-sector managers make greater qualitative efforts to negotiate and consult. However, although their statutory responsibilities do not require them to set up specific joint decision-making machinery, yet in this respect too, the respondents to the public-sector enquiry reported a much higher incidence of such machinery than did the private-sector respondents. Thus 83 per cent of the public-sector respondents reported specific arrangements relating to safety, compared with 52 per cent in the private sector. In the public sector 70 per cent reported specific arrangements concerning redundancy and 58 per cent arrangements concerning dismissals for disciplinary reasons (compared with 25 per cent in each case in the private sector). As many as 46 per cent of the public-sector respondents reported specific arrangements relating to training and 37 per cent arrangements relating to absenteeism and bad time-keeping.

This evidence certainly suggests that the obligation on nationalized industries to negotiate and consult is an effective means of bringing about machinery for these purposes.

Communication

Participation requires a two-way flow of information that will enable all those who are involved in the participative process to interact in a constructive relationship. In this survey it was possible only to enquire into the methods and extent of the formal means by which management communicated with their employees.

The respondents to the survey were asked to indicate from the following list of possible methods of communicating information generally to their employees which, if any, they used when they wished to communicate information of importance.

Table 10 Methods used by Firms to Communicate Information of Importance

	Numbers of firms	%
Works magazine	238	37
Broadcasting	74	12
Letter in pay packet	362	56
Letters sent to employees at home	107	17
Works or shop meetings	426	66
Notice board	610	94

The four most used methods of conveying information were then analysed according to the size of the firm. As might be expected, size appears to be an important factor in deciding how information is conveyed formally from management to employees.

A works' magazine, for instance, is used by only 63 of the 405 firms employing fewer than 500 people, whereas of the 180 firms employing more than 1,000, 138 used works' magazines. The possibilities of informal contact as a reliable means of passing information are more extensive in the smaller organizations. This, together with the fact that the larger firms are more effectively unionized, is probably the reason why a much greater proportion of the larger firms use formal 'works or shop meetings'. Of the enterprises employing fewer than 500, 55 per cent used such meetings, compared with 84 per cent of the enterprises employing 1,000 or more. A letter in the pay packet had been used by 44 per cent of the small firms and 70 per cent of the larger.

The picture that emerges from the limited amount of information obtained is that a great many firms rely principally on a works notice board, supplemented by an occasional letter in the pay packet and a works meeting to convey particular items of information.

Looked at according to industry, the firms with the most extensive communications practices were found in the vehicles, metal manufacture, and transport sectors.

Respondents were asked to state whether they made special provision to convey information to their employees relating to the following aspects of the firm's activities: (1) financial results of the firm; (2) production achievements, and (3) information about new orders received. Nearly three-quarters of the firms surveyed made no special effort to inform their employees of the financial position of the firm.[1] Over half gave no attention to providing information about the order-book, and half of them made no particular effort to provide information on the firm's productive achievements. When these figures were related to the size of the firm they again showed a marked tendency for the larger firm to be more concerned about making information available on these matters to their employees.

The public-sector survey showed a very much greater provision of information on the same subjects. Between two-thirds and

[1] See Chapter 4, p. 92, 'Financial Decisions'.

three-quarters of the respondents reported making special arrangements for conveying information on financial results, new orders and production achievements. Besides the notice board, considerably more use was made of the works magazine, letters, the pay packet and works meetings to communicate this information to employees, compared with the private sector.

What is not known from this survey is how efficient shop stewards and foremen are in passing on information to employees. It could be the case that in spite of a low level of formal action the information flow through informal channels is very good. This may particularly be the case in the very small firms. However, in so far as the replies indicate an attitude on the part of companies towards the supply of information they suggest that many firms do not take this task as seriously as would be widely regarded as desirable under modern circumstances.

Conclusion

It is clear that the size of an enterprise is a factor of considerable significance in determining the formal structure of industrial relations. The information gathered in this survey amply confirms that larger firms are more highly unionized and are more likely to have formal collective bargaining and joint consultative arrangements than smaller-scale employers. Unfortunately it was not possible to separate the influence of the size of the firm from that of the degree of union organization on the establishment and working of negotiating and consultative machinery; both factors are significantly correlated with the degree of participation through these means.

The extent to which negotiating and consultative machinery exists is also influenced in the public sector by the obligation on nationalized industries to establish machinery for negotiation and consultation.

Whatever might be wrong with British industrial relations, the companies responding to this enquiry were mainly of the opinion that both the consultative and negotiating committees of which they had experience were effective bodies. The larger firms had much more confidence in their negotiating arrangements than the smaller firms. This confidence no doubt reflected the greater degree of managerial expertise and bargaining experience available to the larger firms. The much greater readiness of the larger firm to take steps to keep its employees informed is a reflection both of its greater range of managerial skills, and of the need to overcome problems of communication that in the smaller firm can be solved through face-to-face contact between workers and managers. However, what was perhaps most significant was the relatively low level of effort made even by large firms to ensure that their employees were kept informed on major aspects of company progress.

4 The Pattern of Workers' Influence Upon Managerial Decision-Making

In the previous chapter the survey evidence of the extent to which workers participate in managerial decision-making through formal consultation and negotiation was examined. The relations of these types of participation to the range of decisions that managers are called upon to make in the conduct of a business enterprise are now discussed. The extent to which this decision-making is influenced by the four organizational variables is examined. Other forms of employee influence such as restrictive practices are also considered.

Areas of Decision

Managerial decisions may be classified in many different ways. For the purpose of this study it was found convenient to use a simple classification which grouped a number of typical managerial decisions into four main areas. These areas of decision are not independent of decisions that have to be made in the carrying out of the many other activities of an enterprise; they are, nevertheless, the areas which by common consent are of primary interest to workers. These key areas of decision were grouped under four heads; wages and redundancy, work methods, work discipline, and finance.

The questionnaire sought to elicit from the sample of firms to which it was sent the extent to which over this range of critical issues workers influenced the decisions made by management. The extent of the influence and method of participation was classified on the basis of a continuum ranging from total neglect to total acceptance of employees' wishes on these matters.

(1) *Wages and Redundancy*

The methods of wage payment used by a firm are of basic importance to both workers and management. It was, therefore, somewhat surprising to discover that a relatively large number of firms, 119 out of 649, were apparently prepared to change the method of wage payment without going through any formal process of consultation or collective bargaining (Table 11).

Table 11   Workers' Influence on Decisions to Change Methods of Payment and to Discharge Redundant Workers

Type of decision	Employees have no influence on our decision.		We would not consult but would consider possible reactions before reaching a decision.		We would consult and probably/ possibly adjust our decision in the light of this view, but the decision would be ours.		We would negotiate, but if un- successful would put our decision into effect.		We would negotiate and would not proceed until there was agree- ment.		This is a matter on which we would accept what our employees want to do.	
	Number of firms	%	Number of firms	%	Number of firms	%	Number of firms	%	Number of firms	%	Number of firms	%
To change method of payment	54	8	65	10	175	27	23	4	308	48	23	4
To discharge wor- kers no longer needed	174	27	112	18	212	32	83	13	68	11	0	0

In only 52 per cent of the firms answering was it normal for changes in the method of wage payment to be negotiated. That almost half of the firms completing the questionnaire were apparently prepared to make changes in methods of payment without formal negotiation through any type of joint arrange- ments in the firm suggests either that the situation in a great many companies is quite a long way removed from the common assumption that in an area so central to their interests as the method of wage payment workers invariably participate in change through their union organization, or on an individual basis.

It could be the case that the firms negotiating changes in methods of wage payment were normally in the habit of follow- ing settlements made nationally, or that the changes were dis- cussed informally. Unfortunately, owing to the need to keep the questionnaire to the bare minimum and the small number of interviews with workers and managers that could be made, it was not possible to obtain all the information that would have been necessary to discover the extent to which there was informal consultation and bargaining with individuals and shop-stewards outside a formal structure of negotiating committees.

| The pattern of industrial relations in many companies at the plant level would appear to be one of continuous adjustment to change, which is carried on without recourse to formal procedures. This does not mean that there is no dialogue between management and workers, but that it does not always take place within an easily definable system. The process of participation is part of a complex web of arrangements that have been built up over time and are particular to a company or a department and to specific managers, foremen and shop stewards. This kind of continuous participation is highly dependent upon personal understandings and perceptions. Where these fail to satisfy needs they may result in conflict and open dispute, with a stoppage of work as the ultimate consequence. Some evidence from the United States has been accumulated which shows that without the formal support of an established framework of democratic procedures this style of informal relationship is liable to break down under stress.[1]

The discharge of workers on grounds of redundancy (Table 11) has often given rise to bitter conflict between management and trade unions. At least one major trade union had for some time a declared policy of contesting all redundancies, for whatever reason they might be caused. However, the attitude of most unions towards redundancy has been that they should be given advance warning and an opportunity to discuss the issues with management before any final decision is made. The replies given to the question relating to the discharge of workers no longer required, however, suggest that a substantial proportion of the sample of firms would be prepared to carry out a decision to discharge redundant workers without prior consultation or negotiation. Nevertheless, there was a significant number of firms which would not discharge workers no longer required until there had been negotiations with the unions concerned and an agreement had been reached.

[1] See D. E. Pelz, 'Leadership within a Hierarchical Organisation', *Journal of Social Issues*, Vol. 7, 1951.

D

(2) *Work Methods*

Although the most important causes of industrial conflict are related to disputes over levels of pay, the analysis of unofficial strikes prepared for the Royal Commission on Trade Unions and Employers' Associations shows that during the period 1964–66, of the average number of recorded unofficial strikes (2,196), not very far below a half were attributed to disputes arising from working arrangements, rules and discipline, and redundancy, dismissal and suspension etc.[1]

The right of management to take decisions unilaterally in these areas has been increasingly challenged, and trade-union pressure has brought about a good deal of joint regulation through the development of rules and procedures to govern the making of decisions on these matters.

Table 12   Workers' Influence on Decisions to Change Work Methods

Type of decision	Employees have no influence on our decision.		We would not consult but would consider possible reactions before reaching a decision.		We would consult and probably/possibly adjust our decision in the light of this view, but the decision would be ours.		We would negotiate, but if unsuccessful would put our decision into effect.		We would negotiate and would not proceed until there was agreement.		This is a matter on which we would accept what our employees want to do.	
	Number of firms	%	Number of firms	%	Number of firms	%	Number of firms	%	Number of firms	%	Number of firms	%
To introduce new working methods	54	8	107	17	305	47	28	4	152	24	0	0
To introduce work-study methods	106	16	99	15	198	31	30	5	210	32	6	1

From Table 12 it is possible to ascertain the extent to which the firms in the sample accepted joint regulation of the making of changes in work methods.

The introduction of work study has been a prolific cause of industrial conflict, and though up to one third of firms in the sample was prepared to negotiate and obtain an agreement be-

[1] *Report of the Royal Commission on Trade Unions and Employers' Associations* (H.M.S.O., London 1968), p. 101.

fore introducing changes there was an equally substantial number that was apparently used to making decisions in this area without any kind of formal discussion with the workers or their representatives. However, the extent to which workers have been able to impose limitations on the desire of the employer to introduce new work methods has been highlighted by the development of productivity bargaining.

Recent years have seen attempts through productivity bargaining to involve workers in the improvement of efficiency by the introduction of new machinery and methods of working. Productivity bargaining represents the abandonment of unilateral decision-making by both management and workers. In productivity bargaining management has to accept that workers have rights vested in their jobs, which extend to the way in which they have carried them out by established practice. On their part workers have to be prepared to retreat from defensive practices, which are manifestly uneconomic and imposed on management by their collective strength. The bargain that is struck may, however, be a once-and-for-all change that simply involves the two sides in taking up new strategic positions, both having gained in the movements involved. The important question from the point of view of extending the participative role of workers in decisions relating to the efficient utilization of human resources in the enterprise is whether involvement can be institutionalized so as to be a continuous process.

There is evidence that some managements are attempting to extend collective bargaining from a tactical encounter into a long-term process of strategic discussion. This type of development was first introduced in the United States in the steel industry after the disastrous strike of 1959 with the establishment of a long-range problem-solving committee. Problem-solving committees now exist in a number of situations including mining, chemicals, docks and manufacturing concerns. Experience of such bodies as the Civil Service Pay Research Unit suggests that there is a role for the further development of joint bodies of this kind that enable management and the representatives of workers to define the pure bargaining areas more clearly, and by discussion based upon a common knowledge of the facts to have a foundation of agreed evidence and understanding on the issues involved.

(3) *Work Discipline*

Table 13 Workers' Influence on Decisions about Work Discipline

Type of decision	Employees have no influence on our decision.		We would not consult but would consider possible reactions before reaching a decision.		We would consult and probably/ possibly adjust our decision in the light of this view, but the decision would be ours.		We would negotiate, but if un- successful would put our decision into effect.		We would negotiate and would not proceed until there was agree- ment.		This is a matter on which we would accept what our employees want to do.	
	Number of firms	%	Number of firms	%	Number of firms	%	Number of firms	%	Number of firms	%	Number of firms	%
To alter works rules so as to change disciplin- ary procedures	92	14	105	16	224	35	59	9	166	26	3	1
To set up new pro- cedures to deal with absenteeism	130	21	118	18	219	34	68	11	112	17	2	0.3
To dismiss an in- dividual or group of individuals for disciplinary reasons	244	38	169	26	151	23	57	9	27	4	1	0.2

The figures suggest that in matters of discipline companies tend to be more reluctant to accept a necessity to negotiate than in the case of questions relating to wages or changes in work methods. Consultation is clearly practised extensively, but there is a substantial number of firms that apparently prefer to act unilaterally.

Undoubtedly many firms believe that authority must be exercised by management; that to agree to consult or to negotiate on questions of discipline would be to undermine the responsibility of management to manage. There is a clear distinction in the minds of many firms between the establishment of procedures for the regulation of disciplinary proceedings, about which a substantial number of firms are prepared to consult and negotiate with workers and unions, and the decision to dismiss a worker for disciplinary reasons. Relatively few firms are apparently prepared to agree that dismissals for disciplinary reasons should be a matter for negotiation. However, it is interesting to note that there is a small number of firms which is prepared to give to the workers or union body concerned substantial responsibility in relation to discipline and making the decision to dismiss.

The best-known example of workers exercising discipline over themselves is in the printing industry, where it has been traditional for the chapel to ensure that its members observe rules relating to standards of work performance and behaviour. Members of the chapel can be and often have been fined for infringements of these rules. The exercise of this disciplinary responsibility through the chapel has been closely related to the securing of a closed shop and the limiting of the authority of the foreman and management to the exercise of technical control over the production process. This form of participation in the function of maintaining discipline is an extension of the union's bargaining power developed through a control of entry to the job and its exercise.

A different model in which workers directly participate in maintaining discipline in the work-place is the well-known practice at the Firestone Rubber Company. In this company a committee has been established to handle cases of industrial misconduct. It is composed of three elected trade union representatives, the departmental manager and foreman concerned in the case, and a member of the industrial relations department who acts as chairman. The committee considers cases 'involving bad workmanship, insubordination, smoking in forbidden areas, clocking offences, fighting, etc. but does not normally deal with lateness and absenteeism; neither does it deal with cases of theft'.[1] Discussion of cases continues until a unanimous decision is reached. Minutes of proceedings are posted on all factory notice boards.

There was no doubt a considerable amount of arbitrary dismissal. The evidence from the inquiry suggests that the majority of firms were reluctant to give up their right to 'sack' for infringements of work rules. This enquiry was, of course, carried out before the Industrial Relations Act, 1971, introduced the right of appeal against dismissal, with the possibility of obtaining reinstatement or compensation. Under this kind of pressure employers may find that it is in their interest to involve workers in the decision-making process in disciplinary cases on

[1] J. S. Walton, 'Where Justice is Seen to be Done', in *Industrial Society* (London, February 1966).

similar lines to those pioneered by Firestone and a few other firms.

(4) *Financial Decisions*

Decisions relating to pay, productivity and discipline are clearly of immediate and direct concern to workers. The decisions in these areas are also ones that workers feel they are by experience as well as interest qualified to judge or participate in as experts. There are, however, as most workers would readily admit, a wide range of other decisions in which they are not qualified by knowledge or experience to give an expert's view, but in which nevertheless they may legitimately feel they are directly concerned in terms of consequences for their future employment, career development and general welfare as employees. Decisions in the field of company financial policy are in this category. In order to discover how far management was prepared to take into account the views of its employees in the field of financial policy, questions were asked about decisions regarding the raising of capital and the allocation of profits.

It is clear that the overwhelming majority of companies believe that these questions are entirely matters for management decision. There is a small minority that would be concerned at the

Table 14   Workers' Influence on Financial Decisions

Type of decision	Employees have no influence on our decision.		We would not consult but would consider possible reactions before reaching a decision.		We would consult and probably/ possibly adjust our decision in the light of this view, but the decision would be ours.		We would negotiate, but if unsuccessful would put our decision into effect.		We would negotiate and would not proceed until there was agreement.		This is a matter on which we would accept what our employees want to do.	
	Number of firms	%	Number of firms	%	Number of firms	%	Number of firms	%	Number of firms	%	Number of firms	%
To raise additional capital	626	96	18	4	5	1	0	0	0	0	0	0
To allocate profits between investments, dividends, reserves, etc.	626	96	21	3	2	0.4	0	0	0	0	0	0

reactions of their employees and would at least give this passing consideration. There is an even tinier group that would consult their employees and would perhaps adjust their decision in the light of the views expressed.

These results are not surprising. Although unions have expressed profound concern at specific decisions to close plants, and recently more generally at mergers, they have exhibited little desire to become directly involved in the making of decisions relating to capital developments. They have accepted that this is a responsibility of management. Direct involvement might seriously compromise their position as effective bargainers. On the other hand, there is a growing demand for information relating to a company's commercial and financial situation. The demand from the unions to open the books has been muted in the past by the predominance of industry-wide collective agreements. With the shift from the industry to the company and plant level there has come a rising interest in the financial situation of the firm. For some time the larger unions have been compiling data relating to the profitability of the firms with whom they bargain. The extent of this information is limited by the amount which is published, which is often the minimum, and the research resources of the unions, which could hardly be called large.

The managements of many companies have felt the need to make more information available, and the results of the enquiry into the extent to which they provide information were given in Table 10 in Chapter 3.

The provision of information which would enable unions to bargain more effectively was discussed by the Royal Commission on Trade Unions and Employers' Associations. Subsequently, the Industrial Relations Act 1971 makes provision for it to be obligatory for an employer to disclose to trade-union representatives, in collective bargaining, information appropriately required for the negotiations; also to require the larger firms to make available specified general information on a periodic basis. The limits to the type of information to be supplied will only become clear over the course of time. There will be safeguards against demands for information that might be seriously prejudicial to the interests of the company. The availability of basic financial information has for a long time been written into the statutes of other countries, including France, the U.S.A. and West Germany.

The growth of multi-national corporations has brought new and increasing problems of control and negotiation for trade unions and governments. There is rising concern that the possibility of major sectors of employment coming under the domination of multi-national corporations whose decisions, taken at some remote headquarters, and based on the maximization of corporate profitability rather than on the particular interests of each national element, might be adverse to the public interest. Already unions have begun to respond to this challenge by co-ordinating their bargaining activities across national frontiers. The simultaneous strike against the plants of the St. Gobain glass company in 1969 in several countries may presage a common situation in the future.

An issue on a smaller scale than the closing down of a plant or the transfer of production of a particular product by a multi-national corporation to another country is the decision by the management of any firm to cease manufacturing some item and instead to sub-contract the work to another company. Sub-contracting has been a vexed question in the United States for many years and has produced a number of bitter conflicts between unions and management. It is now not uncommon for American management to agree to limit the extent of sub-contracting to certain defined circumstances. Though their interest has not been as great, the attitude of British unions is not very different from that of their American counterparts. They have protested frequently at the sub-contracting of work, especially when there was a suspicion that the decision had been made because of strong union activity.

It is clear from Table 15 that the great majority of firms do not regard a decision to put work out to sub-contract as one which they ought to discuss as a matter of course with the unions or their workers. So long as the level of unemployment remains low and there is no obvious link between a decision to sub-contract and a decision to lay off workers it is unlikely that the unions will attempt to prevent sub-contracting. Where, however, this practice contains a threat to the existence of the unions, as in the case of labour only sub-contracting, it is likely that they will press employers to agree to abandon their use of it. With the growth of company and plant bargaining it is likely that unions will seek to extend their influence to managerial decisions of this kind.

Table 15   Workers' Influence on Sub-Contracting Decisions

	Employees have no influence on our decision.		We would not consult but would consider possible reactions before reaching a decision.		We would consult and probably/ possibly adjust our decision in the light of this view, but the decision would be ours.		We would negotiate, but if un- successful would put our decision into effect.		We would negotiate and would not proceed until there was agree- ment.		This is a matter on which we would accept what our employees want to do.	
Type of decision	Number of firms	%	Number of firms	%	Number of firms	%	Number of firms	%	Number of firms	%	Number of firms	%
To sub-contract some of the work load outside the organization	347	52	181	28	104	16	5	1	12	2	0	0

Influence of Unionization on Decision-Making

The survey indicated, as might be expected, that the greater the degree of unionization, the greater the extent of joint decision-making.

(1) *Wages and Redundancy*

The following table shows that firms reporting substantial trade unionism among their male manual workers were much more likely to regulate methods of payment jointly with the unions than those firms reporting only a moderate trade-union membership.

Table 16 indicates that the firms which are strongly unionized also tend to be ready to enter into consultation and negotiation with their employees. It is the firms with low levels of unionization that tend to look to formal consultation as an alternative to negotiation. However, some 54 per cent of the firms that report no unionization among their employees would not consult their employees on changes in wage payments. On questions of re-dundancy, 73 per cent of non-unionized firms would not consult, compared with 27 per cent of the 'substantial' member-ship group. The greatest proportion appeared likely to consult rather than negotiate on this topic, but in any case the degree of employee influence increases with unionization.

Table 16   Influence of Unionization on Decisions to Change Methods of Payment

Type of decision To change method of payment. Extent of unionization	Employees have no influence on our decision.		We would not consult but would consider possible reactions before reaching a decision.		We would consult and probably/possibly adjust our decision in the light of this view, but the decision would be ours.		We would negotiate, but if unsuccessful would put our decision into effect.		We would negotiate and would not proceed until there was agreement.		This is a matter on which we would accept what our employees want to do.	
	Number of firms	%	Number of firms	%	Number of firms	%	Number of firms	%	Number of firms	%	Number of firms	%
(i) No unionization	21	29	18	25	20	26	2	3	10	13	5	6
(ii) Small (up to one-third)	11	9	20	17	45	39	5	4	31	27	4	2
(iii) Moderate (one-third to two-thirds)	5	6	15	18	30	36	3	4	26	33	5	4
(iv) Substantial (above two-thirds)	13	4	7	3	51	20	11	4	172	67	7	3
(v) Trade union membership a condition of employment	4	3	5	4	29	25	2	2	68	62	5	4

(2) *Work Methods*

A rather different picture of the response of firms to unionization appears when this factor is considered in relation to the introduction of new work methods. Table 17 shows that few firms with substantial union membership would be prepared to introduce new working methods without either consultation or negotiation. Consultation would appear to be particularly important for all firms in connection with the introduction of new methods of working. Only those firms with a substantial degree of union membership or a closed shop were prepared to commit themselves strongly to negotiation on these issues. Very much the same pattern regarding consultation and negotiation was found concerning the introduction of work-study methods, although more of the unionized firms would be prepared to go ahead without consulting on this matter.

Table 17 Influence of Unionization on Decisions to Change Work Methods

Type of decision To introduce new working methods.	Employees have no influence on our decision.		We would not consult but would consider possible reactions before reaching a decision.		We would consult and probably/possibly adjust our decision in the light of this view, but the decision would be ours.		We would negotiate, but if unsuccessful would put our decision into effect.		We would negotiate and would not proceed until there was agreement.		This is a matter on which we would accept what our employees want to do.	
Extent of unionization	Number of firms	%	Number of firms	%	Number of firms	%	Number of firms	%	Number of firms	%	Number of firms	%
(i) No unionization	19	26	17	22	30	39	1	2	8	10	1	0
(ii) Small (up to one-third)	9	9	29	25	64	55	3	3	10	9	1	0
(iii) Moderate (one-third to two-thirds)	8	11	19	23	46	55	3	3	7	8	1	0
(iv) Substantial (above two-thirds)	14	6	27	11	125	46	18	7	76	29	1	0
(v) Trade union membership a condition of employment	5	4	12	6	46	41	2	2	53	47	0	0

(3) *Work Discipline*

When the degree of union organization is examined for its influence on the behaviour of firms in connection with disciplinary procedures (Table 18) a similar picture to that in Table 17 emerges. There are some differences, but they are not very great.

Similar results were found for other decisions relating to work discipline.

(4) *Financial Decisions*

The number of replies indicated that too few employers engaged in consultation on the making of financial decisions to ascertain whether there was any relationship with union influence. Similarly, when the effect of trade union membership on decisions relating to the sub-contracting of work was examined, only 12 firms out of 649 respondents indicated that they would be prepared to enter into negotiations on this question. It is interesting to note, however, that all twelve firms reported that they had either substantial trade-union membership or a closed shop.

Table 18   Influence of Unionization on Decisions to Change Disciplinary Procedures

Type of decision To alter work rules so as to change disciplinary procedures.	Employees have no influence on our decision.		We would not consult but would consider possible reactions before reaching a decision.		We would consult and probably/ possibly adjust our decision in the light of this view, but the decision would be ours.		We would negotiate, but if unsuccessful would put our decision into effect.		We would negotiate and would not proceed until there was agreement.		This is a matter on which we would accept what our employees want to do.	
Extent of unionization	Number of firms	%	Number of firms	%	Number of firms	%	Number of firms	%	Number of firms	%	Number of firms	%
(i) No unionization	32	44	18	23	17	22	5	6	3	4	0	0
(ii) Small (up to one-third)	22	19	31	27	46	40	5	2	14	12	1	1
(iii) Moderate (one-third to two-thirds)	12	14	19	23	31	36	6	11	13	17	0	0
(iv) Substantial (above two-thirds)	16	5	21	8	103	40	31	12	91	35	0	0
(v) Trade-union membership a condition of employment	9	8	15	13	32	28	15	13	40	36	2	2

It has been suggested that the absence of joint regulation of matters relating to wages, employment and discipline is due mainly to the fact that management tends to view the firm as a unitary institution and is hostile to negotiating with unions. There is undoubtedly some truth in this contention, but the evidence given here would suggest that the main reason why management has a unitary rather than a pluralist view of the firm is not because of an ideological commitment but because the unions have frequently failed to increase their organizational strength to a level where they can insist on management accepting a wider field of joint regulation. The response of management to unions is almost entirely pragmatic; if unions are strong and determined to extend the range of their bargaining interests, as the evidence of the United States indicates, they will be able to achieve this goal. Employers are not keen to accept the right of unions to participate in decisions beyond those that have traditionally been the concern of collective bargaining for the very practical reason that this limits their freedom to act and imposes additional costs in time and effort to secure agreement. The reluctance of employers to accept a pluralistic view of the enterprise is based not so much upon a theoretical view of rights and duties, though this is an aspect of the matter, but on a belief that the objectives of the unions are different from those of management and therefore must at some point come into conflict with the achievement of management's goals. The implications of this power conflict will be further examined in the next chapter. It is necessary to note here that the readiness of management to enter into consultation with its employees through formal committees is compounded both of a desire to restrict bargaining to narrowly defined areas of decision-making and a recognition that personal, individual, consultation is virtually impossible in a large-scale, highly structured enterprise.

Influence of Size of Firm on Decision-Making

Size is clearly a factor of significance in determining the pattern of industrial relations in an enterprise. The evidence shows that as firms get larger they are prepared to negotiate on a wider range of topics than when they are smaller. The difference in the extent to which firms employing fewer than 500 people are not unionized and therefore do not enter into negotiations on any issue contrasts sharply with those that employ more than 1,000.

(1) *Wages and Redundancy*

Of the firms employing 1,000 or more employees, 82 per cent accepted negotiation as the normal means of determining changes in the method of wage payment, whereas it was only 36 per cent of those employing fewer than 500 employees. Consultation on changes in methods of wage payments rather than bargaining is of considerable significance in a substantial proportion of all but the very large firms. On questions of redundancy, 26 per cent of firms employing fewer than 500 would consult, compared with 45 per cent of those employing more than 1,000. However, only 18 per cent of these large firms would negotiate and not proceed without agreement.

Table 19   Influence of Size of Firm on Decisions to Change Methods of Payment

Type of decision To change method of payment.	Employees have no influence on our decision.		We would not consult but would consider possible reactions before reaching a decision.		We would consult and probably/possibly adjust our decision in the light of this view, but the decision would be ours.		We would negotiate, but if unsuccessful would put our decision into effect.		We would negotiate and would not proceed until there was agreement.		This is a matter on which we would accept what our employees want to do.	
Size of firm	Number of firms	%	Number of firms	%	Number of firms	%	Number of firms	%	Number of firms	%	Number of firms	%
(i) 0 – 99	26	16	26	16	60	38	4	3	34	21	10	6
(ii) 100 – 499	23	9	33	13	77	31	8	3	98	40	6	2
(iii) 500 – 999	3	5	4	6	15	23	4	6	35	55	3	5
(iv) 1,000 – 1,999	1	1	2	3	16	24	2	3	46	68	1	1
(v) 2,000 – over	2	2	0	0	7	6	5	4	95	85	3	3

(2) Work Methods

The difference in the readiness to accept negotiation as the appropriate method of arriving at decisions is rather less marked between large and small companies when the subject of decision is concerned with working methods and disciplinary procedures. It is worthy of note, however that no firms in the sample were prepared to say that they would accept what their employees might want to do. This is perhaps not surprising since decisions relating to changes in work methods raise fundamental questions of managerial prerogatives. For this reason the apparent readiness of a substantial proportion of management in the larger firms to wait until they had reached agreement with their employees before making changes in work methods suggests that, nevertheless, management is prepared to recognize the right of employees to express concern in changes which affect them directly.

Table 20 shows a pattern that is broadly similar to Table 19, with the number of larger firms ready to decide these questions by negotiation being rather smaller than when the issues are concerned with wages. Some 40 per cent of firms employing 1,000–2,000 would be ready to accept negotiation; the figure for firms with 100–500 was 19 per cent. Consultation assumes a larger role for firms of all sizes, but especially so for the very large firms. On matters relating to work study 61 per cent of large firms would negotiate with employees until agreement was reached, compared with 20 per cent of small firms, but more of those employing fewer than 500 would consult (32 per cent) than of those with over 1,000 employees (24 per cent).

Table 20   Influence of Size of Firm on Decisions to Change Work Methods

Type of decision / To introduce new working methods.	Employees have no influence on our decision.		We would not consult but would consider possible reactions before reaching a decision.		We would consult and probably/possibly adjust our decision in the light of this view, but the decision would be ours.		We would negotiate, but if un-successful would put our decision into effect.		We would negotiate and would not proceed until there was agreement.		This is a matter on which we would accept what our employees want to do.	
Size of firm	Number of firms	%	Number of firms	%	Number of firms	%	Number of firms	%	Number of firms	%	Number of firms	%
(i) 0 – 99	25	16	33	21	74	46	5	3	23	14	0	0
(ii) 100 – 499	27	11	44	18	124	51	3	1	47	19	0	0
(iii) 500 – 999	3	5	9	14	33	52	4	6	24	38	0	0
(iv) 1,000 – 1,999	0	0	12	16	26	35	7	9	29	39	0	0
(v) 2,000 – over	2	2	9	8	63	56	9	8	28	26	0	0

(3) *Work Discipline*

The difference between the large and small firms was less than in the case of work study, when disciplinary questions (Table 21) were at issue. In this case 46 per cent of the larger companies against 17 per cent of those employing 100–500 would normally be prepared to negotiate on these matters. In this area of decision consultation is as important a method of participation as negotiation.

In deciding about procedures to deal with absenteeism, large and small firms showed similar tendencies to consult, but the larger ones were considerably more willing to negotiate (27 per cent compared with 12 per cent); in decisions relating to dismissal for disciplinary reasons the large firms were more likely to negotiate and to consult.

Table 21   Influence of Size of Firm on Decisions to Change Disciplinary Procedures

Type of decision To alter works rules so as to change disciplinary procedures.	Employees have no influence on our decision.		We would not consult but would consider possible reactions before reaching a decision.		We would consult and probably/possibly adjust our decision in the light of this view, but the decision would be ours.		We would negotiate, but if unsuccessful would put our decision into effect.		We would negotiate and would not proceed until there was agreement.		This is a matter on which we would accept what our employees want to do.	
Size of firm	Number of firms	%	Number of firms	%	Number of firms	%	Number of firms	%	Number of firms	%	Number of firms	%
(i) 0 – 99	47	29	22	14	54	34	11	7	24	15	2	1
(ii) 100 – 499	33	13	54	22	90	37	26	11	41	17	1	0.4
(iii) 500 – 999	5	8	12	19	19	30	4	6	24	39	0	0
(iv) 1,000 – 1,999	5	7	7	10	21	31	4	6	31	46	0	0
(v) 2,000 – over	2	2	10	9	40	36	14	13	46	41	0	0

Influence of Type of Industry on Decision-Making

An analysis of the survey was made by industry in order to see whether there were any marked differences between industrial groups covered. Replies on groups of topics were combined and a rank ordering assigned, high rank implying high employee-influence. The results are shown in Table 22. From a combination of all these, shipbuilding and vehicles—the groups with the largest, most highly unionized firms—emerge as having the highest employee-influence, while construction, and textiles and leather, have the lowest.

These findings are close to what might have been expected from commonplace observation. However, it is difficult to disentangle the influence of any specific factor as the primary influence on the pattern of industrial relations revealed by the rank orders in Table 22.

It is possible that the fundamental influence is that of the technological characteristics of the industries examined. Unfortunately it is not possible to give a more precise indication of the extent to which this might be the case. Recent studies attempting to measure technological determinants of industrial relations have shown the problems of disentangling the many variables involved.[1]

Table 22   Analysis of Extent of Workers' Influence by Industry (Private Sector)

	Industrial order	Average no. of workers per establishment	Degree of trade unionization	Strike intensity	Overtime ban	Committees for negotiation and consultation	Committees for negotiation	Committees for consultation	Specific joint bodies	Communications	Influence by workers on certain areas of decision	Overall combined ranking of workers' influence
Vehicles	(VIII)	1	3	2	2	8	6	4	7	1	1	2
Shipbuilding	(VII)	2	1	1	1	6	1	2	1	4	2	1
Chemical	(IV)	3	5	9	5	5	7	1	9	5	5	4
Transport and communication	(XIX)	4	6	7	10	4	2	13	8	3	9	5
Food, drink and tobacco	(III)	5	8	8	9	13	4	3	14	7	12	9
Metal goods	(IX)	6	7	4	6	1	9	8	4	10	8	7
Metal industry	(V)	7	4	3	3	3	2	5	2	2	4	3
Engineering and electricity	(VI)	8	9	5	7	2	5	7	5	6	3	6
Bricks, pottery and glass	(XIII)	9	14	10	15	11	12	10	13	12	14	13
Paper, etc.	(XV)	10	2	13	4	10	8	5	6	9	6	8
Other manufacturing	(XVI)	11	13	6	12	7	11	11	3	8	7	10
Construction	(XVII)	12	15	11	14	15	15	15	15	13	15	15
Textiles and leather	(X)	13	11	14	11	14	10	12	10	14	13	14
Clothing and footwear	(XII)	14	12	15	13	12	14	9	11	11	11	12
Timber, furniture	(XIV)	15	10	12	8	9	12	13	12	15	10	11

The Significance of 'Restrictive Practices'

Unilateral action by workers is a negative form of participation, but in its most extreme form it may impose a powerful constraint on management decision-making. The extent of 'restrictive practices' has been investigated several times in recent years.[2]

[1] Cf. J. Woodward, op. cit., *Industrial Organization: Theory and Practice* (Oxford University Press, 1965); and *Industrial Organization: Behaviour and Control* (Oxford University Press, London 1970).

[2] John Hilton (ed.), *Are Trade Unions Obstructive?* (Gollancz, London 1935); F. Zweig, *Productivity and Trade Unions* (Blackwell, Oxford 1951). More recent studies include J. A. Lincoln, *The Restrictive Society* (Allen and Unwin, London 1967), and G. Roberts, *Demarcation Rules in Shipbuilding and Ship Repairing* (Cambridge University Press Occasional Papers 14, 1967).

In these studies no firm conclusion was reached as to the significance of the limitations imposed collectively by organized workers on production. Two of the investigators were of the opinion on balance that the effect was not as great as is sometimes believed. The other study came to the conclusion that restrictive practices were a serious handicap to industrial efficiency. Since the present enquiry was concerned to discover, so far as this was possible, the influence that workers had on management decision-making through various forms of participative activity, it was decided to ask firms to indicate the extent to which they had experienced a range of different restrictions.

In view of the opinion that has sometimes been expressed by employers' organizations that restrictions imposed by workers are a factor of major importance,[1] the results were somewhat surprising.[2] It could be that persons completing the questionnaires for the respondent firms were not as fully informed as a shop-floor supervisor of the extent or effect of the restrictions mentioned in the questions. It could also be possible that those completing the questionnaire were reluctant for various reasons to indicate the existence of a situation which might give an adverse impression of the level of managerial control or efficiency. Although no evidence came to light to suggest that these possibilities might be a significant cause of distortion of the results, it is necessary to be aware of this limitation to their validity.

It is clear from Table 23 that in the vast majority of cases the restrictions outlined in the questionnaire have apparently generally not been experienced, or if they have, are not thought to have been very significant. Adding together the significant experiences it can be seen that in four of the six cases, fewer than 10 per cent of the firms said that they had experienced significant restrictions. Only two of the restrictions were experienced in a 'fairly significant' or 'very significant' way in more than 10 per cent of the firms. These two restrictions—refusal to work overtime when desired by management, and the limitation of speed of work or volume of output—emphasized the workers' desire for job control and autonomy, and also served to illustrate the

---

[1] Cf. Evidence of the Engineering Employers' Federation to the Royal Commission on Trade Unions and Employers' Associations.

[2] Though perhaps less so when the national enquiry of the late 1950s is recalled. Of 112 industries co-operating in the enquiry, 64 (57 per cent) declared that they had no problems. (White Paper, *Practices Impeding the Full and Efficient Use of Manpower*, H.M.S.O., London 1959).

nature of the sanctions that workers are able to impose upon management. The limitations found in this survey are similar to those observed in Lupton's study of shop-floor activities;[1] they can be interpreted as attempts to maintain control over the job in the interests of employment and the exercise of market pressures.

Table 23   Experience of Restrictive Practices in Public and Private Sectors

	Not experienced		Experienced but insignificant		Experienced and fairly significant		Experienced and very significant	
	Public Sector %	Private Sector %	Public Sector %	Private Sector %	Public Sector %	Private Sector %	Public Sector %	Private Sector %
(i) Refusal to work on piece-work job before the time or price is agreed	83	76	9	18	2	5	6	1
(ii) Refusal to work overtime when desired by management	41	49	45	40	6	9	6	2
(iii) Opposition to work being sub-contracted outside the establishment	57	77	32	19	5	3	4	1
(iv) Demarcation problem	49	73	39	19	10	6	3	2
(v) Opposition to introduction of new machinery and/or techniques	58	76	30	19	7	5	5	1
vi) Limitation of speed of work or volume of output	54	67	22	23	12	9	13	2

The hypotheses that the degree of restriction was related to the size of the organization or the existence of joint machinery, and that the extent of trade unionism can in itself lead to the imposition of restrictive practices, were both examined.

The hypothesis that a high degree of unionization leads to a higher level of resistance to change gains some support—the firms in which a closed shop operated (46 per cent) appeared to be more prone to the imposition of restriction than other firms (16 per cent). Indeed, firms with substantial unionization, or

[1] T. Lupton, *On the Shop Floor* (Pergamon Press, Oxford 1963).

operating a closed shop, appeared considerably more prone to restrictions than the rest of the sample.[1] However, the number of firms in which significant restrictions had been experienced was limited—only 35 of the 375 firms with unionization of more than two-thirds of their male manual workers were in this particular category.

It seems that the large firms (1,000 employees and over) are more likely to have experienced fairly significant resistance to the introduction of new machinery and techniques. There was some evidence that when a joint body for negotiation and consultation existed there was greater experience of restrictions.

Industrial Conflict

Firms were asked whether they had experienced a collective ban on overtime in the past two years, but only 17 per cent (as opposed to 39 per cent of the public sector) had done so, mostly firms in the highly unionized shipbuilding and vehicles industry groups.

In reply to the question of whether they had experienced a strike (undefined) in the past 2 years, 24 per cent of the private sector (and 33 per cent of the public sector) replied that they had done so. As might be expected from other findings in the survey, an analysis of these replies showed a positive connection with the degree of unionization, with size, with the existence of negotiating and consultative machinery, and with the amount of employee influence over decision-making. Similarly, therefore, the industry groups with the highest strike intensity were shipbuilding, vehicles, and metal manufacturing.

No industrial action, then, in the form of a strike or an overtime ban had been experienced by about two-thirds of the firms surveyed. Furthermore, in reply to a general question about how firms viewed their industrial relations, in both the private and public sectors, virtually none considered them 'bad'. About 10 per cent rated them as only 'fair', but in the private sector 39 per cent rated their industrial relations as 'very good', 50 per cent

[1] This is not to say that restriction is only encountered in unionized firms. Mathewson and his colleagues, writing in the United States around 1930, found ample evidence of restriction in non-unionized firms. (See S. B. Mathewson, *Restriction of Output among Unorganized Workers* (South Illinois Press, Carbondale and Edwardsville, 1969) for this and for an interesting consideration of managerial attitudes towards such restrictions.)

as 'good'. In the public sector 19 per cent of the respondents thought their industrial relations were 'very good' and 71 per cent 'good'. Altogether, therefore, 90 per cent of all the respondents in the public and private sector appeared reasonably satisfied with the quality of their industrial relations.

This result appears somewhat surprising and rather at odds with the picture of industrial relations that is obtained by the daily reporting of industrial conflict in the newspapers or the impression conveyed by some employers' representatives in their evidence to the Donovan Commission. The results obtained in this survey probably reflect on the one hand a reluctance to admit to anything less than good industrial relations—in spite of everything—and on the other a genuine belief that at bottom relations between managers and workers are reasonably good. There may also have been an element of ambiguity in the question and the answers given arising from a view that would appear to be widely held, though not tested in this survey, that the problem is not the relations between workers and managers, but the intransigence of the unions and a small group of shop stewards.

Influence of Ownership on Participation

The advocates of profit-sharing have argued that having a stake in the company where a worker is employed is likely to have a positive effect on his attitude and behaviour in relation to the achievement of the goals of the enterprise. It has generally been assumed that companies having profit-sharing schemes will favour and promote participation in management decision-making. The proportions of formal negotiation and consultative committees in firms with some form of profit-sharing support this suggestion.

It has also been strongly argued that the effect of profit-sharing has in fact been minimal, and that it is bound to be so, since the return on the shares is usually small by comparison with the amount the worker will normally earn in wages or salary, and appears to him remote from his own efforts.

On specific areas of management decision-making the response of 131 firms with profit-sharing schemes was compared with the response of firms without such schemes. The results are shown in Table 24.

The general impression from this table is that the differences in behaviour between profit-sharing and non-profit-sharing firms are for the most part not very great. Columns 5 and 6, which might be expected to show the greatest differences, show responses that are almost identical.

In reply to the questionnaire, 131 firms (20 per cent) indicated that they had profit-sharing schemes, where payments were made otherwise than by share distribution. There were, how-

Table 24   Firms with Profit-Sharing Schemes and Extent of Workers' Influence on Managerial Decisions

	Employees have no influence on our decision.	We would not consult but would consider possible reactions before reaching a decision.	We would consult and probably/ possibly adjust our decision in the light of this view, but the decision would be ours.	We would negotiate, but if un-successful would put our decision into effect.	We would negotiate and would not proceed until there was agree-ment.	This is a matter on which we would accept what our employees want to do.
Type of decision:				Percentages		
To raise additional capital	92(97)	6(2)	2(1)	0(0)	0(0)	0(0)
To allocate profits between invest-ment, dividends, reserves, etc.	95(97)	4(2)	2(1)	0(0)	0(0)	0(0)
To subcontract work-load outside organizations	45(54)	31(27)	21(15)	4(3)	0(2)	0(4)
To introduce new working methods	4(10)	16(16)	53(45)	4(4)	23(24)	0(3)
To introduce work-study methods	8(18)	14(16)	35(30)	6(4)	38(32)	1(4)
To discharge wor-kers no longer needed	16(29)	17(16)	41(32)	16(13)	12(10)	0(3)
To change method of payment	1(10)	17(10)	27(37)	1(4)	40(46)	4(3)
To alter works rules to change disciplinary pro-cedures	6(16)	13(16)	42(33)	14(9)	25(28)	0(1)
To set up new pro-cedures to deal with absenteeism	12(22)	20(15)	42(28)	8(10)	19(25)	0(0)
To dismiss an in-dividual or group for disciplinary reasons	24(40)	37(23)	29(25)	8(8)	2(4)	0(0)

The results for firms with no profit-sharing schemes are shown in brackets.

ever, some limitations imposed upon the type of person eligible for membership of the schemes. In 48 cases, manual workers were excluded and, in an additional 14, administrative, technical, and clerical staff were excluded.

Of the 131 profit-sharing firms, only one had no formal joint machinery of any description. Of the remaining 130 firms, 60 had formal consultative committees, 48 had committees with both negotiating and consultative function, and 22 had committees that were purely negotiating bodies. From these figures, it is fair to conclude that the degree of formalization in the conduct of industrial relations in those firms with profit-sharing schemes is high. Nevertheless, there was no set pattern as to the type of joint machinery adopted. Although the purely consultative committee was the most prominent, more than half of the firms had committees with negotiating functions.

Non-profit-sharing firms are slightly more likely to use negotiations and not to proceed until an agreement has been reached; on the other hand, firms with profit-sharing schemes seem to be a little more prepared to consult. The difference, then, seems to be between a somewhat wider span of consultation in profit-sharing firms, which also seem to put a greater emphasis on managerial independence, and a greater readiness in the non-profit-sharing firms to agree to joint decision-making in the areas of wages, work methods and disciplinary procedures.

There is a slight tendency for profit-sharing to increase with size, but it is greatest for the 1,000–2,000 group, not the very largest. There is no obvious connection with the degree of union membership (the most highly unionized firms and the least unionized having the least profit-sharing).

There is some evidence of better use of communication media among firms with profit-sharing schemes, and slight evidence of fewer strikes.

Participation in the Public Sector

It was shown in Chapter 1 how one strand of thinking in the labour movement about industrial democracy led ultimately to public ownership and the establishment of public corporations, which, particularly as a result of the legislation of the late 1940s, came to account for more than a fifth of total employment in Britain. Nationalization as a basic element in the concept of industrial democracy is discussed elsewhere in this book and it is not intended to duplicate that discussion here. It is, however, appropriate to deal with the pattern of workers' influence upon managerial decision-making as it appeared from the supplementary survey described earlier in Chapter 3, some of the results of which have been shown above. As explained in Chapter 3 differences between the methods of compilation of the private and public sector surveys were such that the replies were not comparable in every respect, but nevertheless the information obtained enabled some comparisons to be made.

Apart from the differences between the present surveys it should, of course, be borne in mind that in making comparisons between the private and the public sectors like is not being compared with like. For instance, industries like electricity, the Post Office, gas, coal and the railways are, within themselves, at the same time much larger and more homogeneous than the largest concerns in private hands. The product or service provided in the public sector does not always have parallels in the private sector. The levels at which decisions are likely to be made also differ, there being a greater degree of centralization in the public sector, on account of the size, unity and statutory responsibilities of the enterprises. Finally, there is a difference, clearly significant in the present context, in that the Boards and Corporations established by the main nationalization Acts were required by statute, unlike private enterprises, to establish machinery for negotiation and consultation with bodies representative of organized workers. Each industry carried out this obligation by joint agreement between Board and unions. From the outset it has been a basic tenet of the industrial relations policies of the industries to support the development of strong and stable unions.

Bearing in mind the statutory obligations, and how they were interpreted, it was not surprising that the supplementary survey found much higher union membership in the public sector than in the private, nor that the extent of formal joint machinery was very much greater in the public sector. Although their statutory responsibilities did not require the nationalized industries to set up joint machinery or particular modes of communication for a specific purpose, the much higher incidence of such machinery in the public sector than in the private suggests a greater concern to satisfy formal requirements to develop effective working relations with the unions and workers.

The public sector as a whole, then, clearly does more than the private sector to involve workers or their representatives in its operations. But does this mean that workers have more influence on managerial decisions in the public sector than in the private? The results of the survey suggest that this is so too.

The results suggest fairly conclusively, therefore, that there is more workers' participation in management decisions, at least through negotiation and joint consultation, in the public sector of British industry than in the private. So far as consultation is concerned, the evidence of the survey can be supported from

Table 25   Workers' Influence on Managerial Decisions in Public and Private Sectors

Type of decision	Employees have no influence on our decision.		We would not consult but would consider possible reactions before reaching a decision.		We would consult and probably/ possibly adjust our decision in the light of this view, but the decision would be ours.		We would negotiate, but if un-successful would put our decision into effect.		We would negotiate and would not proceed until there was agree-ment.		This is a matter on which we would accept what our employees want to do.	
	Public Sector	Private Sector	Public Sector	Private Sector	Public Sector	Private Sector	Public Sector	Private Sector	Public Sector	Private Sector	Public Sector	Private Sector
	%	%	%	%	%	%	%	%	%	%	%	%
To subcontract some of the work-load out-side the organization	30	52	18	28	43	16	2	1	8	2	0	0
To introduce new working methods	0	8	0	16	56	47	5	4	39	24	0	1
To introduce work-study methods	3	15	4	15	31	31	3	7	58	32	2	1
To discharge wor-kers no longer needed	8	26	4	17	50	33	13	13	23	10	2	0
To alter works rules so as to change disciplin-ary procedures	6	14	3	16	38	35	7	9	47	26	0	1
To set up new pro-cedures to deal with absenteeism	7	20	13	18	44	34	13	10	25	17	0	0
To dismiss an in-dividual or group of individuals for disciplinary reasons	20	38	25	26	48	23	8	9	2	4	0	0

other sources. For example the then Ministry of Labour, giving evidence to the Donovan Commission, referred to the 'highly developed' joint consultation in the nationalized industries.[1] It is accepted by both unions and management that the attention given to joint consultation has contributed a good deal to the generally good relations between the two sides.[2] The subject-matter of consultation has been wide: in the G.P.O., for instance, it has extended to discussion with workers' representatives about the design of Post Offices. And the public sector has shown willingness to innovate; the participative use of primary work-groups in electricity supply is noteworthy,[3] and new forms of participation in coal-mines have recently attracted attention.

But has the public sector satisfied the hopes that were entertained for it? These hopes were often very far-reaching indeed. Public enterprise, it was thought, would be more efficient than private in serving the nation. It would provide much better wages and working conditions. Workers would be better satisfied in their work, and their attitude to it would change once the fundamental cause of unrest, the conflict of interest between shareholder or proprietor and workers, had been removed and public accountability through parliament established.

This is not the place to discuss the efficiency of public enterprise, on which widely differing views have been expressed. Comparison of wages and working conditions between public and private sectors is likewise beyond the scope of this enquiry. Suffice it to say that there is no evidence to suggest that the greater amount of participation in the public sector has resulted in more or less efficient operation, and that the conditions of

[1] Ministry of Labour, *Evidence to the Royal Commission on Trade Unions and Employers' Associations* (H.M.S.O., London 1965), p. 24. See also the evidence given by several of the nationalized industries themselves, individually, to the Commission.

[2] As to the contribution of consultation see, for example, L. Tivey, *Nationalization in British Industry* (Cape, London 1966). It should be added that the effectiveness of consultation in the public sector is not universally accepted. Hughes, for instance, has expressed the view that 'in nationalized industry there has been considerable neglect of consultation, from both sides'. (J. Hughes, *Nationalised Industries in the Mixed Economy*, Fabian Society, London 1960.)

[3] For a detailed account of the electricity supply industry's consultative arrangements see R. D. V. Roberts and H. Sallis, 'Joint Consultation in the Electricity Supply Industry', 1949–59, in *Public Administration* (1959), and for the experiments with primary working groups see H. Sallis, 'Joint Consultation and Meetings of Primary Working Groups in Power Stations', *British Journal of Industrial Relations* (November 1965).

employment in public enterprises compare favourably with, but are not exceptionally better than, those in private industry. Obviously, uniformity of treatment across any one industry has increased with nationalization.

On the issue of workers' attitudes it must be said that the present form of public enterprise has not proved what has been called 'a gateway to a new society'.[1] Transfer of ownership seems to have had little if any effect on the outlook or morale of workers. Disputes between workers and management appear to be as common as in the private sector. Nor has there been any appreciable difference in the pattern of behaviour of the trade unions.

In summary, it would seem that the present form of public ownership of industry in Britain has been successful in creating greater opportunities for participation than generally exist in the private sector, and that workers' influence on decision-making is somewhat greater. However, the nationalized industries have not been successful in introducing any radical innovation in forms of participation not already found in the private sector. Nor can it be said that the nationalized industries provide a model for the new industrial society sought by the industrial democrats of old.

[1] W. A. Robson, *Nationalised Industry and Public Ownership* (Allen and Unwin, London 1960), p. 321. See also Tivey, op. cit., and H. A. Clegg, *Industrial Democracy and Nationalization* (Blackwell, Oxford 1951).

5 Participation and the Process of Collective Bargaining

The data presented in the previous chapter indicates that in the context of the British system of industrial relations the collective participation of workers in management decision-making is predominantly achieved through negotiation conducted on a trade-union basis rather than through consultative committees. As the level of trade-union membership increases the range of managerial decisions that become subject to collective bargaining is widened. Nevertheless, while in theory any decision might be the subject of challenge by the unions, the extent to which participation actually takes place varies greatly from enterprise to enterprise and from one level of decision to another.

The attitudes of the unions towards participation are by no means uniform. There is, in fact, an acute division of opinion as to the precise role of the union in relation to the decisions of management and the extent to which unions should be given the right to participate and accept the responsibility for carrying out the decisions when made.

Whatever reservations unions may have in connection with participation they can be expected to favour the strengthening and widening of the scope of collective bargaining. The Donovan Commission gave strong support to this policy, seeing collective bargaining as 'the most effective means of giving workers the right to representation in decisions affecting their working lives, a right which is or should be the prerogative of every worker'.[1]

As a result of the report of the Donovan Commission, the strengthening and extension of collective bargaining has become an object of public policy that is accepted by virtually all con-

[1] *Report* of the Royal Commission on Trade Unions and Employers' Associations, para. 212.

cerned. In 1969, a policy statement by the then Government expressed the view that mature collective bargaining 'represents the best method so far devised of advancing industrial democracy ...'.[1]

Though the Conservative Government which took office in 1970 did not see the task of reforming industrial relations in the same light as did its predecessor, its own industrial relations legislation is intended to provide a framework of which the centrepiece is collective bargaining. Thus the Introductory Section of the Industrial Relations Act, 1971, proclaims its purpose as to promote good industrial relations in accordance with general principles which include:—

'(a) the principle of collective bargaining freely conducted on behalf of workers and employers and with due regard to the general interests of the community;

(b) the principle of developing and maintaining orderly procedures in industry for the peaceful and expeditious settlement of disputes by negotiation, conciliation or arbitration, with due regard to the general interests of the community'.

The Commission on Industrial Relations, established in 1969 and strengthened in 1971, has as one of its aims the fostering of improved collective bargaining procedures.

Provision of Information and Collective Bargaining

The provision of full and relevant information has been accepted in many countries as a necessary requirement of constructive collective bargaining and it has been strongly urged by unions in Britain that companies should be compelled by law to divulge certain kinds of information. In its evidence to the Royal Commission, the Amalgamated Engineering Union suggested that two kinds of information should be made available to union representatives; one relating to manpower costs and the other to the commercial viability of the organization. Under the first heading the union asked for:

(a) an index of labour costs per unit of output;

(b) an analysis of the number and type of workers employed, and

---

[1] *In Place of Strife—A Policy for Industrial Relations*, Cmnd. 3888 (London, January 1969), para. 19.

(c) details about the pay-roll.

Under the second, they wanted:

(a) in diversified product firms and groups, an indication of the financial standing of each major form of production;

(b) an indication of the proportion of total sales being exported, and

(c) a table showing broad disbursement by percentages of total company income.[1]

The A.E.U. based this claim on the view that shop stewards and local officials were at a disadvantage because of a lack of relevant information 'It is common for firms to withhold all financial information from union representatives. . . . It also happens quite frequently that employers deliberately misrepresent the financial and trading position of their company to local officials in the belief that they have not the knowledge to refute them.'[2]

Industrial Democracy, a report produced by a Labour Party Working Party, also considered that the union or unions organizing the labour force in a particularly company should be ensured access to the information they require for effective bargaining and participation. The type of information that this report envisaged as necessary was divided into four main headings.

(i) Man-power and remuneration questions, which include such topics as labour turnover, man-power planning, and labour costs per unit of output.

(ii) control questions, dealing with control and ownership of the company.

(iii) development, production and investment questions, covering the state of the order book, proposed substantial changes in methods, and plans for research and development.

(iv) cost, pricing and profit questions, involving cost and price structures, breakdown by plant or product where applicable, and turnover.[3]

[1] See Amalgamated Engineering Union, *Trade Unions and the Contemporary Scene*: evidence submitted to the Royal Commission on Trade Unions and Employers' Associations (1965), pp. 54 and 56.

[2] Ibid., p. 56.

[3] Labour Party, *Industrial Democracy*, Report of Working Party (London 1967), pp. 52 and 53.

This demand for the disclosure of information was given additional weight in the White Paper *In Place of Strife*,[1] and the Iron and Steel Act, 1967. Paragraph 47 of the White Paper stated that 'If employees' representatives are to participate with management on equal terms in the extension of collective bargaining and consultation at company or plant level, they will need adequate information to allow them to form an independent judgment on management proposals, policies and decisions'. The White Paper accepts that many managements already recognize the need to disclose such information, but considers that other firms take an excessively cautious view when no real risk is involved. Refusal to disclose information by some firms is seen as a 'prime cause of the failure of works production committees and similar bodies',[2] and as a reason for prematurely entrenched positions during negotiations. Subsequently the Conservative Government's Industrial Relations Act included provisions for information to be made available for negotiating purposes.

Although availability of information is a necessary prerequisite for viable collective bargaining, one possible effect of more extensive disclosure could be a change in the balance of power in negotiations. If the non-disclosure of information served the interests of management, by giving it a negotiating advantage over the less well-informed union, the removal of this advantage by the threat of legal sanction would alter the balance of power in the bargaining relation. It is, however, difficult to say with certainty how exactly the balance will be changed. The full facts can probably never be known by either side. It is the hope that more information will improve the climate of negotiations by removing suspicion and permitting a more rational process of decision making. On the other hand, however strong the fundamental case may be for providing more information it may not lead to an easier resolution of the basic issues since it is unlikely to change the fundamental conflicts involved.

Clearly, the possible strengthening of the position of the workers' representatives has not been overlooked by the advocates of workers' control, who regard opening the books as 'no more than a starting point to *evaluating* and *interpreting* a

---

[1] *In Place of Strife—A Policy for Industrial Relations* (Cmnd. 3888, H.M.S.O. London, January 1969).

[2] Ibid., Cmnd. 3888, para. 47.

complex situation in order to work out and fight for a policy of advance towards democratic control of industry'.[1]

The more extensive the information supplied to workers' representatives, the greater is the likelihood that the scope of negotiations would widen to cover new topics. The extension of the subject-matter was regarded by the Donovan Report[2] as one of the essentials for the establishment of orderly collective bargaining within the enterprise.

The scope of collective bargaining has been very limited in Britain by comparison with the United States, though wider than in many European countries. Many matters that have been the subject of unilateral management decision or a process of *ad hoc* discussion with shop-stewards are the subject of bargaining and written agreement in the U.S.A. However, the growth of productivity bargaining has led to plant and company agreements covering such matters as redundancy, labour utilization, manpower planning and industrial discipline.

The evolution of collective bargaining in Britain has brought the unions into the position where it has become common for them to enter into agreements with management that will permit the more efficient utilization of human resources. Here opposition and militancy have to give way to systems of joint regulation and joint determination. Although joint procedures for the determination of issues that used to be decided by management alone give the union an opportunity to influence these decisions for the benefit of their members, not all workers are satisfied with these developments. There is a fear that the unions will become too closely identified with management and will agree to decisions that radical workers may think should have been opposed.

When unions become closely associated with management they may come to be looked upon as not pursuing a vigorous and active opposition to the employers. This danger is less great when joint regulation is the result of specific agreements into which the unions have entered at the conclusion of a bargaining process freely entered and openly conducted.

---

[1] M. Barratt-Brown, *Opening the Books* (Institute of Workers' Control Pamphlet Series No. 4, Nottingham 1969), p. 2.
[2] op. cit., para. 203.

Role of Joint Consultation

In the past, collective bargaining was largely confined to questions of remuneration, hours of work and holidays with pay. The limitation of bargaining to this narrow area was due in the main to the fact that most agreements were made nationally and applied to a whole industry. At the level of the plant or enterprise the function of the union representatives was to ensure that the national agreement was observed, and that issues affecting individuals or groups of workers arising from the agreement were dealt with through agreed procedures of representation and negotiation. Questions concerning matters that were not covered by the national agreement were often the subject of joint consultation. It was believed by both management and unions that it was in their common interest to draw a sharp dividing line between these two different but complementary processes. Full employment and economic prosperity gave the shop-stewards an opportunity which they quickly seized to turn consultation into a bargaining process, and to extend national agreements by workplace negotiations, which vastly improved upon the conditions of employment that applied to an industry as a whole.

Although management still has some confidence in joint consultation, as was apparent from the fact that 207 out of 649 firms[1] answering the questionnaire still had consultative committees, the dividing line between consultation and collective bargaining has become increasingly blurred. Now that the unions have accepted that bargaining will take place at the level of the enterprise or plant as well as at the level of industry, they have virtually ceased to be concerned at maintaining a distinction between consultation and negotiation. What was often a rather dubious distinction has become in many cases a complete fiction. Management would often prefer to maintain the distinction between bargaining and consultation, since in the one case it enters into specific commitments while in the other it maintains in the last resort the right to decide and the responsibility for the decision. There are other arguments in favour of maintaining an element of formal consultation apart from management's perhaps rather limited freedom to make the final decision. One of the most important consideration for management is that the ethos of a consultative committee is very different from that of a

[1] See Chapter 3.

E

collective bargaining session. In collective bargaining the two sides generally approach each other as rivals bent upon securing the best deal for themselves. At its best, collective bargaining can achieve positive gains for both sides, but at its worst it degenerates into a conflict situation which is frequently damaging to both sides. With consultation, management is hopeful that the discussions will be carried on in an atmosphere that is free from the threat of serious conflict if agreement is not immediately reached. Ideas and proposals can be discussed in the light of common goals rather than in terms of ends that are in conflict.

It is of some interest to note that while no distinction between consultation and bargaining is normally made in the United States, where every question is seen as a legitimate bargaining issue, in France, Germany and Sweden, for example, the distinction has been fostered.

In France the *comités d'entreprises*, established by law in 1945 were not intended to have decision-making powers in respect of the economic aspects of the enterprise. The committees were to be consultative, except that they would have decision-making powers in dealing with social institutions of the enterprise. In this welfare field the *comités d'entreprises* are able to administer activities that have a separate organization of their own, such as canteens and libraries.

It must be remembered that the French system of collective bargaining is not as extensive as that in Britain, and therefore inroads into areas of consultation are less likely. In fact, as Gréyfié de Bellecombe has remarked when discussing collective bargaining in France, successive wage increases 'owe more to legislation (which from time to time fixes a guaranteed inter-occupational minimum wage, applicable only to a rather small percentage of wage earners but nevertheless important for its symbolic value) and to decisions by employers (drawn up in the light of market conditions and the current psychological climate) than to formal bargaining.'[1]

In West Germany a number of interesting distinctions are made by the Works Constitution Act, 1952, which requires

[1] See L. Gréyfié de Bellecombe, 'Workers' Participation in Management in France: the Basic Problems', in *International Institute for Labour Studies, Bulletin* 6 (June 1969), p. 79.

Works Councils to be established in nearly all forms of enterprise. The Councils comprise elected representatives of manual and office workers who are usually, but do not have to be, trade union members. Distinctions are made between three areas of decision-making: the social (for example, regulating hours of work, training and safety); the personnel (including engagement and dismissals); and the economic (commercial and production). Within these specified areas the Councils have certain prescribed rights of co-determination or consultation, and rights to information. In the social and personnel fields the Councils have wide rights; in the economic field only certain rights to information. They are not charged with responsibilities for regulating wages and conditions.

In Sweden, with a highly developed centralized and advanced system of collective bargaining, the distinction between collective bargaining and joint consultation is also maintained. 'A Swedish industrial worker would not participate in decisions concerning the type of production, choice of markets, price policy, choice of investments, procurement of capital or allocation of profits.'[1] The functions of Works Councils, established under an Agreement of 1946 (and strengthened in 1958 and 1966), are consultative rather than decision-making, but the Councils work for greater productivity and greater occupational satisfaction. The Swedish agreements emphasize that collective bargaining issues are outside the purview of the Councils.

It also seems that Swedish trade unions share the view of the employers that matters for negotiation can and should be separate from matters for consultation. They do not need to become involved in the management of the enterprises, although they expect their members to be consulted beforehand about decisions that affect them. Managerial prerogatives, at least in the fields of financial, commercial and production decisions, still seem to be of practical significance. In Sweden, for instance, the employer has in principle an unrestricted right to transfer workers from one job to another. Several such prerogatives are buttressed by Labour Court decisions.[2]

[1] L. Ekeberg and S. Lantz, *Blue-Collar Workers' Participation in Management in Sweden* (Swedish Institute for Labour Studies, Stockholm 1968), p. 9.

[2] See R. B. Peterson, *The Swedish Labor Court Views Management Rights* (S.A.F., Stockholm 1968).

These comparisons[1] have served to show that, in several other systems, the distinction between consultation and negotiation is preserved; and indeed, in Sweden, the trade unions support such a preservation, in contrast with the growing desire in Britain for the single channel of representation. What is perhaps most important in all of Europe and indeed also in the United States is that management is firmly determined to maintain a clear line of distinction as to what is its decision-making prerogative. Not only in the commercial and financial field, but in the areas of decisions about directing and assigning work, the European employer has generally been successful in preserving freedom to deploy his resources so as to give maximum efficiency without opposition from workers or trade unions, even though on other, 'social' matters, including the effects on workers of certain managerial decisions, the European manager may have less freedom than his British counterpart. It is noteworthy that there is very little productivity bargaining, as understood in Britain, in European countries. In the United States managerial prerogatives are the subject, at almost every contract negotiation, of bargaining, since rights are established by what is in the contract. But once the contract is drawn, the division is clearly accepted by both sides. By contrast, the situation in Britain is far more fluid, flexible and uncertain. Managerial decisions may or may not be challenged, according to the vagaries of the situation; the determining factor may be convention, power, personality and occasionally written agreement. Whatever the normative situation, there is no longer a common standard from one situation to another. The rules are in a state of flux.

Although the formal process of joint consultation has tended to become much less important than twenty years ago, under the impact of plant and enterprise bargaining, the need to discuss many issues as problems to be solved, rather than bones of contention to be picked, is of continuing importance. Where unions exist representation is likely to be through union organization; where there are no unions, consultative committees can be established on what could well be a more informal constituency

[1] It should be added that the European scene is changing to some degree. Works Councils are being strengthened (for instance there is a new Works Constitution Act in Germany) and in some countries unions are becoming more involved at the workplace and are taking a closer interest in commercial and production decisions. In Sweden managerial prerogatives are coming under attack.

basis. The multiplicity of unions in British industry compels complexity in committee structures. It also gives rise to tensions and difficulties that would not exist in either the absence of unions or single-union jurisdiction.

Problem of Union Participation

One consequence of multi-union representation is that plant and company bargaining are often carried on between management and shop stewards completely independently of higher-level union interference or effective control. This situation is in marked contrast with the nationalized industries, where the structure of participation, whether through collective bargaining or joint consultation, is multi-tiered. Issues unresolved at lower levels are transferred to higher levels. Of course, in a less integrated way this situation has existed elsewhere as, for instance, in engineering under the engineering procedure agreement, but it is not without significance that work-place participation has given rise to growing difficulties as it has grown in importance within a vertical structure of authority.

When a final decision has to be taken at a higher level the problem of participation through representatives becomes more acute. Workers are no longer in a face-to-face relationship with their representatives; representation has now become remote; it has also become professional—thus the distance between workers and their representatives has been multiplied. The problems of union bureaucracy and participation in the processes of trade-union government are well known, and have been well studied.[1] If the union is to be an effective instrument of participation at the higher levels of management decision-making, the problems of representation within its own structure must be solved.

What is perhaps of most fundamental importance, however, is that as unions extend the range of collective bargaining they inevitably become increasingly involved in the determination and achievement of managerial goals. This means that the union must become less responsive to popular demands of the rank and file. This phenomenon has frequently been noted in the past in the attitudes and behaviour of senior union officials who have

---

[1] See B. C. Roberts, *Trade Union Government and Administration in Great Britain* (Bell, London 1956); H. A. Clegg *et al.*, *Trade Union Officers* (Blackwell, Oxford 1961).

had the experience of sitting on high-level committees. The oft-made accusation that union leaders 'get out of touch' is not simply a bureaucratic phenomenon arising out of the internal structural characteristics of unions; it is also caused by the inevitable fact that a union leader finds himself involved in decisions that he must support because he knows that in economic and technical terms it would be folly to oppose them. It is, however, in the nature of many decisions made at the top that they are difficult to explain to those who have not been closely involved and have no background of experience and knowledge of the issues out of which the decisions arise.

There is also the further factor that senior union officials find themselves sharing a common professional status with management, which gives them a kind of mutual dependence. Thus it often seems to the rank-and-file trade unionists that their officials have 'gone soft' on management. Exactly the same feelings are sometimes displayed by production managers, who not infrequently feel that personnel managers have developed too close a relation with trade-union officials and too much sympathy for their problems.

Collective Bargaining and Industrial Democracy

In this study participation has been seen as something that inevitably goes on in any organization in different forms. It has been analysed in terms of collective bargaining, consultation and unilateral regulation and examined in terms of the influence exerted by workers along a continuum ranging from unilateral managerial decisions to unilateral workers' decisions. However, the objective of many advocates of greater worker-participation is not to satisfy the desire of workers to have their views taken into account and to reduce the area of unilateral management decision-making, but to establish a system of industrial democracy.

Industrial democracy was seen by the Webbs as simply a society in which the power of management was constrained by the power of the unions to bargain collectively on any question of importance to workers. Given a balance of bargaining power, the operation of the labour market would satisfy both the economic requirement of allocating labour efficiently and the equitable requirement of a fair reward to skill and effort as between capital and labour.

Clegg,[1] making a political rather than an economic analysis of industrial democracy, saw its essential feature in the existence of an opposition to management. This 'opposition' concept of industrial democracy may be criticized on two grounds. The first is that the role of the opposition in a parliamentary system of government is fundamentally different from the role of an opposition to management in an enterprise. In parliament the opposition is always a potential government; in the firm it is a method of imposing a constraint, and as such may be inclined to act quite differently from the way it would if it might be called upon to take office and to carry out on its own responsibility the policy it was advocating. Opposition, for Clegg, really becomes identical with the role of the union in any collective bargaining relationship, and on all fours with the notion of the Webbs.

The second criticism of the concept of opposition as the fundamental characteristic of industrial democracy is that it may be a necessary, but certainly not a sufficient, condition. A trade union may well be able to exert a powerful opposition to management, but it may itself be anything but democratic. Democracy, whether in the state or in industry, implies accountability to the majority as well as acceptance of minorities selected to lead and administer. It might well be held that a trade union is in structure and purpose a democratic organization, but an essential weakness of the collective bargaining opposition concept of democracy is that it is not accountable to the totality of the enterprise —workers, managers and shareholders. Indeed, this concept of collective bargaining implies independence of the enterprise, and to this extent it is a denial that a union can ever be a representative agency of its members at one and the same time as it accepts a responsibility for carrying out managerial decisions. Nevertheless, responsible collective bargaining must be predicated on the assumption that the outcome of any negotiations between management and trade unions will not destroy the enterprise or seriously impair its ability to provide employment and to conserve and enhance its capital, since this would also prevent the union from achieving its *raison d'être,* the continuous im-

[1] H. A. Clegg, *A New Approach to Industrial Democracy* (Blackwell, Oxford 1960).

provement of the wages and working conditions of its members. To this extent a union must accept responsibility for achieving managerial goals.

Clegg further argues that there is no alternative to the existence of trade unions that are independent of the State and management, since 'only the unions can represent the industrial interests of the workers'. He also asserts that 'the ownership of industry is irrelevant to good industrial relations', and therefore one form or another cannot be an essential condition of industrial democracy.

Clegg's second proposition, that only unions can represent the interests of workers, is bound up with the notion of independence. It assumes that staff associations or an internally structured hierarchy of committees cannot be democratic, because as internal bodies they are not independent. Thus, paradoxically, the analogy with parliamentary democracy is tossed out, since opposition in Parliament is opposition within the State. Clegg's concept of opposition and its link with independence is based upon the fact that management has the right to terminate the contract of employment, thus eliminating the opposition and making a farce of independence. This situation need not prevail any more than in a democracy where the Government may order the army to seize the leaders of the opposition and lock them up. This is not an entirely unknown occurrence, but it is not the normal situation.

Perhaps the most fundamental weakness of Clegg's position is that the right to oppose is only one aspect of a democratic system of government, albeit an important one. It is also essential that the opposition should be prepared to assume the responsibility of office. Without this readiness to accept the duties of government, opposition must confine itself to a role of protest. This role may be much less effective as a means of protecting the interests of union members than could be achieved by entering into a participative relationship with both State and management. Accepting a participative role need not destroy this ability to protest, though it will in some respects be a limitation on the degree of organic involvement.

As was said in the Introduction, the analogy between industrial and political democracy raises a number of difficulties, but there is no reason in principle why, as in the democratic state, it should not become a convention of management that decisions are only made with the concurrence of representative bodies or individuals. This situation in fact already exists in a number of well-known cases of industrial self-government. The fact that in none of these instances does the system work in terms of active worker-participation as well as was hoped is not due to management abusing its power.[1]

There is also evidence from other countries that effective institutions of participation and regulation of management decision-making can be established outside, and not dependent upon the collective bargaining process; the German Works Councils are a case in point. Moreover, it has become apparent that even in Britain, where the unions are stronger than in most countries, in important instances they have been unable to protect the interests of their members without statutory assistance, as a panoply of legislation from the Factories Acts and Wages Council Acts to the Redundancy Payments Act bears witness. In other cases, as in the development of plant and enterprise bargaining, power was with the workers within the plant, and depended only little on their membership of a national trade union. The arguments advanced by Clegg do not constitute a proof that a considerable degree of industrial democracy could not be created outside the collective bargaining system.

The mainstream of demand for industrial democracy has followed two separate courses. One has been based upon the conception of the enterprise as an organic unity, in which the divisions between managers and workers arise from functional differences rather than differences in social and economic interest. Many of the most famous schemes of industrial democracy, such as those of the John Lewis Partnership and the Scott Bader Commonwealth, are based upon such a concept.

The other source of support for industrial democracy has been based upon the belief that collective bargaining could be extended to the point where the workers were in control of the enterprise. The advocates of workers' control have rejected joint consultation and the concept of participation as calculated to weaken the bargaining power of the unions and undermine the

---

[1] E. Jaques, *The Changing Culture of a Factory* (Tavistock Publications, London 1951), and A. Flanders *et al.*, *Experiment in Industrial Democracy: A Study of the John Lewis Partnership* (Faber, London 1968).

demand for full workers' control.[1] This argument was vigorously debated in the trade-union movement in the period following the second World War, when it was ultimately rejected by the unions, which showed a preference for joint consultation, as a form of limited participation that did not compromise their independence.

The problem of the role of unions in relation to their collective bargaining functions and the achievement of the right to participate in, if not to control management, was raised acutely by the nationalization of industry. In the event the unions preferred not to compromise their bargaining role, and achieved this by insisting that trade unionists should be on the boards of management, but not as representatives of the unions.

Ownership, Participation and Control

The democratization of the ownership of private enterprise, whether through nationalization or the distribution of shares to the employees, leaves a dilemma for the unions unresolved. The experience of the nationalized industries in Britain suggests that a change of ownership, as Clegg argues, does not of itself involve a change in the function and role of management in relation to the role of workers. If, then, at the same time the unions have no wish to change their function, it is apparent that the pattern of industrial relations will remain in basic terms the same as under private ownership. The gain the unions have made is in a slight addition to their security, and perhaps a marginal advantage in their bargaining relations, but these advantages may well be offset by the cramping effect of being called upon directly to take the public interest into account.

The advocates of workers' control have seen the social ownership of industry as an essential condition of achieving industrial democracy. However, the experience of social ownership suggests that it is compatible with either an authoritarian style of management or a democratic one. In the U.S.S.R. the plant director is given considerable freedom to make decisions without the constraint of collective bargaining or the interference of powerful workers' councils. In Yugoslavia, on the other hand, the workers' council elected for two years by direct and secret ballot from

[1] See K. Coates and A. Topham, in K. Coates (ed.) *Can the Workers Run Industry?* (Sphere Books Ltd, London 1968).

and by the workers in the enterprise, has far-reaching authority. The council is empowered to decide such matters as the rules of the enterprise, its plans and accounts, the election and recall of the management board, the appointment, rights and duties of the director, and the current use of the enterprise's funds, its distribution of income after tax, investment programme and wage structure, its internal discipline, and the engagement and dismissal of its labour force.

Against this background of an extensive degree of worker self-management, and the existence of social ownership, Kolaja,[1] endeavouring to estimate the extent to which workers felt the enterprise to be their own property, found a high level of identification, rising according to skill and responsibility, with executives having the highest sense of personal participation in ownership.

In spite of this active democratization of ownership and indeed of management, the power of the plant director is not negligible. Moreover, the Yugoslav government, acutely concerned by the need to raise the efficiency of industry more rapidly than was being achieved, has recently taken steps to give plant directors greater authority and to encourage a more positive managerial direction that will inevitably reduce the power and effectiveness of the workers' council.

Democratization of the terms of employment is clearly not necessarily limited to democratization of either ownership or the government of the enterprise. The most advanced systems of collective bargaining in the world, in Sweden, the U.S.A., and the United Kingdom, which effectively limit the power of management, have developed within the context of a market economy in which the bulk of enterprises are privately owned. It is not without significance that it is in socialized economies that collective bargaining has virtually ceased to exist. In economies in which wages and the allocation of capital resources are determined by an economic plan, unrestrained collective bargaining would create an incompatible situation. Strikes are practically inadmissible since they would bring workers and the State into conflict, thus creating a contradiction of ends and means that by definition socialist planning exists to prevent.

The role of unions as collective bargaining agents fits un-

---

[1] J. Kolaja, *Workers' Councils: The Yugoslav Experience* (Tavistock Publications, London 1965).

comfortably into the socialist states, as the Webbs[1] and the founders of the Soviet Union recognized fifty years ago.[2] Nevertheless the advocates of workers' control in Britain argue that trade unionism and collective bargaining are indispensable even when industry is socially owned. There would still be clashes of interest between different groups of workers under a system of workers' control, and it would, therefore, be necessary to have independent unions that would defend the interest of these groups.[3] However, it is difficult to conceive that in a system in which the unions were responsible for making the decisions they could also be responsible for fighting them.

Yugoslav experience may be relevant in this respect, since it offers the possibility of examining the role of unions in a system of workers' self-management. Yugoslav unions retain a wide range of functions, though these are somewhat different from those discharged by unions in Western Europe and North America. Yugoslav unions would certainly claim to have protective functions, although they act on behalf of the State. The role of the unions in workers' management, though indirect, is quite an important one, both centrally and through trade-union branches, established in the enterprise. Trade unions can and do intervene when it is judged that things are going wrong. They can propose the recall of members of the workers' management bodies or the dismissal of the enterprise director. The distribution of income within the enterprise must also meet with trade-union approval both as to its equity and to ensure that the workers are not overpaying themselves. Nevertheless, the major sources of power within the Yugoslav enterprise are the Workers' Council and the Director. In these circumstances the role of the union is a difficult one and it is perhaps not surprising that the union is sometimes seen as an agent of management. This may be contrasted with the role of the workers' councils, which were intended as instruments of management, but which in some cases have taken on the functions of a trade union in conflict with the plant director and the established trade unions.

The difficulties concerning the role of the unions which have

[1] S. and B. Webb, *A Constitution for the Socialist Commonwealth of Great Britain* (Longmans, London 1920).

[2] See debates in *All Union Central Council and Communist Party Conferences in Soviet Union 1918–1927*.

[3] K. Coates and A. Topham, 'Participation or Control?' in K. Coates (ed.) op. cit., p. 234.

arisen in Yugoslavia do not seem to have troubled the unions or workers in Germany. Under the German system of *mitbestimmung* the unions are represented on the supervisory board and have a crucial role in the selection of the personnel director of certain enterprises. This has not had the effect of undermining the strength of the unions. Indeed, an important reason why the unions demand the extension of equal trade-union and worker representatives on the board of all public companies, instead of merely in the coal, iron and steel industries, is that they believe that this would greatly increase their collective bargaining strength. Because they believe the unions are correct in this, and for ideological reasons, the employers in Germany equally strongly oppose this extension of the co-determination system.

Pluralism and Participation

In societies with a pluralist political system and in which economic decisions are based primarily on market criteria, collective bargaining is likely to remain of fundamental importance as a method of ensuring the effective participation of workers in the making of a range of decisions relating to terms and conditions of employment. However, it is apparent that in spite of the extension of the range and scope of the bargaining process, participation through a system of representation which is predicated on notions of conflict between the goals of the union and the goals of the managers of the enterprise is limited by this dichotomy of interest. This limitation is accepted by those who see in the power-democratic pluralistic divisions of society and its sub-systems the best safeguard of the interests of workers. The limits of pluralism are, however, influenced, if not entirely determined, by technological, economic and social changes, which in modern society are increasingly giving rise to pressing problems of the power and responsibility of private and public organizations.

The technological and economic developments that are taking place, which in some instances are meaning the end of long-established occupations and the rapid decline of entire industries, are giving rise to a growing tension and a manifestation of conflict between workers and management. In these circumstances workers are aware that they are both increasingly vulnerable and increasingly powerful. The traditional modes of collective bargaining, while valuable both as a protection of the interests of workers and as an instrument of stable management, are nevertheless felt by many to be an inadequate means of regulating and deciding on the right course of action in plants and enterprises in contemporary circumstances.

The desire to participate more effectively thus arises as a felt need by trade unionists, who wish to exercise a greater degree of control over the decisions of management acting under the pressure of changing technological and economic circumstances. The objective of this policy is, however, primarily to constrain management and to achieve the goals of the union as against the other partners in the enterprise. Not every union leader in Britain would accept that involvement in the making of decisions through the appointment of worker-directors, which now enjoys some support in the trade-union movement, would give the unions greater bargaining strength or increase the efficiency of management.

The appointment of worker-directors as a method of democratizing management and involving workers both directly and through trade unions will be examined in the next chapter.

6 Participation at Directorial Level

Participation in the making of management decisions may take place at all levels, but the representation of workers on a board of directors has particular significance, since it offers an opportunity to .influence fundamental policy decisions.\ It is for this reason that worker representation on boards of directors has been sought. Since, however, the appointment of directors to represent the interests of the workers gives rise to problems of acute concern both to trade unions and to the remainder of the board who have been appointed by the shareholders it arouses considerable controversy.

Workers' Directors

As was discussed in Chapter 1, the question of worker representation on the boards of nationalized industries was debated for many years before it was finally resolved in such a way as to avoid the problem of direct links with the trade unions. Demands for workers' representatives on boards of directors have not been confined to representation on boards of nationalized industries. A persistent campaign has been conducted by various groups including the Liberal Party, who have urged that the boards of all public companies, including those privately owned, should include workers' representatives. There is in fact no legal reason to prevent a company from appointing a worker as a director. Under the present law such a director would be in exactly the same position as any other director and would assume all the obligations of a director as prescribed by company law. The law would, however, need to be changed to make the appointment of workers' directors a legal requirement.

The question of the appointment of workers' directors in privately owned companies has shifted during the past few years from the publication of occasional articles and pamphlets recommending this step towards an alternative concept of the enterprise as an organic unity embracing the workers as well as the shareholders. Under prevailing social theory, and in law, the primary responsibility of the board of directors of an enterprise is to the shareholders. If there is a conflict between the social interest of the employees of the company and the economic interest of the shareholders, unless prior rights are established by statute, the shareholders come first. This situation inevitably gives rise to conflicts of interest between management and employees; it is the fundamental dichotomy on which the pluralist system of industrial relations is founded. It is not, however, the only reason for divisions of interest between managers and employees. Conflict is an endemic feature of any organization, and is the product of a great variety of factors that influence the behaviour of managers and workers. In every organizational structure conflict must be institutionalized if the organization is to survive, in such a way as to minimize its effects. What is at issue in the debate about the merits of workers' directors is the extent to which such a development will advance the interests of workers without damaging the interests of the other groups involved. These include on the one hand the trade unions, on the other the shareholders, and, further, the interests of all those who are not directly members of the organization, either as employees or shareholders, but who as customers, taxpayers and members of the community, are affected by the way in which enterprises are conducted.

Attitudes of T.U.C., Labour Party and Liberal Party

Impetus was given to the discussion on workers' representation on boards of directors, when the T.U.C., in presenting written evidence to the Donovan Commission in 1966, expressed themselves in favour of legislation of a discretionary character 'to allow companies to make provision for trade union representatives on the boards of directors'.[1] In the public sector '... provision should be made at each level in the management structure for trade union representatives of the workpeople employed in these

[1] *Trade Unionism* (Trades Union Congress, London 1966), para. 290.

industries to participate in the formulation of policy and in the day-to-day operation of these industries'.[1]

Giving oral evidence before the Commission, in 1967, the T.U.C. explained that they had in mind the election of trade-union members to the boards of companies by the workers; such directors might not have the duties of present directors to the shareholders, though they would be concerned with every aspect of the business and have all the information available to other directors.

While the Donovan Commission were deliberating, interest in workers' representation was also being taken in political quarters. *Industrial Democracy,* the Report of a Working Party of the Labour Party, speaking of private industry, thought that new developments in worker representation in company decision-making bodies might emerge from the further development of bargaining and joint regulation. They considered 'it would be dangerous to abstract the question of worker representation on company boards of directors, etc., from this more fundamental question of the strengthening and co-ordination of collective bargaining within the company'.[2]

As to the public sector, the Working Party took a different view: 'We think that there should be experiments in placing representatives of the workers directly concerned on particular boards.'[3] The following year, a statement by the National Executive Committee of the Party was made to the Annual Conference. Much of it followed closely on the Working Party Report. It was silent about workers' representation on boards in private industry but favoured experiments

in placing representatives of the workers in a nationalized industry on the board of that industry. This representation should not be confined to union officials; nor should it divert attention from the need to involve worker representatives in decision making at every level in an industry, and especially at the various points of production.[4]

The Liberal Party's Assembly in 1968 called for participation

[1] Ibid., para. 262.
[2] Labour Party, *Industrial Democracy,* Report of Working Party (London 1967), para. 92.
[3] Ibid., para. 101.
[4] Labour Party, *Industrial Democracy,* A Statement by the National Executive Committee (Labour Party, London 1968).

by workers in the selection of the boards of all companies over a certain size, on the basis of parity with shareholders. They had been debating the Report of their Industrial Partnership Committee, *Partners at Work*,[1] which recommended that workers in companies employing more than 50 people should be given the right to exercise, collectively, a quarter of the votes cast at General Meetings. Certain key decisions, such as amalgamation and fresh share issues, would have to have the support of more than three-quarters of the votes cast at the General Meeting. The workers' voting power, acquired through share distribution, would achieve parity with that of shareholders and could go beyond it. As the directors would be elected jointly by workers and shareholders none would be representing sectional interests only.

Some Proposals

The Donovan Commission, too, devoted some attention to workers' representation on Boards.[2] A minority of the commissioners felt that the present exclusive right of shareholders to elect directors was inappropriate, as workers were more involved in the well-being of a company than the shareholders; they felt, therefore, that there was a need for directors to be appointed 'to act as guardians of the workers' interest at the stage when company policy is being formulated'.[3]

Two members of the Donovan Commission,[4] while subscribing to the view that there is a need for the interests of workers to be represented at directorial level, felt that this could be best achieved by legislation making the appointment of workers' directors[5] compulsory in companies over a certain size.[6] The same two commissioners also set out in some detail what they envisaged as the method of appointment, and the type of person to be appointed.

[1] Liberal Party, *Partners at Work*, Report of the Industrial Partnership Committee (Liberal Party, London 1968).

[2] Royal Commission on Trade Unions and Employers' Associations, *Report* paras. 1000–5.

[3] Royal Commission on Trade Unions and Employers' Associations, *Report*, para. 1005.

[4] Shonfield and Wigham.

[5] Workers' directors would not be employees of the company to whose board they were appointed.

[6] 5,000 or more employees.

The power of appointment should rest with the trade unions active in the company concerned, who would consult the T.U.C. It is envisaged that those chosen would be more likely to be men with industrial or financial experience or knowledge, or trade union officials, than workers from the bench. (Any trade union official appointed would of course be barred from any collective bargaining involving the company while he was a director of it.)[1]

Once appointed, workers' directors would 'exercise the rights and responsibilities of non-executive directors of companies to which they are appointed'.[2]

Subsequently the White Paper *In Place of Strife* indicated that the Government favoured experiments in the appointment of workers' representatives to the boards of undertakings.[3]

A further refinement to the concept of workers' directors which has been suggested[4] would be to replace the present board of directors by a two-tier structure, responsible respectively for the 'government' and 'management' of the enterprise. The 'government' of the enterprise would be by a representative council appointed on a proportional basis, the representation of workers and shareholders perhaps being based on the net output of the firm attributable respectively to the equity capital and labour employed, and calculated on the net profits, and wages and salaries, or a more complex basis. The principal functions of the representative council would be:

(a) to establish and amend the principal objects of the firm;
(b) to appoint and remove directors and auditors;
(c) to approve amendments of the rules and any proposed changes in the capital structure of the firm;
(d) to receive such financial and other reports as may be necessary to indicate policy and progress.

So, it would be at the 'government' level of the two-tier board that workers would be able to participate through their representatives.

The idea of the representation of workers at board-room level has been the subject of sharp criticism for different reasons by both management and trade-union leaders. The Chairman of

[1] Royal Commission, *Report*, para. 1005.
[2] Ibid., para. 1005.
[3] Cmd 3888, para. 49.
[4] N. Ross, Workers' Participation and Control, *Scientific Business*, Vol. II, No. 8 (February 1965).

Shell Transport and Trading Ltd has suggested that nothing would be gained 'by adding the inexperience of workers' representatives to the incompetence of bad management'.[1] The late Leslie Cannon, then President of the Electrical and Plumbing Trades Union, underlined this point of view by suggesting that if a worker has the ability to be a member of the board that is what he ought to be doing, not continuing as a worker and sitting on the board on a part-time basis.[2]

For those trade unionists who feel that participation necessarily involves a loss of independence, the idea of worker-directors is approached with great caution. It is quite clear that, although worker-directors are supposedly representatives of the workers, they must be involved at times in management decisions. This necessary duality of responsibility was strongly criticized both in the specific context of the appointment of worker-directors, and with regard to the wider concept of participation, by the Electrical and Plumbing Trades Union in their evidence to the Donovan Commission.

A line must be drawn, however, at participation by workers in management. It is our view that little can be gained by such participation. If trade union representatives are in control of an undertaking they will require, quite properly, to take into consideration the views of other interests, in the process of decision-making. They will, in other words, be acting as managers. They will, therefore, no longer be acting as trade unionists. ... The likelihood is that they would receive the odium of being obstructionists from their management colleagues and the odium of being collaborators from their trade union colleagues.

At the risk of sounding banal, it must be said that management has a duty to manage. ... It is not the duty of trade unionists to participate in management. Their duty, quite clearly, is to protect and advance the interests of their members. Frequently this will necessitate the closest collaboration with management. At other times it will require them to say, quite unequivocally, that a certain course of action is not in the interests of their members; this is in the ultimate interest of both parties. Nothing can be gained by attempting to disguise this fact.[3]

[1] D. H. Barran, Chairman of Shell Transport and Trading Ltd, speaking at the conference of the Institute of Personnel Management, October 1967 (as reported in the *Institute of Personnel Management Digest*, 31 November 1967).
[2] On the occasion of *The Times* Management Lecture, March 1970.
[3] Royal Commission on Trade Unions and Employers' Associations, *Minutes of Evidence*, 57, 2469, paras. 161, 162.

Experience of Nationalized Industries in Britain

Until the experiments in the British Steel Corporation, there were two main sources of experience of workers' directors in Britain. One was in certain gas companies and the other was in the industries nationalized during the period of the 1945–50 Labour Government. These two main schemes were different in fundamental respects. In the gas companies workers employed by the companies were elected to the boards. In the nationalized industries persons with experience of trade-union work were eligible to be appointed by the Minister concerned as members of the boards on the same basis as any other member and on condition that all actual connection with the union to which the person had previously belonged had been given up.

The South Metropolitan Gas Company was empowered by Act of Parliament in 1896 to make provision for the election of directors by its workers, who were shareholders under a share distribution scheme.[1] To qualify for election a worker-director would have to have lengthy service and a substantial holding of stock under the co-partnership scheme. Three worker-directors were appointed, it being provided that one should be a 'salaried officer'. The directors retired annually by rotation. They received their normal wage or salary while on directorial duties, together with fees for attendance at meetings. Similar schemes operated in the Commercial Gas Company and the South Suburban Gas Company until nationalization under the Gas Act 1948. The worker-directors on the boards of these companies seem to have functioned in the same way as other directors. No special difficulties seem to have arisen, but the virtue of these schemes in this respect must be seen against the exceptional background of these companies, which had successful co-partnership arrangements, were able to provide a high degree of job security, and at the time had little labour turnover and faced a low level of militant trade-union activity.[2]

[1] See Chapter 1, p. 25.

[2] This evaluation is based on personal communications from directors of the companies concerned. Other information is given in C. Carpenter, *Industrial Co-partnership*, 4th Edition (Labour Co-partnership Association, London 1927). A personal view is expressed by D. Hunter Johnson, *Worker Representation on Company Boards* (Industrial Educational and Research Foundation, 1968), pp. 28 and 29.

The appointment of senior trade-union leaders to the boards of nationalized industries has created no problems for the trade unions other than to deprive them of the services of able and experienced officers. However, since the numbers involved have been small and the age of the appointees has generally not been very far off that at which they would have been compelled to retire from their union posts the effect has been minimal.

Once appointed to the boards of nationalized industries trade-union leaders have rapidly adjusted to their new role. Where they have been given responsibility for personnel administration and industrial relations, which because of their experience and skills has commonly been the case, they have carried out their duties in the same way as any other board member. The fact that they have previously been trade-union leaders does not seem to have had any marked effect on the way in which they have functioned. The nature of the task they have been called upon to carry out and the organizational structure into which they have had to fit seems to have ensured a smooth transition to their new role.

The attitude of the unions towards their erstwhile colleagues as union leaders has helped to prevent any confusion of roles and duality of responsibility. So far as the unions have been concerned the previous experience of the board member responsible for industrial relations has been largely irrelevant. Union leaders might have expected from ex-union leaders a greater degree of understanding of their claims and their organizational problems, but they have not looked upon an ex-colleague as different in any way from other members of the board. They have expected that an ex-union official would carry out his duties in the interest of the board and not in the interest of the union. They have, therefore, acted in exactly the same way towards nationalized industries as they have towards private employers. Although most trade unionists are strong supporters of nationalization and of the appointment of trade-union officials to board membership, they have not allowed this support to influence their actions as bargainers on behalf of their members. It is possible that in particular cases they have been more co-operative and less suspicious of managerial motives than they would otherwise have been, but the over-all effect of this type of consideration has been small.

It is impossible to measure the effect of the appointment of trade-union leaders to the boards of nationalized industries in terms of better industrial relations, or any other criteria that might be used. It would be difficult to claim that these appointments had made any marked difference one way or the other. Other factors than the appointment of trade-union leaders to the boards have been responsible for determining the pattern of industrial relations in nationalized industries.

One of the most important benefits to flow from the appointment of union leaders to the boards of nationalized industries has been the advantage to the individuals concerned. Appointment to a board has given a union leader an opportunity to enjoy a much larger salary, and the distinction of being selected for the limited number of these posts as the crowning achievement of a professional career. The status and prestige carried by the appointment is perhaps of much greater significance to most union leaders than the material rewards, which are an essential element of the posts at this level of responsibility.

Whatever advantages the nationalized industries may have gained from the appointment of experienced and able union leaders to their boards, or whatever benefits might have accrued to the individuals concerned, there is little evidence to show that the workers or the unions have been significantly affected. The workers have largely viewed these appointments with indifference; if they have expressed opinions these have often been somewhat cynical. There have been some cases where positive distrust of ex-union leaders has been expressed by shop stewards. Problems have arisen when the members and leaders of a particular type of union have believed that the board member, because of his previous background, has favoured a particular type of union organization that would be at the expense of their own organization.

The net effect, then, on industrial relations of the appointment of former senior union leaders to the boards of nationalized industries has been extremely small. Its greatest significance, apart from producing some very able managers, hardly distinguishable from any other members of the boards, has been in providing a final rung on the career ladder of union officials that might in an intangible way have inclined them to a greater degree of responsibility, while in union office. This advantage, if such it be counted, might well have been offset by adverse responses the appointments may have generated in the attitudes and behaviour of the rank-and-file union members and their local leaders.

Appointment of Worker-Directors in the Steel Industry

With the establishment of the British Steel Corporation a new development started in 1968. The re-nationalized steel industry was required, following the pattern adopted in the legislation of the 1940s, to enter into arrangements with appropriate workers' organizations for 'the negotiation of terms and conditions of employment', and also for 'the promotion and encouragement of measures affecting efficiency'. The Corporation was also required to promote measures dealing with the safety, health and welfare of persons employed, and to make available, to workers' representatives, information that appeared necessary to enable them to participate effectively in discussions.[1]

Against this background, the Steel Corporation envisaged three methods by which workers would participate in the management of the industry. Two of the methods involved the traditional areas of consultation and negotiation, the third, concerning worker-directors, constituted a major innovation.

The initial proposals, relating to the appointment of workers as part-time directors, provided for up to three worker-directors to be appointed to each of the four group boards,[2] for a period of three years. The workers appointed were to act in a personal capacity and not as representatives, and they were to receive an additional sum of £1,000 a year and expenses above their normal wage or salary. Certain limitations were initially imposed to make certain that they did not act as representatives—the appointees were not expected to serve on the boards of the groups in which they were employed, and were expected to give up any trade-union offices they held.[3] These proposals were modified after discussion with the T.U.C. Steel Committee,[4] to allow appointees to become directors upon the board of the groups which employed them. Later still, the constraint relating to union office was

[1] Iron and Steel Act, 1967, Schedule 4, Part V.
[2] See below.
[3] However, the worker-directors were to be encouraged to attend trade-union branch meetings.
[4] A body set up by the T.U.C. in 1967 from representatives of unions recognized nationally in the industry.

eased to permit directors to retain forms of office which did not involve them in, for example, the conduct of negotiation.

The mechanics of appointment are of particular interest. The Steel Corporation, through the T.U.C., asked unions[1] active in the industry to put forward nominations. There were no suggestions that election by the workers themselves might be considered appropriate. These nominations went through a vetting process before twelve worker-directors were finally appointed by the Corporation. The criteria used in appointment have not been published in any detail, but it is likely that candidates had to satisfy the following conditions. Firstly, they had to have the ability and personal qualities likely to be required; secondly, they had to have considerable trade-union experience; and thirdly, they had to command the respect of fellow employees. What is not known is how much 'horse-trading' went on in the making of these appointments, and how far it was felt necessary to satisfy the realities of power arising from the distribution of trade-union membership, and the occupational groups within the industry, There is no way of knowing without investigation how far the appointments met with the approval of the workers they were appointed to represent.

The organization of the Steel Corporation provided for the establishment of four groups—Midlands, Northern and Tubes, Scottish and North, and South Wales—which reflected a combination of geographical factors, product links, and technical and economic considerations. It was anticipated that the group boards would compete in costs, service, quality and productivity, although not in price, and would be accountable to the Corporation for results. The boards were conceived of as advisory bodies, and authority was vested in the group managing director. Though active only within the prescribed framework of the Corporation policy, group boards are clearly influential in the application of that policy.

At the beginning of 1970 the group structure underwent some considerable changes. The existing group boards were disbanded and regrouped on a product basis, the six new product divisions being special steels, general steels, strip mills, tubes, chemical engineering, and constructional engineering.[2] This re-organization caused the distribution of worker-directors on the boards

---

[1] The Electrical Trades Union refused to participate.
[2] The new structure came into operation on 29 March 1970.

to become uneven. This, however, was adjusted in a way which took account of the size of the division. The total number of worker-directors is now sixteen. In the light of the first two years of operation of the scheme, a job description was worked out for the worker-directors. The job description suggests that the worker-directors will, in an atmosphere of complete confidence and access to all facts, figures and arguments, bring to the divisional board the point of view of the great mass of people in the industry. Such a function, however, would not be expected in any way to duplicate the existing machinery for negotiation and consultation. Nor would the worker-directors be vested with any managerial function or executive responsibility. It is as yet too early to make any appreciation of the way in which this cautious experiment in worker representation has in fact worked out.[1]

General Considerations

In discussing and evaluating workers' participation schemes in general, and worker-director schemes in particular, it is important to distinguish between the two different concepts of workers' representation. In the appointment of former trade-union leaders to the boards of nationalized industries representation is indirect, and through individuals who have an expert knowledge of the needs of workers and experience of bargaining on their behalf. The appointment is not made by the workers concerned themselves, nor is the representative a worker drawn from the workers involved. The British Steel Corporation scheme was an important shift towards the appointment of directors who were drawn from the ranks of the workers themselves and who remained in principle workers, though not direct representatives chosen by fellow workers. The more ambitious schemes of workers' representation exemplified by the John Lewis Partnership, the Scott Bader Commonwealth and the Glacier Metal Company, have all been based upon the concept of direct repre-

[1] For a journalistic appreciation of the employee directors' scheme, see Giles Radice 'Worker Directors lose Touch with the Men', *Financial Times*, 24 January 1969, and Elsbeth Ganguin, 'BSC's worker directors take stock of their first year', *Financial Times*, 25 June 1969. A research team, sponsored by the British Steel Corporation based at the Universities of Bradford, Cardiff, Sheffield and Strathclyde, has been engaged in research on the worker-directors' scheme.

sentation of the employees on the councils of government of the companies. As pointed out elsewhere, this concept of overall directorial policy-making must be distinguished from that which involves active day-to-day management of the enterprise.

Much of the argument about the desirability of workers' representation at the directorial level turns on the issue of workers' representatives who are chosen by and from the workers themselves, or are experts appointed to ensure that the interests of workers are effectively taken into account when managerial policy is made.

For those who view the role of worker-directors in functional terms, their appointment is valid only if it contributes to the efficiency of the enterprise, through the improvement of industrial relations and the more effective performance of the board itself. For those who see the organization of an enterprise in terms of the distribution of power, the primary role of a worker-director is to protect the interests of those whom he represents rather than add to the efficiency of the corporate body.

In carrying out their study of workers' participation in Norway, Emery and Thorsrud examined the nature of the directorial board and its functions. They came to the following conclusions:[1]

(1) The primary function of the board is to conserve and ensure the growth of the company's capital *per se*. This function is distinct from that of management, which 'is primarily concerned with the efficient operation of the concrete resources at its disposal and with the efficient exploitation of ... markets ...'

(2) The board is the only body properly placed to make decisions relating to the conservation and growth of the company's capital.

(3) Membership of the board of directors is only justified 'in so far as their competence contributes to achieving optimal conditions of security and growth for company capital'. The board will seek to obtain (with some qualifications) the skills that are critical to decisions about the security and growth of its capital, and will tend to insist that its members shall be primarily concerned with its main function.

[1] F. E. Emery and E. Thorsrud, *Form and Content in Industrial Democracy*, Chapter 6 (Tavistock, London 1969). The inquiry related to a small number of enterprises in the public, or quasi-public sector, having workers' directors. It was not found that the institution of such directors had had any appreciable value.

(4) Unless the board clarifies and agrees upon its functions there is no basis for arriving at a policy that will effectively relate company interests to other interests. Members of the board must therefore act together to achieve the goals of the enterprise, and not as representatives of special interests.

(5) As the suppliers of the capital of the company, the shareholders stand in a special relation to the board, since without capital there can be no organization.[1] In the case of other interest groups, such as workers, customers and the government, their relationship to the enterprise is one that is determined by negotiation and mutual consideration.

It is possible to argue that if the primary function of the board is to 'conserve and ensure the growth of the capital of the company', then the achievement of such a goal might be facilitated by having the benefit of workers' experience at directorial level. There can be no doubt that a lack of understanding of industrial relations problems can prove to be a costly weakness in the managerial policy of an enterprise, and it is possible that a workers' director might be an important factor in remedying this situation.

If as a result of the appointment of workers' directors it were possible to achieve a greater degree of understanding of the goals of the enterprise and the conditions that have to be satisfied to achieve them, then all the parties might well benefit. The critical question to be answered is whether the involvement of workers in the process of decision-making through having a representative on the board of directors is more likely to achieve a positive benefit for workers' interests as well as management interests than a clear-cut negotiating relationship. Those who believe that the results will be positive will favour the appointment of worker-directors; unfortunately there is no way of establishing any certain causal connections between the appointment of worker-directors and improvements in industrial relations.

Moreover, it is not necessary, as Emery and Thorsrud conclude, for a board of directors to include representatives of the various interest groups to satisfy social needs. These can be met,

[1] Compare Lord Cole: 'Consumers, the government, workers, managers, are all special interests. It is only the shareholders' interests which really span them all'. *The Future of the Board* (Industrial Educational and Research Foundation, London 1968).

and may well be best met, by the board not being representative of any group but the shareholders, since it is then easier for it to weigh justly the claims of the differing groups on its resources. Representation within the board may lead to internal conflict and a weakening of the ability of the enterprise to achieve its goals. If this were to be the outcome of the appointment of workers' directors the results might be negative for the enterprise as a whole and the workers might well suffer the most.

There are those who see the enterprise as a cockpit, in which opposing sides fight each other, and for them it is desirable to strengthen the power of the workers by their being directly represented on the boards of directors. For those who think of the enterprise in pluralistic power terms, the issue of workers' representation on the boards of directors clearly becomes one of whether this will alter the power balance in the workers' favour. There is a strong and growing belief among the trade unions that it might well do so. If it were to be clearly and decisively shown that workers' directors were not able to achieve a substantial measure of influence and control, which would be to their benefit, it would be undesirable on grounds of self-interest for workers to seek such representation.

The appointment of workers' directors could have implications for collective bargaining if either of the bargaining parties were as a result strengthened or weakened. Worker-directors might feel that it was their duty to give support and encouragement to the trade unions and the shop-stewards, or at least to ensure that their case was fully understood and given sympathetic consideration. On the other hand it is also possible that by being involved in the process of board decision-making they would become completely identified with and feel loyal to the corporate policy of the board. In these circumstances the influence of worker-directors might serve to weaken the unions' case and limit their endeavour. On balance it is likely that the influence of worker-directors would probably make little difference to the traditional working of the collective bargaining system.

Only if the industrial relations system were to be fundamentally changed, and centred on an enterprise system in which the traditional boards of directors in private and public enterprise were replaced by a workers' council, as in Yugoslavia, would collective bargaining cease to play a dominating role. In this respect it is interesting to examine the working of co-determination in Germany, especially since collective bargaining is less firmly established and the unions are less militant than in Britain.

German Experience of Co-Determination

The German Co-determination Act, 1951, requires a labour director to be appointed to the management board of companies in the mining, iron and steel industries; seventy-one such directors were working under the provisions of this Act in 1968.[1] These directors cannot be appointed or dismissed against the wishes of the majority of workers' members on the supervisory board. German law, not only in the industries mentioned but generally, provides for both a supervisory board and a management board. The supervisory board, which is likely to meet quarterly, has the duties of appointing the management board and approving the annual accounts. It has the right to information to enable it to supervise the management board's activities. In mining, iron and steel, half of its members represent workers, directly or indirectly. Members of the supervisory board may not be members of the management board, and vice versa. The actual operation of the company is carried out by the management board, which may comprise a commercial director, a technical director and the labour director.

German co-determination has been the subject of extensive research and considerable controversy. At the same time it seems to have made very little difference to efficiency, industrial relations or workers' satisfaction in their jobs. Studies reported by Fürstenberg found that, although about three-quarters of the workers knew that co-determination had been introduced into their enterprise 'only half of the interviewed workers had any concrete ideas about the actual meaning of co-determination and most of these just knew the name of their labour director'.[2]

[1] F. Fürstenberg, 'Workers' Participation in Management in the Federal Republic of Germany', International Institute for Labour Studies *Bulletin* No. 6 (June 1969), p. 120.

[2] Fürstenberg, op. cit., p. 130. Interestingly, one of the studies quoted suggested a correlation between knowledge of co-determination among workers and level of skill (77 per cent of skilled workers, 68 per cent of semi-skilled and 55 per cent of unskilled had knowledge). The study by G. Hespe *et al. An investigation into communication and participation in the Bar and Rod Mill* (Sheffield 1969), p. 3, found that only five out of forty workers knew of the existence of the worker-directors in the British steel industry.

The position of the labour director has been the subject of numerous surveys. Neuloh's survey found that 64 per cent of the workers saw him as their representative, 21 per cent thought he represented both management and workers, while 6 per cent regarded him as a representative of management. Nearly a half saw his main task as a form of arbitration between the conflicting influences to which he was subject.[1] A survey of labour directors reported by Blume found their contacts with workers to be good. As to the qualities needed for the job, more than a half stressed professional skill and almost half emphasized character. Blume's study also elicited that about two-thirds of the labour directors were in charge of the entire personnel organization in their enterprise.[2]

The Germans recognize the problem of the dual allegiance of the labour director, as combining the functions of effective management and effective representation of the workers' point of view. Fürstenberg considers such dual allegiance is not uncommon in modern life and stresses that the service the directors devote to their managerial role has not prevented 'a greater consideration of the social needs of employees when major changes in technical equipment and plant layout are being planned'.[3] A problem that sometimes develops, however, arises from the director becoming so closely identified with the management that he becomes remote from the workers.

As has been stated, workers and shareholders have equal representation on the supervisory boards of companies in mining, iron and steel. In an eleven-man board one manual and one office worker are nominated by the Works Council from among employees of the firm, with the concurrence of the trade unions. The unions propose three other members, one of whom cannot be a representative of the union, nor an employee, nor have any considerable financial interest in the enterprise. The 'eleventh man' is nominated by the other ten. In the private sector, outside mining, iron and steel, the Works Constitution Act, 1952, calls for a third of the supervisory board members to be repre-

---

[1] O. Neuloh, *Der neue Betriebsstil* (Tübingen 1960). Neuloh found that only sixteen out of ninety-six directors came directly from being workers, and only six had been trade-union officials. Many had pursued studies after leaving school: ten were graduates.

[2] In E. Potthoff, O. Blume and H. Duvernell, *Zwischenbilanz der Mitbestimmung* (J. E. B. Mohr [Paul Siebeck], Tübingen 1962).

[3] Fürstenberg, op. cit., p. 123.

sentative of workers. If, as is often the case, there are only two such members, one must be a wage-earning employee and the other a salaried one. While the employers are now content with the provisions of the Act of 1952 concerning board membership, the unions maintain that the minority representation of the workers means that no transfer of power takes place and that it is easy for the other members to ensure that the workers' representatives are ineffective.

In the co-determination industries in 1960, 578 out of 1,250 members of supervisory boards were workers' representatives. Of these, 28 per cent were, or had previously been manual workers, 28 per cent were trade-union officials, and 17 per cent clerks.[1] The scope for participation by the workers' representatives in board work varies according to the rules adopted and the relationship between board members, labour directors and the statutory works councils. A study by Voigt suggests that there are differences in outlook between the representatives appointed from within the enterprise and the outside representatives; the former complain that they do not get time to inform themselves properly on matters to be discussed and feel that the outside representatives are not well prepared; the outside members do not seem active in making contact with the workers in the enterprise. 'Inside' members are said to be too parochial. The neutral members appear to fulfil a mainly mediatory function.

In relating German co-determination to the British framework, one cannot ignore the fact that the German labour director is only a part of a comprehensive industrial relations system, which includes the works councils and workers' representation on both management and supervisory board. Nevertheless, the experience is relevant in relation to the structure of the company, and to the continuing role of collective bargaining, which has grown in strength and significance during the period since the co-determination system was introduced.

Although studies of co-determination in Germany indicate that the system has not brought about dramatic changes in the relation of workers to management, it is nevertheless generally strongly supported by the trade unions. The two-tier structure of supervisory board and management board has attracted widespread interest as a practical method of equating the need for

[1] E. Potthoff, O. Blume and H. Duvernell, op. cit.

managerial initiative and independence in day-to-day decision-making with an element of social control in which unions and workers are able to participate.[1] A number of British writers have suggested that company law should be revised to permit the establishment of a two-tier board structure in this country. Such a step would make possible a much greater degree of participation, with little danger to either the unions or management, but perhaps with positive benefit to both.

[1] For instance, two reports (by Sanders and Lyon-Caen), relating to the proposed European company to operate throughout the Common Market, have recommended a two-tier structure. The Report of the Verdam Commission in Holland also made a similar recommendation.

7 Management and Participation

In previous chapters we have examined the concept of participation, the extent to which it is practised through existing methods of consultation and collective bargaining, and the possible effects of the development of formal systems of participation on the established institutions. In this chapter the focus will be on management as a decision-making institution essential to the realization of the goals of an enterprise, and as a process through which the variety of interest groups that are vitally involved in the activity of the enterprise, namely the shareholders, workers, suppliers, customers, the local community, and the nation at large, are harmoniously integrated.[1] Management as a structural element with an identifiable group interest of its own is subject to the constraints which these participating elements impose on its decisions. Our concern is with the role of workers as a participative element and the effect of different types of participation on the carrying out of the managerial function.

The frame of reference traditionally employed by management has limited the role of workers to the carrying out, within the competence of their occupational roles, of decisions made by those charged with the task of management. Managerial authority, in the eyes of most managers, has been grounded not only on a functional requirement, but even more fundamentally on the exercise of an inherent right. Since the emergence of the trade unions the right to manage has been subject to continuous challenge, and under the pressure of the unions the decision-making prerogatives of management have been greatly

[1] These interest groups have been called 'the stakeholders' by E. Rhenman, in *Industrial Democracy and Industrial Management* (Tavistock, London 1968). For a sociological analysis of the decision-making process in the modern firm, see T. D. Weinshall, *Conceptual Schemes of Organisational Behaviour and their Possible Application*, a paper presented at Ashridge Management College (September 1968).

whittled down. Though the concept of participation through consultation and collective bargaining has been generally accepted in principle, if not completely in practice, management is still acutely concerned to maintain what it considers to be the essential foundation of its authority, namely, the moral right to take certain decisions without challenge from the unions.

It is clear that the way in which management perceives the enterprise, as, equally, the way in which the union perceives the enterprise, influences the responses of either side to each other. The notion,[1] however, that the main factor preventing a higher degree of workers' participation is management's unitary frame of reference is probably exaggerated, since it is quite clear that management cannot successfully achieve the goals of the enterprise unless it is capable of reconciling the conflicting interests of shareholders, workers, suppliers, customers, and the wider community within which it exists. It has, in fact, been argued that the maintenance of the co-operation of these essential interests is the principal function of management, and in this respect all enterprises must be pluralistic unless they have an outright monopoly situation and exist in a totalitarian society.[2] What is at issue for management is how far it could and should permit the process of participation to go in respect of the role of workers, as individual employees and as members of trade unions, or of other collective associations. If management were to accept the goals of the workers or the unions, at the expense of the other elements that comprise the total organization, this would be to subscribe to the particular unitary concept of workers' control that in a pluralistic society would lead to a breakdown of the organization. The constraints on management grow out of its fundamental task of managing, and if workers are to participate in the process of decision-making they must be prepared to accept goals which maintain the organization as a co-operative venture.

The readiness of management to accept formal consultation and collective bargaining has been brought about by technological developments and social change. These factors are continuing to push back the extent of managerial authority and

---

[1] A. Fox, *Industrial Sociology and Industrial Relations*, Research Paper No. 3 (Royal Commission on Trade Unions and Employers' Associations, 1966).

[2] T. D. Weinshall, op. cit.

advance the range of workers' participation both horizontally, in terms of carrying out the job task, and vertically, in terms of making decisions relating to the enterprise as a whole. The problem for management, whose task is to achieve the goals of the enterprise by harmonizing the conflicting associated interests, is to develop institutional arrangements that will make this possible.

Profit-Sharing, Co-Partnership and Co-Ownership

Among the earliest efforts to achieve a closer association between workers and the achievement of the goals of the enterprise are profit-sharing, co-partnership and co-ownership, whose development was sketched in Chapter 1 and some of whose characteristics were discussed in Chapter 4. As previously stated, such schemes are generally limited to participation in the profitability of the enterprise, and rarely carry with them any right to participate in managerial decision-making. Moreover, the financial stake of the worker in the success of the enterprise through these means is likely to be much less than through increases in pay and improvements in conditions of employment. It is, however, interesting to note that recently suggestions have been put forward that would have the effect of giving workers a much more substantial holding in the capital of enterprises in the private sector.[1] Such schemes would not of themselves bring about a much greater degree of participation in management decision-making. Most of the relatively small number of enterprises that are at present owned by their workers are not of sufficient size to be representative of industry as a whole, but two, the large John Lewis Partnership and the medium-sized Scott Bader Commonwealth, are so well established and of such a nature as to permit certain inferences to be drawn. These examples seem to suggest that ownership by the workers has surprisingly little relevance to participation in the managerial decision-making process.[2]

[1] See for instance Bow Group, *Cutting the Cake* (London 1968); Liberal Party, op. cit. (1968); and H. A. Turner, Evidence to the Royal Commission on Trade Unions and Employers' Associations, 1967 (reported in *Financial Times*, 10 March 1967).

[2] See Flanders *et al.*, op. cit. (1968), and F. H. Blum, *Work and Community: The Scott Bader Commonwealth and the Quest for a New Social Order* (Routledge and Kegan Paul, London 1968).

Probably the smaller the size of the enterprise the easier it is to achieve participation.[1] It is perhaps not without significance that most of the members of Demintry—The Society for Democratic Integration in Industry—are very small firms.

The need for expertise, the professionalization of the management process and growth in scale of organization, and the diffusion of capital holdings, have served to weaken the control of the shareowners over the appointed managers, whether they be members of the public or employees. While the pressure for participation arises in part from the fact that workers have no say in decisions that significantly affect their interest, since they are taken for the advantage of shareholders, in practice shareholders exert little control over management. A board of directors, acting in the name of the shareholders, is, so long as it is maintaining the capital of the company and securing reasonable growth according to circumstances, largely free to determine its own managerial policies.

The Influence of the Behavioural Scientists

Another form of approach to participation which has had a strong influence on management derives from the 'scientific management' school of thought associated with F. W. Taylor[2] and from later management and organization theorists. 'Scientific management' theorists believed that workers' tasks should be simplified and broken down so far as possible; that close supervision was essential, and that virtually the only motive for working was economic. Workers' social groupings were not taken into account very much. The approach to work processes was from the point of view of systematic observation and measurement, and it seems to have been taken for granted that someone other than the worker is best fitted to decide how a job should be done and that the worker's area of judgement should be reduced to the minimum. On the other hand, Taylor sincerely believed that the adoption of scientific management would do much to eliminate causes of dispute. No system of management should be considered 'which does not in the long run give satis-

---

[1] Accounts of endeavours to achieve particular forms of industrial democracy in, for example, Rowen Engineering Ltd, Glasgow, and Landsman's (Co-Ownership) Ltd, are included in P. Derrick and J. F. Phipps, *Co-ownership, Co-operation and Control* (Longmans, London 1969).

[2] See F. W. Taylor, *Scientific Management* (Harper, New York 1947).

faction to both employer and employee, which does not make it apparent that their best interests are mutual, and which does not bring about such thorough and hardy co-operation that they can pull together instead of apart'.[1]

Other writers express the desire to bring more objectivity to the conduct of the work-place. Mary Parker Follett argued that decision-making could be depersonalized: in cases of apparent conflict the joint study of facts would throw up the 'law of the situation', from which the course to be followed would become self-evident. Managerial decisions would be seen to derive from objective requirements, and not be based on the personal wishes of managers.[2] Later, Simon saw the task of administration as being to design the environment in such a way that decisions would be made rationally in terms of the goals of the enterprise.[3]

But these approaches were concerned with the formal organization rather than with the human beings who make up the organization. Around 1930, the famous Hawthorne experiments showed the importance of informal work-groups, and, inspired particularly by Elton Mayo,[4] the view spread that good management necessitated far greater attention to human relations than it normally received. As Bendix put it: 'Failure to treat workers as human beings came to be regarded as the cause of low morale, poor craftsmanship, unresponsiveness, and confusion'.[5] Organizational structure, external economic factors, technology, trade unions and the power balance between managers and workers, were largely ignored by the human-relations school. It was assumed that there was a considerable measure of identity of purpose within the enterprise and that high morale would automatically lead to high productivity.[6]

After the work of Mayo and his associates the task of labour-management relations came to be seen as 'the removal of barriers to collaboration and the reconciliation of both efficiency

---

[1] Ibid., p. 21.

[2] H. C. Metcalfe and L. F. Urwick, *Dynamic Administration* (Pitman, London 1941).

[3] H. A. Simon, *Administrative Behaviour* (Macmillan, New York 1947).

[4] See particularly his *The Human Problems of an Industrial Civilisation* (Macmillan, London 1933), and *The Social Problems of an Industrial Civilisation* (Routledge and Kegan Paul, London 1942).

[5] R. Bendix, *Work and Authority in Industry: Ideologies of Management in the Course of Industrialisation* (Wiley, New York 1956), p. 294.

[6] For a review of Mayo's contribution to managerial ideology see ibid. pp. 308–27.

and social satisfaction within the ambit of common purpose provided by the goals of the enterprise'.[1] To this end, participation could be viewed as a managerial tool. It was seen as a means of increasing efficiency rather than as creating industrial democracy. The advantages that could stem from the use of participation as a managerial device were, it was suggested, likely to be considerable, including a higher rate of output and increased quality of product; a reduction in turnover, absenteeism and tardiness; a reduction in the number of grievances; more peaceful manager-subordinate and manager-union relations; and a greater readiness to accept change.[2]

One of the results that flowed from the awakening of interest in the human aspects of the enterprise that accompanies the popularization of the ideas of the human-relations school was the stimulation of the study of the behavioural sciences, and particularly of their industrial application. This in turn led to the development of managerial practices of a participatory character. Some of them genuinely involved workers in decision-making, albeit usually only at the level of the job; these are discussed later in this chapter as horizontal forms of participation. Others cannot be regarded as genuinely participative but as a means of facilitating the management of the enterprise by taking account of the views of workers and anticipating any likely opposition to managerial policies. Good communications, and the use of attitude surveys and techniques of motivation were among the devices used to this end. Full employment, with its emphasis on the need to retain and attract workers, and the growing power of trade unions, and particularly of working groups, spurred on the development of such techniques.

In respect of its implications for participation it is useful to review the development since Mayo of thought about the human structure of the enterprise.

Undoubtedly the most influential contributor to the development of modern management thinking on human relations has been Douglas McGregor.[3] McGregor saw that industry was a

[1] J. Child, *British Management Thought, a Critical Analysis* (Allen and Unwin, London 1969), p. 118.

[2] R. Tannenbaum and F. Massarik, 'Participation by Subordinates in the Managerial Decision-Making Process', *The Canadian Journal of Economics and Political Science* (1950), p. 412.

[3] See D. McGregor, *The Human Side of Enterprise* (McGraw-Hill, New York 1960), and *The Professional Manager* (McGraw-Hill, New York 1967).

long way from realizing the potential represented by its human resources: there should be a greater understanding of human behaviour in organizational settings, and new managerial styles needed to be evolved.[1] McGregor contrasted two managerial styles. One, 'Theory X', epitomized the traditional beliefs that basically people disliked work (and must therefore be coerced to achieve organizational objectives) and preferred direction to thinking for themselves. The other, 'Theory Y', took into account that in modern industrial societies most people's basic needs had been satisfied, so that new motivations were needed. 'Theory Y' sought to provide for an integration of individual and organizational goals and epitomized a style of management based on assumptions that it is as natural for man to work as to play or to rest; that he will exercise self-direction and self-control in the service of objectives to which he is committed; that commitment is a function of the rewards associated with the achievement of objectives; that the average man accepts and even seeks responsibility; that imagination and creativity are more widely distributed than is commonly supposed; and that workers' intellectual capacities are only partially utilized.[2]

Almost equally influential has been the work of Likert, and others associated with the Institute for Social Research at the University of Michigan. Studying the styles of high- and low-producing managers and supervisors Likert found that greater productivity, higher earnings and lower costs were achieved by those who were most effective in the human aspects of their work and who built up highly motivated work-groups. Likert postulated four styles of management ranging from an autocratic form to a participative form in which leader and subordinates, as a group, tackle problems and solve them. Leadership is supportive and the group is geared to high performance goals. The participative form of management was clearly the most successful.[3]

---

[1] In later work McGregor (*The Professional Manager*, 1967, chapter 6) put it even more strongly. 'I become steadily more persuaded that perhaps the greatest disparity between objective reality and managerial perceptions of it is an underestimation of the potentialities of human beings for contributing to organisational effectiveness'.

[2] D. McGregor, op. cit. (1960). McGregor made it clear that he was not viewing Theory X and Theory Y as 'right' or 'wrong', nor as mutually exclusive, but merely as indicative of two basic forms of managerial attitudes.

[3] R. Likert, *New Patterns of Management* (McGraw-Hill, New York 1961).

Likert emphasized the value of the human resources of an enterprise, a theme which was elaborated by R. E. Miles. Commenting that the typical modern manager rejects autocratic concepts of leadership, Miles suggested that the human-relations approach represents only a slight departure from autocratic tradition and does not bring out the point that participation may be useful for its own sake. The human-resources approach, on the other hand, is based on assumptions that people want to help creatively; that the majority of the labour force can so help; and that it is management's task to create the right environment and to encourage self-direction. In the human-relations model Miles sees participation as producing improved satisfaction and morale, which in turn lowers resistance to managerial acts and increases compliance with formal authority, while the human-resources approach leads to improved decision-making and control and improved satisfaction and morale among subordinates. Managers should recognize and make more meaningful use of the skills, talents and creativity of the people whom they direct.[1]

A further development in the behavioural sciences with relevance to participation came from Frederick Herzberg.[2] Herzberg and his associates, in investigations which have since been replicated in several different countries and for several different occupations, with consistent results, asked people to recall what was happening in their jobs at times when they felt particularly satisfied and times when they felt particularly dissatisfied. Analysing the results, it was found that satisfaction at work was associated with achievement, recognition of achievement, interesting and challenging work, responsibility, and scope for advancement. The unhappy experiences related to times when company policy and administration, human relationships, technical supervision, working conditions or pay were felt to be poor or inadequate. From these results it was deduced that the first set of factors represented the features of a job with the greatest power to motivate people, while the second set, termed by Herzberg the 'hygiene factors' (which were rarely mentioned in the responses concerning satisfying experiences) did not have the

[1] R. E. Miles, 'The Affluent Organization', *Harvard Business Review*, May–June 1966 (see also 'Human Relations or Human Resources?', *Harvard Business Review*, July–August 1965).

[2] See F. Herzberg *et al.*, *The Motivation to Work*, 2nd edn. (Wiley, New York 1959), and F. Herzberg, *Work and the Nature of Man* (World Publishing Co., Cleveland, New York 1966).

power to motivate but were important in that they created dissatisfaction if they were less than adequate. Participative styles of management provided the right framework for good motivation.

The ways in which the personal goals of the individual at work could be reconciled with the goals of the enterprise were studied by Argyris. Neglect of the individual's needs created apathy on his part. Job enlargement could be a palliative, but the real need was for workers to have more control over their environment by greater participation in, and control over, decisions most closely related to them. To this end leadership should become more democratic.

So far in this chapter some of the main influences on managerial thought and practice that are relevant to our subject have been reviewed. It will have been noted that though some of them involve genuine participation by workers in at least some types of decision, on the whole they assume that managerial policies should be directed towards taking account of workers' needs and views, or possibly encouraging participation by workers in the decisions most closely concerning their work, rather than towards participation in the broad conduct of the enterprise.

It will also have been noted that though the present study relates to Britain, all of the influences described have emanated from the United States. This is not to say that British behavioural scientists have ignored the subjects discussed—the work of Woodward, Burns and Stalker, and Lupton, for instance, is of considerable importance to understanding the human structure of the enterprise, but it is not in the main stream of thought about participation. (The work of the Tavistock Institute will be discussed later in this chapter.) Possibly the greater emphasis placed on participation, in the forms discussed, by American writers on management and industrial relations reflects the American emphasis on inter-personal relationships in industry, as opposed to the British—and West European—emphasis on institutional forms. Whatever the reason, the work of the American writers has had an appreciable impact on British management thought[1]—and not only through American-owned companies in Britain.

But how soundly based is the work described? It has not

[1] See J. Child, *British Management Thought* (1969).

been without its critics. The human-relations school has been heavily criticized, on the grounds already mentioned.[1] Even the validity of the original Hawthorne experiments has been questioned.[2] Some of the criticism of the human-relations approach has also been applied to what has been called the 'neo-human relations' school, including the work of McGregor, Likert and Argyris.[3]

> It shares with human relations a solidary view of the enterprise and a stress upon employees' social needs. Its orientation remains primarily social psychological. Moreover, the aim of neo-human relations continues to be the further integration of employees with the goals and social network of the enterprise, and the reconciliation of individual motivation with organizational purpose. It rarely makes any clear distinction between managerial and operative level employees, except to state that the lack of self-actualization opportunities is normally most acute at the lower end of the industrial hierarchy. As with human relations, it accords little attention to technology, economic interests, or organizational environment as factors influencing employee orientations and hence behaviour. . . . Phenomena such as output restriction and loyalty to trade unions still tend to be seen mainly as indications of employees' desires to reduce a psychological feeling of submissiveness.[4]

On the other hand, the newer school no longer believes that workers' co-operation can be won simply through social and participatory policies: it is accepted that organizational structures need to be reshaped and rigid hierarchical levels replaced by less formal systems of groups.

Not only has neo-human-relations teaching been criticized, but much of the experimental evidence on which it is based has been found wanting. Thus, Strauss has criticized the research as being sometime suspect methodologically; as disregarding the fact that what works well in one set of circumstances does not necessarily work well in another; and as disregarding technological considerations, the need for quick decision-making in

---

[1] For a summary of such criticism see H. A. Landsberger, *Hawthorne Revisited* (Cornell University Press, Ithaca, New York 1958).

[2] See A. Carey, 'The Hawthorne Studies: a Radical Criticism', *American Sociological Review*, Vol. 32, 3 (1967), pp. 403–16, and A. J. M. Sykes, 'Economic Interest and the Hawthorne Researches', *Human Relations*, Vol. 8, 3 (August 1965), pp. 253–63.

[3] See Miles, op. cit. (1965, 1966), and G. Strauss, 'Human Relations—1968 Style', *Industrial Relations* (May 1968).

[4] Child, op. cit. (1969), p. 178.

many industrial situations, the difference between different workers' needs and personalities, and the impact of trade unionism. 'Only a relatively trivial amount of participation,' says Strauss, 'is feasible in many industrial situations'.[1]

Herzberg, too, has come in for criticism. His research has been criticized on methodological grounds by Levine and Weitz.[2] In their own work Blood and Hulin found that job satisfaction varied according to social class,[3] and the same researchers later criticized Herzberg's work on the grounds that both the location of the plant and the cultural background of the workers are neglected.[4] Southgate has made the point that none of the Herzberg experiments take account of variables laying outside the job context.[5] The finding of Goldthorpe et al. that their sample of workers were more interested in economic reward than in opportunities for job satisfaction strengthens the point.[6]

Though the views of the neo-human-relations school may not be beyond criticism, and some of the evidence on which they rely may be suspect, there can be no doubt about the increasing influence that the behavioural scientists are coming to exercise in industry. In that their work has led to a more realistic appreciation of the human structure of the enterprise, and of the forces creating conflict and making for co-operation, its influence must be judged wholly beneficial. It has discredited traditional but unsound assumptions and provided management with new and effective techniques of personnel administration. Some of these have provided considerably greater opportunities for workers to influence their work, and the conditions under which it is done, than have been usual in industry in the past. The participative techniques adopted have themselves varied from

[1] G. Strauss, 'Participative Management: a Critique', ILR Research, Vol. xii, No. 2 (1966), p. 6. See also the criticism of D. McGregor and R. Likert by G. Odiorne in Michigan Business Review (Ann Arbor, November 1967).

[2] E. L. Levine and J. Weitz, 'Job Satisfaction Among Graduate Students' Journal of Applied Psychology, Vol. 52, 4 (August 1968).

[3] M. R. Blood and C. L. Hulin, 'Alienation, Environmental Characteristic and Worker Responsibility', Journal of Applied Psychology, Vol. 51, 3 (1967)

[4] C. L. Hulin and M. R. Blood, 'Job Enlargement', Psychological Bulletin Vol. 69, 1 (1968).

[5] J. Southgate, 'The Dependence of the Herzberg Theory of Job Satisfaction upon the Social Context in which it is Tested', North-Western Polytechnic Research Paper No. 1 (London 1969).

[6] J. H. Goldthorpe et al., The Affluent Worker: Industrial Attitudes and Behaviour (Cambridge University Press, 1968).

motivational techniques that have been described as manipulative,[1] to others that provide for free decision-making by workers, or joint decision-making by workers and management.

Some motivational techniques can hardly be called participative, but the greater stress now being laid on managerially induced forms of participation by management theorists with some successful practical experience of participative management[2] seems likely to produce a marked increase in participative styles. The increased attention being given to the human-resources approach is also likely to extend participative practices.

Participative management has been described as:

> ... the discipline whereby an organization learns how to tap something of the latent potential of its members. It involves entirely new skills of behaviour; it requires from managers a whole new understanding of the processes that happen both within and between groups of people. It is, in fact, the gradual, stressful, risk-taking process of experience by which management matures from its outmoded role of directing, controlling and governing to its new role of enabling, encouraging, assisting and reinforcing achievement by others.[3]

It must, however, be added that though participative management, as at present practised, regards the wishes and views of workers as important, its focus is upon the range of decisions that are related to the carrying out of the tasks different groups of workers are called upon to perform.

As a matter of principle participative management could be extended to cover the full range of decisions taken by management, including those of the board of directors, thus extending the concept of participation to the conclusion of a complete system of democratic control. The evidence, however, seems to suggest that the majority of workers are more concerned with having a say in managerial decisions related to their specific tasks than with the running of the enterprise. They are concerned with such major issues as the decision to close down or reduce the

---

[1] See Strauss, op. cit. (1968), p. 264, and discussion in G. H. Litwin and R. A. Stringer, *Motivation and Organisational Climate* (Bailey Brothers and Swinfen, 1968).

[2] See Likert, op. cit. (1961); *The Human Organization: Its Management and Value* (McGraw-Hill, New York 1967), and A. J. Marrow *et al.*, *Management by Participation* (Harper and Row, New York 1967).

[3] K. Robertson, 'Managing People and Jobs', *Personnel Management* (September 1969), p. 24.

scale of an enterprise when this will result in the loss of employment or lower wages. The concern here, however, is with the impact of such decisions upon themselves, not with participating in the management process as an occupational activity *per se*. Only a very small minority of workers wish to be managers and to accept the responsibility of carrying out a managerial role.

One of the ways in which the interests of workers who may wish to contribute to the efficiency of the enterprise in which they are employed may be channelled in a limited way, but one that is mutually profitable to enterprise and worker, is the suggestion scheme.

Suggestion Schemes

The suggestion scheme is a form of participation that has obvious attractions to management and has been quite widely adopted in Britain. Suggestion schemes were known as long ago as the nineteenth century, but it was not until the second World War that they achieved popularity. The basis of such schemes is the offer of a reward, usually financial, for suggestions for improving the efficiency of the enterprise. As an example cited in an Industrial Welfare Society report made clear, such schemes make available 'the great potential source of improved methods represented by the interests of the company's employees, not only in their particular work, but also in the more general problems affecting the company as a whole'.[1]

There seems to be no limitation upon the topics that can be raised in a suggestion scheme, although people with certain specialized skills, or whose jobs are centred upon an ability to bring forward new ideas, are often disqualified from participating. Again, in the Industrial Welfare Society survey, some schemes suggest matters on which suggestions are invited. So, in one particular case, the following topics are specified:

(a) New methods capable of saving time, labour or material, of increasing production and clerical efficiency, or improving the quality, design or appearance of the company's productions.
(b) Improvements leading to better or more comfortable working conditions;

[1] Survey No. 17, *Suggestion Schemes—Extracts from Firms' Schemes* (Industrial Welfare Society, London 1954), p. 2. See also *Successful Suggestion Schemes* (Industrial Welfare Society, London 1958).

(c) Improvements leading to greater efficiency in any department of the company's factories or offices;

(d) Means of extending the sales and uses of the company's products;

(e) Means of reducing waste or scrap.[1]

The survey conducted as part of the present inquiry sought to ascertain the extent of suggestion schemes, and the degree of satisfaction with them. No attempt was made in the survey to discover detailed information about such schemes.

It was found that 40.3 per cent of the respondents had a formalized suggestion scheme. Some comparisons can be made with the data collected by the National Institute of Industrial Psychology in the late 1940s. Of their 408 respondents, 70 per cent had formal suggestion schemes. This might suggest a relative decline in formal suggestion schemes. Whereas the availability of a suggestion scheme appeared to be independent of the degree of unionization, Table 26 shows the distribution of suggestion schemes by size of firm.

Table 26   Distribution of Suggestion Schemes
Related to Size of Firm

Size	With a Scheme Number of Firms	%	Without a Scheme Number of Firms	%
0 – 99	24	15	136	85
100 – 499	72	29	173	71
500 – 999	36	56	28	44
1,000 – 1,999	36	53	32	47
2,000 – and over	94	84	18	16

As might be expected, the larger the firm the more likely it is to operate a suggestion scheme. Not only are the informal contacts that exist so easily in small firms more difficult in large firms, but large firms, with their well-developed personnel departments, can more readily service such schemes.

Of the respondents with suggestion schemes 43.5 per cent expressed dissatisfaction with the working of their schemes. Only 22.7 per cent of *all* respondents had a suggestion scheme with which, to a greater or lesser extent, they were satisfied. The level of dissatisfaction compares fairly closely with that found

[1] Industrial Welfare Society, op. cit.

by the N.I.I.P. In that case, 61 per cent of the firms with suggestion schemes were dissatisfied with the quantity of suggestions,
and 59 per cent with the quality.

As noted above, there seems to have been something of a
decline in the popularity of suggestion schemes. Some of the
criticisms made of joint consultation have also been made of
suggestion schemes, and Gorfin has referred to causes of failure
as including indifference on the part of management, supervisory resistance, too small rewards, red tape and delay, in-
competent or incorrect answers, poor promotion, and refusal to
reconsider a question.[1] To this list might be added a reluctance
on the part of workers to become involved in managerial problems—a feeling that such involvement might lead to mistrust
and suspicion among fellow workers and that a successful suggestion might even create redundancy. Yet another factor could
be that, with the growth of productivity bargaining, improvements are seen as having a cash value, to be bargained about
rather than left to the discretion of the management or to a
committee.

Workers' suggestions are often sought as part of Scanlon and
Rucker Share-of-Production Plans,[2] in which participation is regarded as an important ingredient. Scanlon-type schemes have
often provided for (1) shop-floor Production Committees, to consider more efficient production methods, means of reducing
waste, and departmental production schedules, and (2) Screening
Committees, to survey the operation of the plan and suggestions
emanating from the Production Committees. Individual awards
for suggestions are not usual, but all workers share in the benefits of improved productivity.

[1] C. C. Gorfin, 'The Suggestion Scheme: A Contribution to Morale or an
Economic Transaction?', *British Journal of Industrial Relations* (November
1969), p. 370.

[2] It will be recalled that these Plans are based on the relationship existing
between the sales value of a product and the material value. The difference
between these values, the added value, may be called the production value,
of which in practice productive wages form a nearly constant proportion for
an enterprise. If, by efficient working, workers can increase the value of
production, the increase is paid into a fund and divided between company,
workers and reserves. Such schemes have proved too radical or complex for
most enterprises, and though they have aroused some enthusiasm their success
rate has not been high. See R. B. McKersie, 'Wage Payments Methods of the
Future', *British Journal of Industrial Relations*, Vol. 1, No. 2 (June 1963)
and Industrial Relations Counselors Inc., *Group Wage Incentives: Experience
with the Scanlon Plan* (I.R.C., New York 1962).

Task-Based Participation

As mentioned in the early part of this chapter, increasing use is now being made by management of the behavioural sciences. Nowhere is this more apparent than in the greater care being taken to design jobs with the human aspect in mind as well as the technical, and in the extent to which managements involve workers in decisions concerning their work and immediate working environment.

In an early study of work group leadership White and Lippitt wrote that a democratic leader:

1. Permits all members to discuss policy formation. He encourages the group to make necessary decisions.
2. Permits discussion on future as well as present activity. Does not try to keep members in the dark about future plans.
3. Permits members to define their own job situation as much as possible. For example, the defining of the way to accomplish the tasks and the divisions of the tasks is up to the group.
4. Focuses on obtaining 'objective' facts on 'human problems'. Tries to base any necessary 'praise' or 'discipline' upon these objective facts and not upon his personal needs.[1]

Likert has argued that 'Supervisors with the best records of performance focus their primary attention on the human aspects of their subordinates' problems and on endeavouring to build effective work groups with high performance goals'. Such supervisors Likert refers to as 'employee centred'.[2]

Miller and Form have commented that 'If work is to be satisfying, the formal organization structure must be changed so that employees experience more activity than passivity and greater relative independence than dependence, use more than their surface abilities, have a longer time perspective, and are involved in decision-making'.[3]

Job enlargement, job rotation and job enrichment have been suggested as contributing to workers' satisfaction. Advances in industrial psychology have led to a reversal of the traditional belief that jobs should be so designed as to give the worker the

[1] R. White and R. Lippitt, 'Leader Behavior and Member Reaction in Three Social Climates', in D. Cartwright and A. Zander, *Group Dynamics* (Harper, New York 1953), p. 487.
[2] Likert, op. cit. (1961), p. 7.
[3] D. C. Miller and W. H. Form, *Industrial Sociology* (Harper and Row, New York 1964), p. 630.

simplest possible task, making the minimum call on his resources. Routine jobs are therefore now increasingly being designed to extend the pattern of operations by adding further
similar operations. Job rotation enables workers to have a change
of work, acquire additional skills and versatility, and enhance
their understanding of the work of their department. Job enrichment commonly gives workers greater responsibility by in-
corporating elements of supervision and control in the job.

As thus described, none of these techniques could be classed
as participative. It cannot even be said that they invariably
produce greater job satisfaction: indeed, many operators resent
the extra calls on them and the interference with their working
rhythm. However, two examples can be given where the techniques have been developed in a participative form.

The Philips electrical firm have developed the concept of work-
structuring, which they have defined as 'The organization of
work, the work-situation and the conditions of labour in such a
way that, while maintaining or improving efficiency, job content
accords as closely as possible with the capacities and ambitions
of the individual employee'.[1] Much of the re-structuring has
been done on the basis of working groups. The Philips experience
suggests that work-structuring requires a considerable degree
of commitment at all levels of management, extensive study and
training, and a great deal of consultation and communication.
The results of the changes made show improvement in job
satisfaction and in productive efficiency. Workers are, of course,
involved in deciding the new groupings and methods of work,
but the extent of the involvement of management and industrial
engineers in re-structuring does limit the autonomy of the work-
group.

Other work on job enrichment has been carried out in I.C.I.,
where a series of controlled studies took place—in various parts
of the business and in different functions and levels of seniority
—in 1967 and 1968.

The changes made by I.C.I. have been summarized:

---

[1] *Work-Structuring: a summary of experiments at Philips—1963 to 1968*
(N. V. Philips' Gloeilampenfabrieken, Eindhoven, Holland, N.D.—1969),
p. 4. This booklet describes briefly some of the experiments carried out in
Philips' Dutch works. For a description of changes made in the firm's works
in Hamilton, Scotland, see D. H. Thornely and G. A. Valentine, 'Job
Enlargement: Some Implications of Longer Cycle Jobs on Fan Heater Production', in *Philips' Magazine*, May 1969.

'. . . foremen were made responsible for the selection, training, development and discipline of their men; they were given control of certain budgets and more technical responsibility. Process operators were allowed to fix their own breaks; they were encouraged to make certain decisions connected with the running of the plant and to initiate maintenance work directly.

Design engineers were given a more independent role; within a sanctioned project, limits on their capital expenditure authority were removed; they were given fuller managerial control of their junior staff. Draughtsmen set their own target completion dates and played a more active part in costing, specifying equipment, initiating indents, assessing tenders and liaising with vendor firms.

Junior laboratory staff were encouraged to write the final 'research minute' on any project for which they had been responsible; they were given time to follow up their own ideas, even if these went beyond the department's planned framework of research; they were authorized to requisition materials and services on their own signature.

Sales representatives were allowed to decide their own calling frequencies; reporting on customer visits was left to them; they were given more say in technical service and more authority to negotiate directly with the customer.'[1]

The changes made seem to have given decidedly good results in respect of improved performance and fairly good results in respect of job satisfaction.

Again, however, the extent of workers' participation in the decision-making involved in these changes was limited. As Paul, Robertson and Herzberg commented, 'experimental constraints . . . dictated that there could be no participation by job holders themselves in deciding what changes were to be made in their jobs. The changes nevertheless seemed to be effective. On the other hand, when people were invited to participate . . . results were disappointing'.[2] None the less, the job-enrichment approach seems to offer possibilities for participation, and suggests a new and realistic role for management. To quote Paul, Robertson and Herzberg again,

'. . . management becomes a service, its purpose to enable, encourage,

---

[1] K. Robertson, op. cit., p. 23. Further details of some of the I.C.I. studies, and studies in other British companies, are given in W. J. Paul, K. Robertson and F. Herzberg, 'Job Enrichment Pays Off', in *Harvard Business Review* (Boston, Mass., March/April 1969), and in W. J. Paul and K. Robertson, *Job Enrichment and Employee Motivation*, Gower Press, London 1970.

[2] Ibid., p. 75.

assist and reinforce achievement by employees. Task organization and task support are the central features of the manager's new role. In task *organization* two complementary criteria emerge (1) tasks have to be authentic—i.e. the more opportunity they give employees to contribute to business objectives, the more effective they are likely to be motivationally; (2) tasks have to be motivational— i.e. the more they draw upon the motivators, the more likely they are to produce an effective contribution to business objectives. In task *support,* factors such as company policy and administration, technical supervision, inter personal relations and working conditions all have to be pressed into the service of the motivators. Control of the job is achieved by providing people with the tools of their trade, with the information they require, with training as appropriate, and with advice when sought.[1] . . .

As to the role of participation, the same authors say:

participation is indeed the best route to motivational change, but only when it is participation in the act of management, no matter at what level it takes place. And the test of the genuineness of that participation is simple—it must be left to the subordinate to be the prime mover in consultation on those topics where he carries personal responsibility. For the manager, as for the subordinate, the right to be consulted must be earned by competence in giving help. Therein lies the only authority worth having.[2]

Autonomous Work-Groups[3]

As has been noted, from the pioneering work of Lewin, Lippitt and White[4] on leadership styles, behavioural scientists have contributed a great deal towards an understanding of the behaviour of work-groups.[5] In 1954, Thelen suggested the development of autonomous work-groups, responsible for organizing work, setting goals and training. One semi-autonomous work-group—limited in its powers of decision about such matters as work allocation and time of breaks—was studied by Morse and Reimer, who, finding that workers' interest declined after

[1] Ibid., p. 77.
[2] Ibid., p. 76.
[3] It may be noted that autonomous work-groups have been common in Britain since the eighteenth century, on the basis that the employer has paid a group of workers on sub-contract terms, the work to be organized and carried out by the working group itself.
[4] Op. cit., p. 167.
[5] For a review of the research, see M. Bucklow, 'A New Role for the Work Group', *Administrative Science Quarterly*, Vol. 11, No. 1 (June 1966).

their attempts to extend their authority were denied by management, concluded that the 'granting of "safe" areas of decision-making and the withholding of "hot" ones is not likely to work for long'.[1] Later, Non-Linear Systems Inc., of California, replaced assembly-line production by small self-paced groups of seven members with responsibility for complete assembly, and found that this gave an increase in productivity. The researcher concluded that much of the motivation for the improvement came from the increased opportunities to use skills, to learn and teach, and to take responsibility, though some came from gregariousness.[2]

Some of the most interesting experiments concerning working groups have been carried out by the Tavistock Institute of Human Relations, of London. The Institute was interested in participation as long ago as the 1940s, when it acted as consultant to the Glacier Metal Company. It became interested in group work, which it developed considerably in an Indian textile mill.[3] In Britain the Institute undertook a study of the development of techniques of coal extraction.[4] Coal-getting had originally been carried out by teams of men possessing several skills. The introduction of longwall mining, conveyor belts and 'factory' methods of labour deployment was expected to show a considerable improvement in productivity, but proved disappointing: output and morale were both low. The research team worked out a new form of production organization in which jobs were rotated and the workers accepted more responsibility for operations: the management provided supporting services rather than direct supervision. The success of the method adopted confirmed the researchers' belief in the superiority of the composite organization.

The principle emerged from the Tavistock studies that the

[1] N. Morse and E. Reimer, 'The Experimental Change of a Major Organisational Variable', *Journal of Abnormal and Social Psychology*, Vol. 52 (1956).
[2] A. M. Kuriloff, 'An Experiment in Management—Putting Theory Y to the Test', *Personnel*, Vol. 40 (1963).
[3] A. K. Rice, *Productivity and Social Organisation—the Ahmedabad Experiment* (Tavistock Publications, London 1958); *The Enterprise and its Environment* (Tavistock Publications, London 1963).
[4] E. L. Trist and K. W. Bamforth, 'Some Social and Psychological Consequences of the Longwall Method of Coal-getting', *Human Relations*, Vol. IV, No. 1 (1951); and E. L. Trist, G. W. Higgin, H. Murray and A. B. Pollock, *Organisational Choice: Capabilities of Groups at the Coal Face under Changing Technologies* (Tavistock Publications, London 1963).

enterprise could not be looked on simply as a social system, or as a technical system. Attempts to optimize either system as an entity would result in sub-optimization for the enterprise as a whole. The enterprise was really a socio-technical system, and what was needed was joint optimization of the correlative systems. Responsible autonomy was seen as necessary for effective productive systems. In the words of Bucklow, 'it gives the work group a central role in the production system, not the peripheral supporting role envisaged by Mayo and Likert, and has successfully motivated rank-and-file workers to a greater co-operative effort than other methods'.[1] What often happened in normal industrial practice, as Emery has described it, was that 'men are perceived as building blocks and the engineers seek to make them as homogeneous as possible by tying them down as tightly as they can to the job, so that there will be as little variance as possible. They then lash the blocks together with a stout supervisory system'.[2] The Tavistock Institute concluded: 'The requirements of the individual in an industrial setting are such that the most potent form of engaging the worker's interest, and the only alternative to the reward and punishment procedure, is to move towards a design that can cope with the tasks arising from the technology and, in addition, to design these jobs in such a way as to create conditions for what we call task involvement.'[3]

In recent years the Institute have been involved in three further important studies in participation. In Norway they were associated with a study of industrial democracy, with particular reference to workers' representation at top management level, and with a second study concentrating on direct participation in the work-place—a study which led to three field experiments involving successful reconstruction of working operations.[4] Thirdly, the Institute collaborated with the Shell Company in that company's evolution of a participative philosophy.[5]

[1] M. Bucklow, 'A New Role for the Work Group', *Administrative Science Quarterly*, Vol. 11, No. 1 (June 1966), p. 73.

[2] F. E. Emery, 'Democratisation of the Work Place (a historical review of studies)' (T.I.H.R., Doc. No. T 813, June 1966), p. 6.

[3] Ibid., p. 8.

[4] For a summary of these studies see E. Thorsrud, 'Socio-technical Approach to Job Design and Organisational Development', *Management International Review*, Vol. 8 (1968).

[5] The Shell experience has now been written up in P. Hill, *Towards a New Philosophy of Management*, Gower Press, London 1971.

Recent developments in the British coal industry of self-managing teams of coal-face workers, who meet together in conference and decide in common how the work is to be carried out, have been extremely successful and provide empirical support for the concept of the democratic work-group.[1]

Consultative and Decision-Making Councils

Both the John Lewis Partnership and the Scott Bader Commonwealth provide interesting and well-documented examples of consultative machinery, but most interesting of all are the arrangements operating at the Glacier Metal Company.

The arrangements at Glacier illustrate what can happen when joint bodies are given a great deal of responsibility. The long-established Works Council at Glacier is a body carefully designed to be representative of the main interest groups in the works—seven hourly-paid workers, three weekly- and three monthly-paid staff, and the chief executive or his nominee. The Chairman is elected from outside the Council and the employee representatives are elected by a larger Works Committee, itself elected from section committees. The Council meets monthly and exercises considerable authority in dealing with problems concerning the running of the works. Decisions are required to be unanimous. The Council is the principal legislative organ in a comprehensive framework of four systems—legislative, executive, representative and appeals. It is maintained that acting with the sanction of all groups within the enterprise, as represented by the Works Council, managers have greater real authority than managers in other enterprises, rather than less. Indeed, there is considerable emphasis on the command structure of management as an essential aspect of its role.[2]

Current Views

Participation through works councils, such as that at Glacier Metal, participative styles of management which do not increase workers' decision-making powers, and participative techniques which give workers a measure of control over their work and

[1] C. Shephard, National Coal Board, statement at *The Times* Management lecture, *Industrial Democracy: Fantasy, Fiction or Fact*, March 1970.

[2] J. Kelly, *Is Scientific Management Possible?* (Faber, London 1968).

working environment, have all been tried with some success. It has been demonstrated that these limited forms of participation have at any rate neither significantly lessened managerial authority nor weakened the bargaining position of the workers.

Though numbers of British enterprises practise, or have shown interest in, participative styles of management, employers have made relatively few public comments about participation generally. The Confederation of British Industry did, however, express a view in their evidence to the Donovan Commission. They did not consider that experience of co-ownership and worker participation in management was sufficient to suggest that general development along such lines was possible. The aim of producing a satisfying job for the individual, and general recognition of the workers' role, was best furthered by the application of sociological research, the proper allocation of managerial responsibility for labour matters, training, development or revival of joint consultative machinery, improved communications, and the development of sickness, pensions and redundancy programmes.[1] Subsequently the C.B.I. set up a study group to look at the long-term implication of worker participation.[2]

On the whole, employers and their spokesmen have evinced deep mistrust as to the value of participation, particularly in integrative forms, such as the appointment of workers' directors, though they reflect a widespread belief in the desirability of prior consultation with workers on matters that concern them. Mr. John Davies, then Director-General of the C.B.I., speaking in relation to the Labour Party's publication *Industrial Democracy,* was reported as saying that there was a 'lot of absolute nonsense' talked about worker participation in management. 'The people responsible for enterprises are the decision-makers. It is right that they should be susceptible to a great deal of advice and help, but that is as far as it should go'.[3] Sir Denning Pearson, at the time Chief Executive of Rolls-Royce, laid stress on the level of decisions when he said that 'workers must have adequate opportunities to take part in making decisions which affect their day-to-day work'.[4] Mr. David Barran, Chairman of the Shell

---

[1] Evidence, para 103. For discussion of the Confederation's views see Royal Commission on Trade Unions and Employers' Associations, Minutes of Evidence, 69 (1968).

[2] *Financial Times,* 18 November 1968.

[3] *The Times,* 29 July 1968.

[4] *Financial Times,* 24 August 1968.

Transport and Trading company, discussing ways and means of bringing management and unions closer together, was 'convinced that the answer does *not* lie in workers' representation on the boards of companies. Nothing will be gained by adding the inexperience of workers' representatives to the incompetence of bad managements. Workers, however, must be brought into consultation at every level short of the board room'.[1] Sir Reay Geddes, Chairman of Dunlop, said that 'if worker participation meant sharing responsibility over business decisions it would not be good for business, for those in it, nor would it be in the best interests of a strong trade union movement'. However, he expressed himself in favour of far more consultation with worker representatives at shop-floor level and for improvements in the channels of communication.[2]

The British Institute of Management, the Industrial Society, the Institute of Personnel Management, the Industrial Co-Partnership Association and several other bodies active in the field of management have held conferences concerned with participation; the B.I.M. have issued an occasional paper on its implications,[3] and the Industrial Society published the results of Sawtell's work.[4]

There can be no doubt that during the coming years there will be important developments in the organization of enterprises, the role of management and the degree of worker participation. As yet it is impossible to say what will come to be accepted as the normative pattern of industrial relations in the enterprise, but it is extremely likely that the present boundary line between workers and management will become less sharply delineated.

[1] *Institute of Personnel Management Digest* report, No. 31, November 1967.
[2] *The Times*, 19 November 1969.
[3] B.I.M., *Industrial Democracy: Some Implications for Management*, B.I.M., London 1968.
[4] R. Sawtell, *Sharing Our Industrial Future* (Industrial Society, London 1968).

8 Looking Toward the Future

The Changing Form of Industrial Society

It may be thought a paradox that at a time when it has become commonplace to speak of a growing demand for workers to participate there is evidence of apathy in respect of participation by workers in their trade unions, and in respect of an instrumental approach to at least some types of work. Yet the paradox may be more apparent than real. It seems likely that what is at issue is not so much a positive desire by the great majority of workers to be involved in running an enterprise but a growing expectation that decisions affecting them will not be made without their concurrence, or at least without their having had the opportunity of expressing their view.

Such expectations are a far cry from the normal expectations current as recently as the 1930s. But much has changed since the 1930s. Firstly, we have experienced unprecedented rates of technological and organizational change, which have been a prerequisite of the rapid improvement in material standards of living in much of the world. Such changes must be expected to continue, and with them will come change in the nature of workers' jobs.[1]

To the worker such changes have often proved disruptive and a threat to his livelihood. In part the threat has been countered by the ease with which other work may be found, by improved unemployment benefits, and what by traditional standards are very generous redundancy arrangements. But these have not proved enough to satisfy the worker, who has not unnaturally continued to respond with resentment to the disruption of his life by deci-

[1] See, for instance, Blauner's prediction that in continuous process industry automation increases the worker's control over his job and results in more meaningful work. R. Blauner, *Alienation and Freedom* (University of Chicago Press, 1964), p. 182.

sions made outside his control, sometimes by unknown men and in the light of knowledge which he does not have. Major disruptions apart, the increasing size and complexity of industry have in themselves tended to result in decisions being made further away from the worker: a factor hardly likely to decrease alienation from the purposes and organizational processes of industry.

Secondly, while industry has changed, so has the social environment. The worker is likely to be better educated than his father, and his education will probably have taught him to think of self-development and to question what he finds in his environment—a far remove from the age in which, for the majority, education commonly amounted to little more than the inculcation of facts. Then, too, there has been a realization by workers of the political power that they can exercise through the electoral process, and through the achievements of the Labour Party. Even more importantly they have come to recognize the industrial power that they can wield in many enterprises, particularly as a result of continued full employment, to oppose decisions that they do not like.

These developments have made workers unwilling to accept authority when it is exercised arbitrarily and in a way that offends their sense of what is right. As one sociologist put it: 'Again and again we discover that men living in the last third of the twentieth century will obey orders in a more than merely mechanical manner only if these orders have also been explained and justified'.[1]

It is not only the worker who has changed over the years. Managers too have adjusted,[2] more or less, to the same kind of stimuli, and in the process managerial ideology has undergone adaptation. Both in industry and in society generally, institutions are being remodelled increasingly in forms that take more account of people's views. In industry collective bargaining has undergone a remarkable decentralization. Some major British trade unions are following policies designed to make them more

[1] Richard F. Behrendt: *Autonomous and plural strategies of development*, p. 33. (Quoted here from Jean de Givry, 'Developments in Labour–Management Relations', *International Labour Review*, January 1969, p. 5.)

[2] For a detailed consideration of managerial adjustment see J. Child, *British Management Thought* (Allen and Unwin, London 1969), and in relation to the wider setting of business, *The Business Enterprise in Modern Industrial Society* (Collier-Macmillan, London 1969).

responsive to the wishes of their rank and file, even though this diminishes the authority traditionally exercised by union leaders.

That the human side of enterprise has changed and is changing, any manager will admit. In the words of de Givry: 'Just like the monarchies of the past, the modern undertaking is now gradually evolving from absolutism to a "constitutional" system under which authority is exercised in accordance with a set of principles, criteria and rules that have all been discussed and agreed on beforehand.'[1] A century ago it was taken for granted that the overriding purpose of an industrial or commercial enterprise was to make money for its owners. Subject to such protective provision as the law might introduce, the place of the worker in the enterprise was basically a contractual one, in which work was done in exchange for a wage. Today, on the other hand, though the formal structure of the enterprise has changed remarkably little, it is increasingly accepted that an enterprise has two main goals. It should perform the economic function of producing goods and providing services as efficiently and economically as possible: and it should perform the social function of providing satisfactory conditions of employment, just government, meaningful work and the maximum opportunity for self-fulfilment to those employed in it.

Sometimes the pursuit of one of these goals helps achievement of the other: sometimes it impedes it and there is conflict. Society is becoming less willing to tolerate pursuit of the economic goal without due regard to the social goal, but except in very special circumstances it is not prepared to permit the enterprise to be run in the interests of the workers to the detriment of its economic function, since that would be at the expense of the broader social interest. Lack of vigour in pursuing the economic goal and overmuch emphasis on the immediate interests of their members were clearly the cause of the downfall of the nineteenth century self-governing workshops. If economic progress is desired it seems certain that decisions that workers do not like will sometimes be necessary. This is as true under Yugoslav workers' management and in the Soviet Union as it is under western capitalism.

Put together these factors suggest that workers are less ready

[1] J. de Givry, 'Developments in Labour–Management Relations', *International Labour Review* (January 1969).

to accept arbitrary authority, but that it will continue to be necessary that they should accept such authority as may be required to give a just balance in the pursuit of the two goals. This would suggest (a) that authority exercised must flow from the technological and organizational (including the economic and social) demands of the situation, and (b) that it must be perceived by workers as required by the situation—which in turn suggests extensive provision of information, and consultation and other forms of participation.

Looking to the future the desirable form of the industrial enterprise would seem to be one in which that authority, which in the nineteenth century was considered justified by ownership and which in the first half of the twentieth century was seen as a right exercised by managers because they were the appointees of the owners who were the sole judge of their ability, as well as the sole source of their right to manage, will increasingly be seen to spring from an objective and accepted appraisal of functional requirements in which all concerned are recognized to have a legitimate interest.

But, it may be said, the industrial relations system in Britain does not rest on what is functional; it rests on the balance of industrial power between management and workers. There is much truth in this contention, but if our society is to function to the best advantage in terms of economic efficiency and social stability, order will have to count for more and sectional power for less. Power exercised arbitrarily from the shop floor may be neither more nor less desirable than power exercised arbitrarily by management. In a highly developed functional society in which a wide range of decisions are increasingly determined by technology, dependence on power to solve problems of social equity seems increasingly anachronistic.

The Demand for Participation

The survey reported was not such as to reveal changes over time, but it seems incontrovertible, speaking generally, that workers are directly participating more deeply, in a wider range of managerial decisions than used to be the case. The growing, if not yet clearly articulated, demand for greater personal participation, and the other factors discussed above, seem likely to accentuate this trend. Increasing complexity of organizations, and the external changes already referred to, suggest a greater need for workers to be involved in decisions taken at their place of work, if increased alienation and discord are to be avoided and economic growth to be unimpaired. It should not be overlooked that a spread of participative practices may create a greater desire to participate and that improved education and changed attitudes can add to the contribution that workers can make within their enterprise.

At present the trend to greater participation is expressed in the strengthening and extension of collective bargaining that has been developing and that has been commended by, amongst others, the Donovan Commission. Joint consultation, as we have seen, has weakened, at least on a formal basis, rather than strengthened over recent years. Other forms of participation, such as by means of workers' directors, have been more talked about than practised. But present practices do not necessarily reflect the most desirable forms of participation, whether viewed from the standpoint of workers' aspirations or from that of efficient operation of the enterprise.

The Forms of Participation

(1) *A Constitution for the Enterprise*

In the Introduction it was explained why profit-sharing, and the kind of co-ownership and co-partnership schemes normally encountered, were not regarded as of much significance in relation to participation in management. But ownership has some relationship to control, and it is possible that, as Turner has suggested,[1] 'Workers participation in management requires, if it is to go beyond mere formal devices, a basis of perceivable interest (in both senses of that word)'. We need to consider whether a share in ownership might increase the workers' sense of identification with the purpose of the enterprise and/or carry with it a stake in decision-making.

Apart from the attempts of the Wider Share-Ownership Council to encourage the purchase of equity generally, there have been a number of suggestions put forward to provide workers with shares in the companies that employ them. The Liberal Party's

[1] H. A. Turner, *Evidence to the Royal Commission on Trade Unions and Employers' Associations* (1967).

Assembly of 1966 called for workers to have the right to share in any profits and capital increase and to have such voting rights as to give them, after an interim period, equal rights with shareholders. The Party's Industrial Partnership Committee's Report *Partners at Work*[1] recommended a scheme whereby after equity shareholders had received 5 per cent on the equity of a company, any residual net annual profit after tax should be shared equally between workers and shareholders, to be distributed in cash, or shares, or both. Workers could exercise the full voting rights carried by their shares, which would, however, be held by elected Trustees, at least for the first five years. It has been suggested[2] that a proportion of company profits earmarked for re-investment should be capitalized as 'workers' shares', the sales of which would be restricted. Such shares would carry voting rights which would, however, be exercised by workers' representatives. In 1968 the Conservative Bow Group produced a scheme[3] for companies to 'buy in' a proportion of shares each year, until 35 per cent of the voting equity had been achieved, and to hold the shares in trust for the workers.

Such ideas are not confined to Britain. In France[4] the Order of 17 August 1967, under Article 33 of the Finance Law of 12 July 1965, provided for companies employing more than 100 to make available a share of profits on a specified basis. Shareholders are allotted 5 per cent return on capital from the net profit gained. The balance of the net profit (if any) is then divided in proportion to salaries and wages spent on goods and services, and half of the resultant figure is distributed among workers in proportion to their remuneration. The worker has to wait, however. It is five years before he receives any gain from the arrangement, which also restricts the form of payment to one of three ways, one form being share distribution. Only a minority of workers are expected to benefit from the scheme, under present conditions, and the amounts involved are mostly likely to be small.

[1] Liberal Party, *Partners at Work* (Liberal Party, London 1968).
[2] Turner, op. cit., paras. 30 and 31, reported in the *Financial Times*, 10 March 1967.
[3] *Cutting the Cake* (Bow Group, London 1968), p. 16.
[4] See P.E.P. (M. P. Fogarty), 'A Companies Act 1970?', *Planning* No. 500 London, October 1967, pp. 112–15; J. Ladreyt, 'De Gaulle's new pan-capitalism', *Personnel* (March 1968); and 'French Worker Participation in Profit-Sharing', *French Embassy Press and Information Service*, London 1970. See also *Workers' Negotiated Savings Plans for Capital Formation*, O.E.C.D., Paris, 1968 and 1970.

Only 2.4 per cent of the firms covered by our survey reported having schemes for distributing shares to workers without payment on their part as distinct from other forms of participation in profits. Distribution did not extend to manual workers in the case of one in eight of these firms. The survey did not ascertain the value of the shares distributed, but it is known that in most employee shareholding schemes in operation the value of employees' shares is small in proportion to workers' earnings or to the profits of the firm, and that sometimes the shares do not carry voting rights. It is commonly believed that such schemes have no more than a vague motivational value.[1]

But suppose that proposals to distribute a part of company profits to employees through the issue of shares in the equity capital were put into effect. Suppose[2] that workers came to own 35 per cent, half, or the whole of the equity of their enterprises, with voting rights. What would be the consequences for workers' participation in management? To some extent this might depend on the size of the enterprise. Obviously much would depend on whether the workers were able to use their voting power collectively or not, particularly if their total interest were a minority one. A tiny interest, used collectively, might be influential if it were directed by a trade union so that it could be effectively represented at General Meetings. The impact of an interest that was appreciable, but less than 50 per cent, would depend on the distribution of the balance of the equity. However, even where the interest might be considerable, it is necessary not to forget that in practice shareholders' powers are limited and can rarely be used to interfere with the day-to-day conduct of the enterprise.

Public ownership (and for that matter trade-union ownership)[3] seems to have little effect on the attitudes of workers. The view

[1] See Acton Society Trust and G. Naylor, *Sharing the Profits* (Garnstone Press, London 1968).

[2] We leave aside the many practical problems associated with implementing such an arrangement. Also the problems of principle: why should workers who happen to be employed in a growing and profitable firm enjoy benefits denied to their fellows employed in socially necessary but unrewarding enterprises? why should people who have invested their life savings in shares have to hand over a proportion of its fruits to workers who may not have bothered to save anything?

[3] M. Derber, 'Worker Participation in Israeli Management', *Industrial Relations*, Vol. 3 No. 1 (1963), pp. 51–72.

has been expressed[1] that ownership is irrelevant to industrial democracy. It would appear that there is much in this view. Ownership by the workers in the enterprise would not necessarily produce greater participation in management. In the situation where competition was lacking, or the working group held a strategic position, it could then have undesirable effects.[2] Where workers held a partial share in ownership it might either be meaningless (if the share were small), or open to the disadvantages of full ownership if the share were large.

(2) *The Form of the Company*

From the form of ownership we turn to the status and structure of the enterprise that is predominant in employing power in our society, the joint-stock company.

The traditional form of joint-stock company is merely a device whereby a number of people can pool their capital to fulfil a common economic purpose through an organization which at the same time limits their liability. Incorporation as a company is a legal privilege and Parliament exacts conditions to be met before incorporation is granted and lays down rules to govern the company's operation.

In its basic concepts, company law remains as it was worked out between 1840 and 1862. Its concern is almost entirely with protecting the interests of the share owners. The standing of workers in companies is virtually neglected and there is no requirement on the company, leaving aside such protective legislation as the Factories Act, 1961 and the Redundancy Payments Act, 1965, to have regard to the well-being of workers or, for that matter, of the community at large. But circumstances, and with them the social significance of the company, have changed since the mid-nineteenth century. Companies are much larger, and the largest may employ tens or even hundreds of thousands of workers and have a budget equal to that of a fair-sized country. The social significance of the modern industrial corporation can no longer be defined in terms of the rights and duties of the owners of its share capital. This has been recog-

---

[1] H. A. Clegg, *A New Approach to Industrial Democracy* (Blackwell, Oxford 1960), p. 21.
[2] There is evidence for this possibility in the history of the co-operative movement.

nized in the development of regulation of the external activities of corporate enterprises. However, it may be asked, is there adequate reflection in law of the concept that a company is being entrusted by the community with some of its resources,[1] and should be accountable to the community for the use it makes of them? A number of aspects of company law have been the subject of some debate in recent years, including, to mention those that most concern participation, the status of the worker in the company; the representation of interests other than those of the shareholder; the constitution of the board of directors; the disclosure of information, and the recognition of trade unions for the purpose of collective bargaining.[2] The last two of these aspects bear on participation only in so far as they are aids to collective bargaining, whereby workers participate, directly or indirectly, in regulating wages and working conditions. The other aspects call for closer consideration.

The feeling of dissatisfaction with the legal position of the worker in the enterprise has been stressed by a number of writers.[3] Should not the relationship of the worker to his enterprise, it is argued, now be represented by more than a contract of employment? Surely the worker should have some form of membership of his company, as a matter of social justice, either by direct entry onto the firm's register of members (which would require a change in the law) or by entry through becoming a shareholder.

But what, from the point of view of participation, would be the effect of workers becoming members of their companies—which is already possible for any worker who cares to spend a small

---

[1] Cf. '. . . The human association which in fact produces and distributes wealth, the association of workmen, managers, technicians and directors is not an association recognised by law.' Eustace Percy, *The Unknown State: A Plea for the Study of Government*. University of Durham (London 1944).

[2] See, for instance, M. P. Fogarty, *Company and Corporation—One Law?* (Chapman, London 1965), K. W. Wedderburn, *Company Law Reform* (Fabian Society, London 1965); L. C. B. Gower, *Modern Company Law* (Stevens, London 1957); and C. de Hoghton (ed.), *The Company Law Structure and Reform in Eleven Countries*, PEP, London 1970. The then President of the Board of Trade said (House of Commons Debates, 14 February 1967, col. 359) that the Government would bring in a Companies Bill which would 're-examine the whole theory and purpose of the limited joint stock company, the comparative rights and obligations of shareholders, directors, creditors, employees, and the community as a whole'. In the event this was not pursued, but a report in the *Financial Times*, 20 July 1970, suggested that the new Conservative Government proposed to re-examine the form of the company.

[3] op. cit.

sum of money on purchasing the necessary qualifying share? It is argued that workers would thereby enhance their status, and would come to identify with their enterprise. But workers are usually hard-headed practical people, more moved by fact than form, and the fact is that membership status would, of itself and under present arrangements, be likely to have no more than a very slight motivational effect and give workers a chance of speaking at general meetings and voting, for what their votes would be worth, in the election of directors and passage of the annual accounts. How many would do so?

There would seem to be no reason why workers should not be classed as members of companies, but, as experience of the John Lewis Partnership has shown, such membership cannot be seen as necessarily leading to participation in management to any significant extent.

The legal position with regard to the purposes of the company presents sterner problems. Why should companies not have to pay attention, it is argued, to the interests of workers, customers, suppliers, the local community, and indeed the community at large? In practice, of course, companies do pay regard to these interests, but it has been suggested that an obligation should be laid upon them. In Fogarty's words, 'The ideal formula is probably one which begins by emphasizing a company's key role as a market enterprise for producing goods and services on economic terms, but then goes on to make clear, on German and Dutch lines, that subject to this main purpose a wide range of public and social considerations have also to be taken into account.'[1]

Elsewhere Fogarty has reminded us[2] that German Law used to provide that the executive board of a company 'Shall on its own responsibility manage the company as the good of the business and its staff and the common good of the nation require'.[3] This provision is not included in the German Companies Act of 1965, but the accompanying official commentary, which in German practice is taken into account by the Courts in interpreting the law, indicates that the executive board must

[1] P.E.P., op. cit., p. 120.
[2] 'Co-determination and Company Structure in Germany', *British Journal of Industrial Relations*, Vol. II, No. 1 (March 1964), p. 81.
[3] *Aktiengesetz*, 1937, Section 70, as quoted by Fogarty, op. cit.

take account of the interests of shareholders, employees, and the community.

The Verdam Commission's Report, in Holland, has proposed that directors should 'fulfil their task, within the framework of the public interest, on behalf of the totality of interests in the company and of the enterprise attached to it'.[1]

In Britain, it has been suggested that workers, customers and the community should each nominate a director who would be required to report at the annual general meeting on their custody of their constitutents' interests. Company memoranda and articles of association should be required to set out objectives, which would include provisions in general terms relative to the interests of the three groups mentioned.[2]

Here we are concerned only with the workers employed by a company, and at present there is no obligation on a company to have regard to their interests, beyond satisfying the law of employment and protective legislation. The company must operate to further the interests of the shareholders: 'there are to be no cakes and ale, except such as required for the benefit of the company'.[3] When the *News Chronicle* was sold, the directors proposed to give a large portion of the proceeds to the employees, as redundancy pay. As the company was not likely to continue operations the payments proposed could not be regarded as benefiting the shareholders by encouraging remaining or prospective employees. Accordingly a shareholder's challenge to the board's decision succeeded[4] (though a large sum was later made available to the redundant employees by agreement).

The argument for a statutory requirement that companies should have regard to the well-being of their workers has been countered on several grounds. In practice companies do have (and given full employment and the existence of trade unions,

[1] P.E.P., op. cit. (1967), p. 120. (The reference is to p. 115 of the Verdam Commission's Report, 1965.)

[2] G. Goyder, *The Future of Private Enterprise* (Blackwell, Oxford 1951), and *The Responsible Company* (Blackwell, Oxford 1961).

[3] Bowen, L. J., Hutton v. West Cork Railway Co. 1883, 23 CL, D 654 CA.

[4] Parke v. *Daily News*, 1962, Chancery Reports, p. 927. Compare: 'It can hardly be denied that industry is in practice a joint enterprise in which management and workers participate as well as shareholders, and indeed participate rather more actively, and the law, by investing the shareholders alone with legal rights, does not merely fail to reflect the reality—it turns it upside down.' C. A. R. Crosland, *The Future of Socialism* (Cape, London 1956), pp. 351–2.

have to have) regard to the well-being of their workers; their attention to this matter is not likely to increase by their being subject to a statutory requirement. Cases such as Parke v. *Daily News* are very rare. But the most weighty argument is that such a requirement on directors might 'dilute and diffuse that concentration upon profit which is necessary, not merely for the sake of their own Company, but I should have thought in present circumstances for the sake of the community at large'.[1] Or in Lord Cole's words:

> These suggestions stem from the idea that the shareholders are only one among many interests that the Board should serve. At the heart of this theory lies the idea that a Board does not concern itself as much about other interests—the workers, the customers, the government and even the suppliers—as it does about the shareholders, ignoring the fact that unless proper weight is given to all these interests, the Board will not have served its shareholders properly.... Consumers, the government, workers, managers, are all special interests. It is only the shareholders' interests which really span them all.[2]

The Board's prime function, on this view, is 'the proper allocation of resources in order to produce the most desirable profits'.[3] No country has in fact been prepared to give to private companies an untrammelled freedom to determine their affairs, since the evidence of their behaviour has shown it to be necessary in the public interest to regulate the way in which they use their power and resources.

On balance it would seem that to make statutory provision that companies should have regard to workers' interests might have practical effect, though it would not necessarily involve workers in decision-making. The idea remains one that cannot be ignored in any consideration of the place of the worker in relation to the enterprise in which he works.

It is not proposed to repeat here the arguments about workers' representation on the boards of companies, or about the possi-

---

[1] W. G. McClelland, *The Creation of Wealth and its Distribution: a dual responsibility* (Industrial Co-Partnership Association, London 1968), p. 11.

[2] Lord Cole, *The Future of the Board* (Industrial Educational and Research Foundation, London 1968), pp. 14, 15. It may be added that the absence of a statutory requirement need not prevent a company spelling out its view of its obligations to workers, as in the case of Shell UK Ltd, reported in Chapter 7.

[3] Ibid., p. 13.

bilities of a two-tier board structure, that have been set out in Chapter 6. It is, however, appropriate to refer to participation through formal Committees or Councils within the enterprise.

(3) *Formal Committees*

Formal consultative committees have been discussed in several preceding chapters. In Chapter 5 there was reference to the form of committee established in the enterprise in France, Germany and Sweden. Much more could have been said about European practice in this respect.[1] Though formal consultative committees are uncommon in the United States, Britain and Ireland are virtually the only countries in Western Europe in which the setting up of a committee or council, either of workers alone or jointly with management, in an enterprise of any size is not required by collective agreement (as in the Scandinavian countries) or by law (as in most other countries). Another difference between British and European practice is that though, as in Britain, most continental forms of committee are excluded from dealing with matters normally the subject of negotiation, their scope, rights and duties are generally much wider than those of British committees, which tend to be somewhat production-centred. Yet a further difference is that in many of the continental countries the committees have been strengthened from time to time,[2] over the very period in which British consultative committees have been declining. However, it must be said of the continental committees that despite a great deal of effort in several countries, including the extensive provision for the training of committee members,[3] they have met with no more than modest success, and their formal rights have not always been borne out in reality. Such success as they have had has tended to be in the social and personnel aspects of the enterprise; though they have some achievements to their credit in

[1] A summary is to be found in I.L.O., *Participation of Workers in Decisions within Undertakings*, Labour–Management Relations Series, No. 33, I.L.O., Geneva 1969; and *Workers' Participation in Western Europe*, Institute of Personnel Management Information Report 10 (New Series), Institute of Personnel Management, London 1971.

[2] It is noteworthy that in 1970 the Danish Works Committees were considerably strengthened by national agreement and in 1971 Austria, Germany and Holland strengthened their works councils by legislation.

[3] Something almost unknown in Britain, though the practice of training shop-stewards in responsibilities associated with negotiation is increasing.

improving productive efficiency they have had little impact in the commercial and economic areas of decision-making. But they have proved a useful instrument for requiring employers to observe certain standards, particularly in the social and personnel fields. It does seem that British neglect of this type of machinery, partly attributable perhaps to equating it with the traditional type of production committee, is unjustified. Would compulsory committees, with similarly wide terms of reference to those of the continental committees, be successful in Britain?

In the present British climate of opinion, the introduction of compulsory committees would probably be strongly resisted by both employers and unions, and accordingly such committees would stand little chance of success, dependent as they are on the effort put in to them. Neither do the T.U.C. and the C.B.I. have the power or the inclination to provide for such committees by national agreement. Nevertheless, if only as a form of expression of managerial accountability, the idea would appear to deserve more consideration than it has received hitherto.[1]

As for voluntary committees, the encouragement of consultative machinery by the Code of Practice, under the Industrial Relations Act, 1971, may have positive results, but it is highly unlikely that bodies with authority, such as the Glacier Works Council described in Chapter 7, will be much copied voluntarily.

Yet, despite the decline in the use of formal consultative machinery and the fact that, particularly in highly unionized firms, many of the customary subjects of joint consultation have come to be dealt with by negotiating machinery, both the survey made in the present inquiry and European experience suggest that given enthusiasm and effort on the part of senior managers a well-designed consultative committee can in many cases provide a form of participation beneficial to management and workers alike. If the same stress were placed on developing such forms of co-operative machinery as has been placed in Britain in recent years on machinery for collective bargaining,[2]

[1] So far consideration has been mainly political. For instance, Mr. Harold Wilson, when Prime Minister, at one time advocated compulsory production committees (*The Times*, 1 November 1965), and Mr. Robert Carr, in a speech to the Conservative Party Conference, proposed the establishment of elected councils (*The Financial Times*, 9 October 1969). The Liberals have long advocated compulsory works councils.

[2] *Vide* the Report of the Royal Commission on Trade Unions and Employers' Associations, which deals extensively with collective bargaining but devotes only two paragraphs to joint consultation.

the results in terms of industrial relations might be surprising.

(4) *Collective Bargaining*

As stated in earlier chapters, collective bargaining is the main form of participation in Britain, and its likely strengthening and extension will bring about an increase in participation through unions. The trend towards work-place bargaining and particularly the practice of productivity bargaining imply substantially increased involvement of workers, primarily in the regulation of wages and conditions but also in the organization and method of performance of work. It may also involve, or at least interest, workers to a greater extent in the broad conduct of the enterprise. Unfortunately there is little evidence that involvement through collective bargaining increases identification with managerial decisions. The trend towards work-place bargaining may have positive implications in respect of the aspects of the decision-making that are of immediate and direct concern to workers, but may inhibit participation beyond this point.

Not all of the consequences of strengthening collective bargaining are necessarily favourable, at least if 'strengthening' is equated, as it was by the Donovan Commission, with strengthening trade unions' power to negotiate. As pointed out in Chapter 5, collective bargaining is most effective when there is a balance of power between management and workers. When superior power is in the hands of workers it may provide participation to an extent that, by making it possible to block decisions important to the efficient conduct of the enterprise, efficiency is inhibited. Conversely, where the management remains strong and the workers weak, collective bargaining cannot be relied upon to provide very much participation. A fundamental failing of collective bargaining is that it favours the industrial strong at the expense of the weak: it is in many respects an imperfect instrument of participation since its primary purpose is to persuade management to satisfy the requests of the unions.

Extension of the field of collective bargaining also has other weaknesses. It may well result in a raising of the level of conflict. If the subjects of bargaining are extended to include those in which decisions depend on technical factors, and relate to matters on which urgent decisions are required for operational reasons, participation through unions may give rise to conflicts which could have extremely serious effects.

The rapid growth of one particular form of collective bargaining, productivity bargaining, has been noted in earlier chapters. Its growth has probably owed most to the pressures of governmental incomes policies between 1966 and 1969, but it has certainly introduced a new dimension to traditional collective bargaining by involving workers in aspects of the operation of the enterprise with which they had not usually been associated previously, and making a greatly increased amount of information available to them. Government pressure apart, there seems no doubt that where it has been properly carried out, productivity bargaining has improved the quality of industrial relations,[1] enhanced job satisfaction, and also produced useful improvements in efficiency. But leaving aside certain sections of industry in the United States, productivity bargaining is rarely encountered outside Britain, mainly because many of the decisions which in Britain have been the subject of bargaining are in other countries within the exercised prerogatives of management and would not have a price put on them. Whether the freedom of decision enjoyed by management in other countries yields better overall results in the economic field than British productivity bargaining is not susceptible of proof.

(5) *Participative Forms of Management and Participation in the Job*

Participative forms of management, some of which were described in Chapter 7, have achieved increasing support in recent years, and have found favour with some notably progressive and successful companies. Sometimes the practice amounts to no more than the careful inculcation of a participative managerial style, ensuring that there is genuine consultation and that due account is taken of workers' views before managerial decisions are finalized. Periodic attitude surveys may be made to ensure that workers' views are known, the results being thoroughly and openly discussed and taken into account. As in the case of I.B.M., a participative form of management may be supplemented by devices designed to introduce a degree of managerial account-

[1] See W. W. Daniel, *Beyond the Wage–Work Bargain* (P.E.P., London 1970).

ability to workers.[1] There has been criticism that some participative managerial policies and practices, including the use to
which attitude surveys may be put, are aimed at keeping unions
out by eliminating grievances, and that they may seek to manipu-
late individuals to serve the organization's ends, as opposed to
the more socially acceptable end of harmonizing individual and
organizational goals.

Such forms of participative management usually apply at all
levels and relate to a wide range of decisions. Another type of
participation based on managerial initiative relates more especially
to the work process immediate to the worker. Essentially it involves the decentralization of decision-making in that area
(though decisions made must fit into the overall policies of the
enterprise). It may take the simple form, practised for centuries,
of sub-contracting work to working groups on a lump-sum basis,
leaving the group to organize the work—as in the old Guild
Socialist idea of the collective contract.[2] Another form is job
enrichment, as described in Chapter 7. And lastly, combining in
a way both job enrichment and some elements of the collective
contract, is the autonomous work-group, also discussed in
Chapter 7.

Of all the forms of participation discussed, those just described (short of the manipulative form) seem among the most
immediately fruitful. Though they call for a certain sophistica-
tion on the part of management they are readily realizable without structural change; they provide participation in areas in which
workers are most interested; they seem likely to add to workers'
satisfaction in their jobs; and the evidence seems to suggest
they are likely to increase operational efficiency.

This can hardly be said of the other form of direct participation in the work process, that of restrictive practices. Rapid
technological change, and the concomitant blurring of divisions
of skill, coupled with the security of continued full employment
and supported by active man-power policies, seem likely to have
some impact on restrictive practices, but so long as participation

[1] Apart from sophisticated provision for pursuing grievances through
successive levels of management, I.B.M. has a procedure—the 'speak up'
procedure—for criticisms of management to be dealt with confidentially, at
higher level than the complainant's immediate superior, by a kind of
ombudsman.
[2] See also H. A. Clegg, *A New Approach to Industrial Democracy* (Blackwell,
Oxford 1960), pp. 121–8.

is primarily through collective bargaining it is unlikely that restrictive practices will be entirely eliminated. Positive participation would seem to offer a means of dissolving this largely negative form of participation, but it could only be fully effective as an alternative to collective bargaining.

The Task Ahead

This book has sought to show the complexity of the subject of participation and to demonstrate the importance of clarity in defining the purposes for which participation may be desired, the levels at which (and type of decision in which) it is envisaged, and the forms that it may take. It should have become clear that it is meaningless to say that participation is good, or bad, without reference to these characteristics. It also seems clear that there can be no simple solution that will meet the apparent need for greater participation by workers in decisions at their place of work. Some courses advocated seem more promising than others, some less; what seems most likely is that changes in the enterprise will provide a combination of means of participation.

Perhaps there may be change in the formal structure of the enterprise and some increase in managerial accountability; perhaps more sensitive use of collective bargaining and joint consultation and certainly more examples of direct participation in management.

In the British environment it seems unlikely that the direct participation of workers in management decision-making at middle and high levels will rapidly increase. Though in important respects legislation could assist in bringing about participation of a formal nature, this of itself would not necessarily change the attitudes of managers and the processes of management. Nor would the formal right of participation in senior management through the concept of worker-directors ensure that workers developed a greater understanding of the needs of an efficient enterprise and the willingness to make a greater contribution. However, it is possible that a growth of participation at the department level might provide a foundation for the subsequent evolution of much more extensive forms of participation embracing the whole enterprise.

A fully participative system of industrial government is, however, not likely to be achieved or even perhaps closely approached without the development and widespread acceptance of a general theory of participative industrial democracy. It can be argued that the failure to make work a meaningful and satisfying activity under contemporary conditions has made this an urgent need. It is possible that the only effective antidote is the creation of a society in which an individual can find a wider opportunity to participate in the making of decisions of all kinds that affect his well-being. The ordinary individual may be satisfied to leave the taking of many decisions to others so long as he is entitled to protest when he finds they bear upon him onerously. The right to protest is, however, alone not enough. A negative check is a vitally necessary safeguard against any kind of tyranny, but the positive involvement in the making of decisions of as many of those affected by them as posible is at bottom one of the essentials of democracy, and the only way to satisfy the minority who feel this need to be active participants. How this is to be achieved while ensuring that efficiency is not impaired is the task that lies ahead.

Bibliography

SECTION I
Official Publications and Publications of the International Institute for Labour Studies

I PUBLICATIONS OF H.M.S.O., LONDON

A. Committee of the Ministry of Reconstruction on the Relations between Employers and Employed (The 'Whitley' Committee) 1916–18.
    1. *Interim Report on Joint Standing Industrial Councils* Cmd. 8606, 1917.
    2. *Supplementary Report on Works Committees* Cmd. 9001, 1918.
    3. *Second Report on Joint Standing Industrial Councils* Cmd. 9002, 1918.
    4. *Report on Conciliation and Arbitration* Cmd. 9099, 1918.
    5. *Final Report* Cmd. 9153, 1918.

B. Ministry of Labour, *Attitudes to Efficiency*, 1966.

C. Royal Commission on Trade Unions and Employers' Associations 1965–68.
    1. *Report*, Cmd. 3623, June 1968.
    2. *Minutes of Evidence*
        20 Engineering Employers' Federation.
        21 Electricity Council.
        24 Amalgamated Engineering Union.
        30 Transport and General Workers' Union.
        57 Electrical Trades Union.
        61 and 65 Trades Union Congress.
        69 Confederation of British Industry.
    3. *Research Papers*
        1. *The Role of Shop Stewards in British Industrial Relations*, W. E. J. McCarthy (1966).
        2. (Part 1) *Disputes Procedures in British Industry*, A. I. Marsh (1966).
        (Part 2) *Disputes Procedures in Britain*, A. I. Marsh and W. E. J. McCarthy (1968).

3. *Industrial Sociology and Industrial Relations*, A. Fox (1966).
4. 1. *Productivity Bargaining*. 2. *Restrictive Labour Practices*. Written by the Commission's Secretariat (1967).
6. *Trade Union Growth and Recognition*, G. Bain (1967).
9. *Overtime Working in Britain*, E. G. Whybrew (1968).
10. *Shop Stewards and Workshop Relations*, W. E. J. McCarthy and S. R. Parker (1968).

  4. Government Social Survey, *Workplace Industrial Relations*. An enquiry undertaken for the Royal Commission on Trade Unions and Employers' Associations in 1966, 1968.

D. Central Statistical Office, *Standard Industrial Classification*, 1968.

E. White Paper, *In Place of Strife. A Policy for Industrial Relations* Cmd. 3888, 1969.

II INTERNATIONAL LABOUR OFFICE PUBLICATIONS

A. I.L.O. Studies and Reports. Series A (Industrial Relations) No. 42. *Joint Production Committees in Great Britain* (Montreal 1943). No, 43. *British Joint Production Machinery* (Montreal 1944).

B. Workers' Management and Labour Relations in Yugoslavia (Geneva 1958).

C. Workers' Management in Yugoslavia (Geneva 1962).

D. Participation of Workers in Decisions Within Undertakings, *Labour–Management Relations Series*, No. 33 (Geneva 1969). Report on the International Seminar on Workers' Participation in Decisions Within Undertakings (Belgrade) (Geneva 1969).

E. Lerner, S. W., 'Factory Agreements and National Bargaining in the British Engineering Industry', *International Labour Review* (Geneva, January 1964).

III PUBLICATIONS OF THE INTERNATIONAL INSTITUTE FOR LABOUR STUDIES, GENEVA

'Workers' Participation in Management', *Selected Bibliography*, 1950–1970, The Institute (Geneva 1971).

Bulletin 2. Feb. 1967, pages 64–125, *Workers' Participation in Management*.

  I R. W. Cox, 'A Fruitful Field for Enquiry'.

  II K. F. Walker and L. Gréyfié de Bellecombe, 'The Concept and its Implementation'.

  III A Research Project.

Bulletin 5. Nov. 1968, pages 138–220, *Workers' Participation in Management*.

  I K. F. Walker, 'Conceptual Framework and Scope of National Studies'.

II Country Studies Series: *India* (No. 1), *Poland* (No. 2).
Bulletin 6. June 1969, pages 54–186, *Workers' Participation in Management*.
Country Studies Series: *France* (No. 3), *Federal Republic of Germany* (No. 4), *United States* (No. 5).
Bulletin 7. June 1970, pages 153–285, *Workers' Participation in Management*.
Country Studies Series: *Israel* (No. 6), *Japan* (No. 7), *Spain* (No. 8).

IV ORGANIZATION FOR ECONOMIC CO-OPERATION AND DEVELOPMENT, PARIS
A. *Workers' Attitudes to Technical Change: an integrated survey of research*, A. Touraine et al., 1965.
B *Workers' Negotiated Savings Plans for Capital Formation*, D. Robinson and S. Barkin, 1968 and 1970.

V EUROPEAN ECONOMIC COMMUNITY, BRUSSELS
A. *Proposed Statute for the European Company*, 1970.
B. Sanders, Pieter, *Projet d'un Statut des Sociétés Anonymes Européenes*, Etudes Série Concurrence, No. 6, 1967
C. Lyon-Caen, Gérard, *Contributions à l'Etude des Modes de Représentation des Intérêts des Travailleurs dans le Cadre des Sociétés Anonymes Européennes*, Etudes Série Concurrence No. 10, 1970.

VI NETHERLANDS PUBLICATIONS
Rapport van de Commissie ingesteld bij beschikking van de Minister van Justitie van 8 April 1960 (Verdam Commission), Herziening van het Ondernemingsrecht (Staatsuitgeverij/'s-Gravenhage 1968).

SECTION II
Books

ACTON SOCIETY TRUST and NAYLOR, G., *Sharing the Profits* (Garnstone Press, London 1968).
ARGYRIS, C., *Personality and Organisation: The Conflict between System and the Individual* (Harper and Row, New York 1957).
ARGYRIS, C., *Understanding Organisational Behaviour* (Tavistock Publications, London 1960).
ARGYRIS, C., *Integrating the Individual and the Organisation* (John Wiley, New York 1964).
BAKKE, E. WIGHT, 'The Function of Management' in HUGH-JONES, E. M. (ed.), *Human Relations and Modern Management* (North Holland Publishing Co., Amsterdam 1958).
BANKS, J. A., *Industrial Participation—Theory and Practice: a Case Study* (Liverpool University Press, 1963).

BANKS, O., *The Attitudes of Steelworkers to Technical Change* (Liverpool University Press, 1960).

BARNARD, C. I., *The Functions of the Executive* (Harvard University Press, Cambridge, Mass., 1938).

BENDIX, R., *Work and Authority in Industry: Ideologies of Management in the Course of Industrialisation* (John Wiley, New York 1956).

BENNIS, WARREN C., *Changing Organisations* (McGraw-Hill, New York 1966).

BLAU, P. M., and SCOTT, W. RICHARD, *Formal Organisations* (Chandler, San Francisco 1962).

BLAUNER, R., *Alienation and Freedom: The Factory Worker and his Industry* (University of Chicago Press, 1964).

BLOCH-LAINE, F., *Pour une Reforme de l'Entreprise* (Editions du Seuil, Paris 1963).

BLUM, F. J., *Work and Community: The Scott Bader Commonwealth and the Quest for a New Social Order* (Routledge and Kegan Paul, London 1968).

BLUMBERG, P., *Industrial Democracy: The Sociology of Participation* (Constable, London 1968).

BLUMENTHAL, W. M., *Co-determination in the German Steel Industry* (Princeton University Press, 1956).

BOTTOMORE, T. B., *Elites and Society* (Penguin Books, Harmondsworth 1966).

BROWN, PHELPS E. H., *The Growth of British Industrial Relations* (Macmillan, London 1959).

BROWN, WILFRED B. D., *Exploration in Management: a description of the Glacier Metal Company's concepts and methods of organization and management* (Heinemann, London 1962).

BROWN, W. ROBSON, and HOWELL-EVERSON, N. A., *Industrial Democracy at Work: A Factual Survey* (Pitman, London 1950).

BURNS, T., and STALKER, G. M., *The Management of Innovation* (Tavistock Publications, London 1961).

CARTWRIGHT, D., and ZANDER, A. (ed.), *Group Dynamics* (Harper, New York 1953).

CAUTER, T., and DOWNHAM, J., *The Communication of Ideas* (Chatto and Windus, London 1954).

CHAMBERLAIN, N. W., *The Union Challenge to Management Control* (Harper, New York 1948).

CHILD, JOHN, *British Management Thought: a Critical Analysis* (Allen and Unwin, London 1969).

CHILD, JOHN, *The Business Enterprise in Modern Industrial Society* (Collier-Macmillan, London 1969).

CLAY, H., *The Problem of Industrial Relations* (Macmillan, London 1929).

CLEGG, H. A., *Industrial Democracy and Nationalisation: a Study Prepared for the Fabian Society* (Blackwell, Oxford 1951).

CLEGG, H. A., *A New Approach to Industrial Democracy* (Blackwell, Oxford 1960).

CLEGG, H. A., KILLICK, A. J., and ADAMS, R., *Trade Union Officers* (Blackwell, Oxford 1961).

COATES, K. (ed.), *Can The Workers Run Industry?* (Sphere Books Ltd, London 1968).

COATES, K., and TOPHAM, A., *Industrial Democracy in Great Britain* (MacGibbon and Kee, London 1968).

COLE, G. D. H., *Self-Government in Industry* (Bell, London 1919).

COLE, G. D. H., *Guild Socialism Restated* (London 1920).

COLE, G. D. H., *Workshop Organisation* (Clarendon Press, Oxford 1923).

COLE, G. D. H., *Life of Robert Owen* (Macmillan, London 1930).

COLE, G. D. H., *A Century of Cooperation* (Allen and Unwin, London 1944).

COPEMAN, G., *The Challenge of Employee Shareholding, How to close the gap between Capital and Labour* (Business Publications, Batsford, London 1958).

COYLE, DOMINICK J. (ed.), *Industrial Democracy: a Symposium* (Irish Management Institute, Dublin 1969).

CROSLAND, C. A. R., *The Future of Socialism* (Cape, London 1956).

CROZIER, M., *The Bureaucratic Phenomenon* (Tavistock Publications, London 1964).

DAHRENDORF, R., *Class and Class Conflict in Industrial Society* (Routledge and Kegan Paul, London 1963).

DAS, N., *Experiments in Industrial Democracy* (Asia Publishing House, New York 1964).

DERBER, MILTON, *The American Idea of Industrial Democracy, 1865–1965* (University of Illinois Press, Urbana 1970).

DERBER, M., *Labor–Management Relations at the Plant Level Under Industry-Wide Bargaining* (University of Illinois, 1955).

DERRICK, P., and PHIPPS, J. F. (eds.), *Co-ownership, Co-operation and Control: an Industrial Objective* (Longmans, London 1969).

DE SCHWEINITZ, D., *Labor–Management Consultation in the Factory* (University of Hawaii, Honolulu 1966).

DRUCKER, P. F., *The New Society: the Anatomy of the Industrial Order* (Heinemann, London 1951).

DUNLOP, J. T., *Industrial Relations Systems* (Henry Holt, New York 1958).

EKEBERG, L. O., and LANTZ, S. W., *Blue Collar Workers' Participation in Management in Sweden* (Swedish Institute for Labour Studies, Stockholm 1968).

EMERY, F., and THORSRUD, E., in co-operation with TRIST, E., *Form and Content in Industrial Democracy* (Tavistock Publications, London 1969).

ETZIONI, A., *A Comparative Analysis of Complex Organisations* (The Free Press, New York 1961).

FLANDERS, A., *The Fawley Productivity Agreements* (Faber, London 1964).

FLANDERS, A., *Industrial Relations: What is Wrong with the System?* (Institute of Personnel Management, London 1966).

FLANDERS, A., POMERANZ, R., and WOODWARD, J., *Experiment in Industrial Democracy: a Study of the John Lewis Partnership* (Faber, London 1968).

FOGARTY, M. P., *Company and Corporation—One Law?* (Geoffrey Chapman, London 1965).

FOX, ALAN, *A Sociology of Work in Industry* (Collier-Macmillan, London 1971).

FROMM, E., *The Sane Society* (Routledge and Kegan Paul, London 1956).

GALENSON, W., and LIPSET, S. M. (eds.), *Labor and Trade Unionism* (John Wiley, New York 1960).

GARCIN, W., *Cogestion et Participation dans les entreprises des pays du Marché Commun* (Editions Jupiter, Paris 1968).

GELLERMAN, S. W., *Motivation and Productivity* (American Management Association, New York 1963).

GELLERMAN, S. W., *Management by Motivation* (American Management Association, New York 1968).

GLASS, S. T., *The Responsible Society: the ideas of the English Guild Socialist* (Longmans, London 1966).

GOLDTHORPE, J. H., *et al.*, *The Affluent Worker: Industrial Attitudes and Behaviour* (Cambridge University Press, 1968).

GOODMAN, J. F. B., and WHITTINGHAM, T. E., *Shop Stewards in British Industry* (McGraw-Hill, London 1969).

GOYDER, G., *The Future of Private Enterprise* (Blackwell, Oxford 1951).

GOYDER, G., *The Responsible Company* (Blackwell, Oxford 1961).

HACKMAN, RAY C., *The Motivated Working Adult* (American Management Association, Bailey Brothers and Swinfen, Folkestone 1969).

HANNINGTON, W., *Industrial History in Wartime* (Lawrence and Wishart, London 1940).

HARBISON, F., and MYERS, C. A., *Management in the Industrial World* (McGraw-Hill, New York 1959).

HARPER, J. C., *Profit-Sharing in Practice and Law* (Sweet and Maxwell, London 1955).

HERBST, P. G., *Autonomous Group Functioning: an Exploration in Behaviour Theory and Measurement* (Tavistock Publications, London 1962).

HERZBERG, F., *et al.*, *Job Attitudes: Review of Research and Opinion* (Psychological Service of Pittsburgh, Pittsburgh, Pa. 1957).

HERZBERG, F., *et al.*, *The Motivation to Work*, 2nd edn. (John Wiley, New York 1959).

HERZBERG, F., *Work and the Nature of Man* (World Publishing Co., Cleveland, New York 1966).

HILTON, JOHN (ed.), *Are Trade Unions Obstructive?* (Gollancz, London 1935).

HOBSON, S. G. (ed. ORAGE, A. R.), *National Guilds: An inquiry into the wage system and the way out* (Bell, London 1919).

HOBSON, S. G., *Pilgrim to the Left, Memoirs of a Modern Revolutionist* (London 1938).

HOMANS, G. C., *The Human Group* (Routledge and Kegan Paul, London 1951).

INSTITUT NATIONAL DE GESTION PREVISIONNELLE ET DE CONTRÔLE DE GESTION, *Vers une Gestion Participative* (Hachette, Paris 1971).

INSTITUTE OF PERSONNEL MANAGEMENT, 'Workers' Participation in Western Europe', *Institute of Personnel Management Information Report* No. 10 (New Series), (The Institute, London 1971).

INTERNATIONAL CONFEDERATION OF FREE TRADE UNIONS, *Workers' Participation in Industry*, Study Guide No. 3 (Brussels 1954).

IRISH MANAGEMENT INSTITUTE, *Industrial Democracy: A Symposium* (Irish Management Institute, Dublin 1969).

JAQUES, E., *The Changing Culture of a Factory: a study of authority and participation in an industrial setting* (Tavistock Publications, London 1951).

JONES, B., *Cooperative Production* (1894).

KAHN, R. L., and BOULDING, E. (eds.), *Power and Conflict in Organisations* (Tavistock Publications, London 1964).

KELLY, JOE, *Is Scientific Management Possible?: a critical examination of Glacier's theory of organisation* (Faber, London 1968).

KELLY, JOE, *Organizational Behaviour* (Richard D. Irwin Inc., Homewood, Illinois 1969).

KOLAJA, J., *Workers' Councils: The Jugoslav Experience* (Tavistock Publications, London 1965).

LANDSBERGER, H. A., *Hawthorne Revisited* (Cornell University Press, Ithaca, New York 1958).

LAPPING, B., and RADICE, G. (eds.), *More Power to the People: Young Fabian essays on Democracy in Britain* (Longmans, London 1968).

LEITCH, J., *Man to Man: The Story of Industrial Democracy* (London 1920).

LEWIS, J. S., *Partnership for All* (Kerr Cross, London 1948).

LEWIS, J. S., *Fairer Shares* (Staples Press, London 1954).

LIBERAL PARTY, *Britain's Industrial Future*—the Report of the Liberal Industrial Inquiry (Ernest Benn, London 1928).

LIKERT, R., *New Patterns of Management* (McGraw-Hill, New York 1961).

LIKERT, R., *The Human Organisation: Its Management and Value* (McGraw-Hill, New York 1967).

LINCOLN, J. A., *The Restrictive Society* (Allen and Unwin, London 1967).

LITWIN, G. H., and STRINGER, R. A., *Motivation and Organisational Climate* (Bailey Brothers and Swinfen, 1968).

LIVERPOOL UNIVERSITY, DEPARTMENT OF SOCIAL SCIENCE, *The Dock Worker: an analysis of Conditions of Employment in the Port of Manchester* (Liverpool University Press, 1954).

LUPTON, T., *On the Shop Floor* (Pergamon Press, Oxford 1963).

MACIVER, R. M., and PAGE, C. M., *Society* (Macmillan, London 1953).

MARROW, A. J., *et al.*, *Management by Participation: Creating a Climate for Personal and Organisational Development* (Harper and Row, New York 1967).

MAYO, E., *The Human Problems of an Industrial Civilisation* (Harvard University Press, Boston, Mass. 1933).

MAYO, E., *The Social Problems of an Industrial Civilisation* (Routledge and Kegan Paul, London 1949).

McCLELLAND, W. G., *The Creation of Wealth and its Distribution: A dual responsibility* (Industrial Copartnership Association, London 1968).

McGREGOR, D., *The Human Side of Enterprise* (McGraw-Hill, New York 1960).

McGREGOR, D., *The Professional Manager* (McGraw-Hill, New York 1967).

MEISTER, ALBERT, *Où va l'autogestion yougoslave?* (Editions Anthropos, Paris 1970).

MELMAN, S., *Decision-making and Productivity* (Blackwell, Oxford 1958).

METCALFE, H. C., and URWICK, L. F., *Dynamic Administration* (Macmillan, New York 1947).

METZGER, B. L., *Profit Sharing in Perspective* (Profit Sharing Research Foundation, Evanston, Ill. 1964).

MHETRAS, V. G., *Labour Participation in Management: an Experiment in Industrial Democracy in India* (Manaktalas, Bombay 1966).

MILLER, D. C., and FORM, W. H., *Industrial Sociology* (Harper and Row, New York 1964).

MILLER, E. G., and RICE, A. K., *Systems of Organisation* (Tavistock Publications, London 1967).

MILNE-BAILEY, W., *Trade Unions and the State* (Allen and Unwin, London 1934).

MORRISON, H. S., *Socialisation and Transport: the Organisation of Socialised Industries, with particular reference to the London Passenger Transport Bill* (Constable, London 1933).

MURPHY, J. T., *Preparing for Power* (Cape, London 1934).

NATIONAL INSTITUTE OF INDUSTRIAL PSYCHOLOGY, *Joint Consultation in British Industry* (Staples Press, London 1952).

NEULOH, OTTO, *Der Neue Betriebsstil* (Tübingen 1960).

NEWMAN, JEREMIAH, *Co-responsibility in Industry* (M. H. Gill and Son Ltd, Dublin 1955).

NICHOLS, T., *Ownership, Control and Ideology* (Allen and Unwin, London 1969).

PATCHEN, MARTIN, *Participation, Achievement and Involvement on the Job* (Prentice-Hall, Englewood Cliffs, New Jersey 1970).

PATEMAN, C., *Participation and Democratic Theory* (Cambridge University Press, London 1970).

PAUL, W. J., and ROBERTSON, K. B., *Job Enrichment and Employee Motivation* (Gower Press, London 1970).

PENTY, A. J., *The Restoration of the Gild System* (Swan, London 1906).

POLE, W. (ed.), *The Life of Sir William Fairbairn, Bart.* (Longmans, London 1877).

POLITICAL AND ECONOMIC PLANNING, *Attitudes in British Management* (P.E.P., London 1965).

POSTGATE, R., *The Builders' History* (N.F.B.T.O., London 1923).

POTTER, B. (later Webb), *The Cooperative Movement in Great Britain* (Allen and Unwin, London 1930 (first published 1891)).

POTTHOF, E., BLUME, O., and DUVERNELL, H., *Zwischenbilanz der Mitbestimmung* (J. E. B. Mohr (Paul Siebeck), Tübingen 1962).

PRIBICEVIC, B., *The Shop Stewards' Movement and Workers' Control, 1910–12* (Blackwell, Oxford 1959).

RECKITT, M. B., and BECHHOFER, C. E., *The Meaning of National Guilds* (Cecil Palmer, London 1920).

RHENMAN, E., *Industrial Democracy and Industrial Management: a critical essay on the possible meanings and implications of industrial democracy* (Tavistock Publications, London 1968).

RHENMAN, ERIC, *et al.*, *Cooperation and Conflict in Organizations* (John Wiley and Sons, Chichester 1970).

RICE, A. K., *Productivity and Social Organisation—the Ahmedabad Experiment* (Tavistock Publications, London 1958).

RICE, A. K., *The Enterprise and its Environment* (Tavistock Publications, London 1963).

ROBERTS, B. C., *Trade Union Government and Administration* (Bell, London 1956).

ROBERTSON, D., and DENNISON, S., *The Control of Industry* (Nisbet, Cambridge 1960).

ROBSON, W. A. (ed.), *Problems of Nationalised Industry* (Allen and Unwin, London 1952).

ROBSON, W. A., *Nationalised Industry and Public Ownership*, 2nd edn. (Allen and Unwin, London 1962).

SADLER, P. J., *Leadership Style, Confidence in Management and Job Satisfaction* (Ashridge Management College, 1966).

SAWTELL, R., *Sharing Our Industrial Future?* (Industrial Society, London 1968).

SCHLOSS, D. F., *Methods of Industrial Remuneration*, 3rd edn. (Williams and Norgate, London 1898).

SCOTT, WILLIAM H., *Joint Consultation in a Liverpool Manufacturing Firm: a Case Study in Human Relations in Industry* (Liverpool University Press, 1950).

SCOTT, WILLIAM H., *Industrial Leadership and Joint Consultation* (Liverpool University Press, 1952).

SELZNICK, P., *Leadership in Administration: a Sociological Interpretation* (Row, Evanston, Illinois 1957).

SENIOR, NASSAU, *Industrial Efficiency and Social Economy* (Henry Holt and Co., New York 1920).

SIMON, H. A., *Administration Behaviour* (Macmillan, New York 1947).

STAGNER, R., and ROSEN, H., *The Psychology of Union–Management Relations* (Wadsworth, Belmont, California 1965).

STURMTHAL, A., *Workers' Councils: a study of Workplace Organisation on both sides of the Iron Curtain* (Harvard University Press, Cambridge, Mass. 1964).

TABB, J. Y., and GOLDFARB, A., *Workers' Participation in Management: Expectations and Experience* (Pergamon, Oxford 1969).

TANNENBAUM, A. S., *Control in Organizations* (McGraw-Hill, New York 1968).

TANNENBAUM, A. S., *Social Psychology of the Work Organisation* (Tavistock Publications, London 1966).

TAYLOR, FREDERICK W., *Scientific Management: comprising shop management, the principles of scientific management, testimony before the special House Committee* (Harper, New York 1947).

THOMPSON, E. P. (ed.), *Out of Apathy* (Stevens, London 1960).

TRIST, E. L., HIGGIN, G. W., MURRAY, H., and POLLOCK, A. B., *Organisational Choice: Capabilities of Groups at the Coal Face under Changing Technologies* (Tavistock Publications, London 1963).

VAN GORKUM, P. H., *Industrial Democracy at the Level of the Enterprise* (The European Association of National Productivity Centres, Brussels 1969).

VAN GORKUM, P. H., *et al.*, *Industrial Democracy in the Netherlands* (J. A. Boom en Zoon, Meppel 1969).

VITELES, M. S., *Motivation and Morale in Industry* (W. W. Norton and Co., New York 1953).

VROOM, V. H., *Work and Motivation* (Wiley, New York 1964).

WALLACE, WILLIAM, *Prescription for Partnership* (Pitman, London 1959).

WALPOLE, G. S., *Management and Men* (Jonathan Cape, London 1944).

WALTON, RICHARD E., and McKERSIE, R. B., *A Behavioral Theory of Labor Negotiations: an analysis of a Social Interaction System* (McGraw-Hill, New York 1965).

WEBB, S., *The Restoration of Trade Union Conditions* (Nisbet, London 1917).

WEBB, S. and B., *Industrial Democracy* (Longmans, London 1920).

WEBB, S. and B., *A Constitution for the Socialist Commonwealth of Great Britain* (Longmans, London 1920).

WEBB, S. and B., *History of Trade Unionism* (Longmans, London 1920).

WHITE, R. K., and LIPPITT, R., *Autocracy and Democracy* (Harper and Row, New York 1960).

WILKEN, FOLKERT, *The Liberation of Work* (Routledge and Kegan Paul, London 1969).

WOODWARD, J., *Industrial Organization: Theory and Practice* (Oxford University Press, London 1965).

WOODWARD, J., *Industrial Organization: Behaviour and Control* (Oxford University Press, London 1970).

WOOTTON, G., *Workers, Unions and the State* (Routledge and Kegan Paul, London 1966).

ZWEIG, F., *Productivity and Trade Unions* (Blackwell, Oxford 1951).

SECTION III

Booklets, Pamphlets and Articles

ALEXANDER, R. J., 'Membership in a Printing Union', *Sociological Review*, New Series, Vol. 2 (1954).

ALLEN, A. J., *Management and Men: a Study in Industrial Relations* (Hallam Press, London 1967).

ANDRIĆ, STANISLAVA, and SEVER-ZEBEC, MARIJA, *Bibliography on Workers' Participation in Management in Yugoslavia*, Ekonomski Institute (Zagreb 1969) (and Appendix, 1970).

ASSOCIATION NATIONALE DES DIRECTEURS ET CHEFS DE PERSONNEL, *Personnel*, Numéro Spéciale, La Participation dans l'Entreprise.

BAKKE, E. WIGHT, *The Impact of Human Relations on Production* (The Industrial Co-partnership Association, London 1954).

BARRATT-BROWN, M., *Opening the Books* (Institute of Workers' Control, Pamphlet Series No. 4, Nottingham 1969).

BATSON, R. W., BIRD, W. J., CLARKE, R. O., HARRIS, L. G., TUCK, G. R., and WILLMOTT, P., *How Far is it Possible to Carry Workers Participation in Company Decisions?*—reports of the discussion of six study groups (Co-partnership, London, July 1969).

BLOOD, M. R., and HULIN, C. L., 'Alienation, Environmental Characteristics and Worker Responsibility', *Journal of Applied Psychology*, Vol. 51, 3 (1967).

BLOOD, M. R., and HULIN, C. L., 'Job Enlargement', *Psychological Bulletin*, Vol. 69, 1 (1968).

BOW GROUP, *Cutting the Cake* (London 1968).

BOYD, JOHN M. *Is Industrial Democracy Compatible with Efficiency?* (The Institution of Production Engineers, September 1967).

BRAYFIELD, A. H., and CROCKETT, W. H., 'Employee Attitudes and Employee Performance', *Psychological Bulletin*, Vol. 52, No. 5 (1955).

BRITISH INSTITUTE OF MANAGEMENT, *Industrial Democracy, Some Implications for Management* (B.I.M., London 1968).

BUCKLOW, M., 'A New Role for the Work Group', *Administrative Science Quarterly*, Vol. II, No. 1 (June 1966).

CAREY, A., 'The Hawthorne Studies: a Radical Criticism', *American Sociological Review*, Vol. 32, 3.

CARPENTER, C., *Industrial Co-partnership*, 4th edn. (Labour Co-partnership Association, London 1927).

CLARKE, R. O., 'The Dispute in the British Engineering Industry 1897-8', *Economica* (London, May 1957).

CLEGG, IAN, *Industrial Democracy. Perspectives on Work, Welfare and Society* (Sheed and Ward, London 1968).

COATES, K., and TOPHAM, A., *Participation or Control?* (Bertrand Russell Centre for Social Research, Pamphlet Series No. 1, 1967).

COCH, L., and FRENCH, J. R., 'Overcoming Resistance to Change', *Human Relations*, Vol. 1 (1948).

COLE, LORD, *The Future of the Board* (Industrial Educational and Research Foundation, London 1968).

CONFEDERATION OF BRITISH INDUSTRY, *Communication and Consultation: report of a Working Party* (C.B.I., London 1966).

CONFEDERATION OF BRITISH INDUSTRY, *Productivity Bargaining* (C.B.I., London, May 1968).

DANIEL, W. W., *Beyond the Wage-Work Bargain* (P.E.P., London 1970).

DAW, J. WARD, 'Profit-Sharing and Co-Partnership', *The Director* (London, July-October 1955).

DAW, J. WARD, *Workers' Participation in Industry* (Co-Partnership, London, January 1969).

DERBER, M., 'Worker Participation in Israeli Management', *Industrial Relations*, Vol. 3 No. 1 (1963).

DERBER, M., *Labor Participation in Management*—Proceedings, Seventeenth Annual Meeting, Industrial Relations Research Association (1964).

DERRICK, P., 'Is Co-ownership the Answer?', *New Society*, No. 31 (2 May 1963).

EMERY, F. E., *Characteristics of Socio-Technical Systems* (Tavistock Doc. No. 572, January 1959).

EMERY, F. E., *Democratisation of the Workplace* (*a historical review of studies* (T.I.H.R. Doc. No. T.813, June 1966).

EMERY, F., and MARCK, J., 'Some Socio-technical Aspects of Automation', *Human Relations*, Vol. 15, No. 1 (1962).

ENGINEERING EMPLOYERS' FEDERATION, Annual Reports.

ENGINEERING EMPLOYERS' FEDERATION, *Productivity Bargaining in the Engineering Industry* (E.E.F., London 1968).

FARROW, NIGEL, *The Profit in Worker–Ownership* (Business, London 1965).

FATCHETT, D. J., *The Machinery of Worker Participation* (Personnel, April 1969).

FEDERATED ENGINEERING EMPLOYERS, *Conditions of Management* (London 1898).

FEDERATION OF BRITISH INDUSTRIES, *The Control of Industry. Nationalised and Kindred Problems* (London 1919).

FLANDERS, A., 'The Internal Social Responsibility of Industry'. *British Journal of Industrial Relations*, Vol. IV, No. 1 (March 1966).

FLANDERS, A., *Managerial Power and Industrial Democracy* (Co-Partnership, October 1967).

FLANDERS, A., 'Collective Bargaining: a Theoretical Analysis', *British Journal of Industrial Relations*, Vol. 6, No. 1 (March 1968).

FOGARTY, M. P., 'Co-Determination and Company Structure in Germany', *British Journal of Industrial Relations*, Vol. II, No. 1 (March 1964).

FRENCH, J. E., ISRAEL, J., and AS, D., 'An Experiment in Participation in a Norwegian Factory', *Human Relations*, Vol. 13, No. 1 (1960).

GANGUIN, ELSPETH, 'B.S.C.'s worker directors take stock of their first year', *Financial Times* (25 June 1969).

GEDDES, REAY, *Industry and Worker Participation* (Industrial Education and Research Foundation, London 1969).

GILMAN, N. P., *Profit Sharing between Employer and Employee* (Houghton Mifflin, Cambridge, Mass., 1889).

GIVRY, J. DE, 'Developments in Labour–Management Relations', *International Labour Review* (January 1969).

GLOBERSON, ARYE, 'Spheres and Levels of Employee Participation in Organizations', *British Journal of Industrial Relations*, Vol. VIII, No. 2 (July 1970).

HENDERSON, JOAN, 'Some Examples of Effective Consultative Committees', *Industrial Society* (London 1970).

HENDERSON, JOAN, 'A Practical Guide to Joint Consultation', *Industrial Society* (London 1970).

HENDERSON, JOAN, 'The Case for Joint Consultation', *Industrial Society* (London 1970).

HESPE, G., *et al.*, *An Investigation into Communication and Participation in the Bar and Rod Mill*, unpublished report (Sheffield 1969).

HOLTER, H., 'Attitudes towards Employee Participation in Company Decision-making Processes, *Human Relations*, Vol. 18, No. 4 (1965).

INDUSTRIAL EDUCATIONAL AND RESEARCH FOUNDATION, *Worker Representation on Company Boards*, Discussion Paper No. 2 (London 1968).

INDUSTRIAL RELATIONS, 'A Symposium: Workers' Participation in Management: an International Comparison', Vol. 9, No. 2 (February 1970).

INDUSTRIAL RELATIONS COUNSELORS INC., *Group Wage Incentives: Experience with the Scanlon Plan* (I.R.C., New York 1962).

INDUSTRIAL WELFARE SOCIETY, *Suggestion Schemes—Extracts from Firms' Schemes* (London 1954).

INDUSTRIAL WELFARE SOCIETY, *Successful Suggestion Schemes* (London 1958).

INSTITUTE OF PERSONNEL MANAGEMENT, Conference Report, *Institute of Personnel Management Digest* (31 November 1967).

INSTITUTE OF WORKERS' CONTROL, *Bulletin*, Vol. 1, No. 1 (Nottingham 1968), Vol. 1, No. 2 (1969).

INTERNATIONAL CONFEDERATION OF FREE TRADE UNIONS, European Regional Organisation, 'Joint Consultation and Co-determination of the Works Councils in Western Europe'. *Report of Springe Seminar*, I.C.F.T.U. (Brussels 1967).

JAQUES, E., *Employee Participation and Managerial Authority* (London 1968).

JENKINS, D., 'Industrial Democracy', *Sweden Now* (January/February 1970).

JONES, J., *Trades Unionism in the Seventies* (T.G.W.U. 1969).

JONES, LLEWELLYN G., 'Guidelines in Productivity Bargaining', reprinted by *Personnel* (Business Publications, 1967).

JOHNSON, D. HUNTER, *Worker Representation on Company Boards* (Industrial Education and Research Foundation, 1968).

JOHNSTON, T. L., *Industrial Democracy Revisited*—Lecture to the Institution of Engineers and Shipbuilders in Scotland (October 1968).

KARSH, BERNARD, 'Human Relations versus Management' (in H. S. Becker, B. Geer, D. Riesman and R. W. Weiss (eds.)), *Institutions and the Person*, Aldine (Chicago 1968).

KERR, CLARK, 'What became of the Independent Spirit', *Fortune* (June 1953).

KURILOFF, A. M., 'An Experiment in Management—Putting Theory Y to the Test, *Personnel*, Vol. 40 (1963).

LABOUR PARTY, *Annual Conference Report*, 1935.

LABOUR PARTY, *Port Transport Industry*—Report of Study Group (Labour Party, London 1966).

LABOUR PARTY, *Industrial Democracy*—Report of Working Party (Labour Party, London 1967).

LABOUR PARTY, *Industrial Democracy*—A Statement by the National Executive Committee (Labour Party, London 1968).

LADREYT, J., 'De Gaulle's New Pancapitalism', *Personnel*, March 1968.

LAMMERS, C. J., 'Power and Participation in Decision-making in Formal Organisations', *American Journal of Sociology*, Vol. 73, No. 2 (September 1967).

LEONARD, JAMES, *Co-Operative Co-Partnership Productive Societies* (Co-Operative Productive Federation Ltd, Leicester 1965).

LEVINE, E. L., and WEITZ, J., 'Job Satisfaction Among Graduate Students', *Journal of Applied Psychology*, Vol. 52 (4 August 1968).

LIBERAL PARTY, *Industrial Affairs*—a Report of the Industrial Affairs Committee (Liberal Party 1962).

LIBERAL PARTY, *Partners at Work*—the Report of the Industrial Partnership Committee (Liberal Party, London 1968).

MANAGEMENT INTERNATIONAL REVIEW (Issue devoted to Industrial Democracy), Vol. 9, 2–3 (Wiesbaden 1969).

MARSH, A. I., *Managers and Shop Stewards* (Institute of Personnel Management, London 1963).

MARSH, A. I., and COKER, E. E., 'Shop Steward Organisation in the Engineering Industry', *British Journal of Industrial Relations* (June 1963).

MATHEWSON, S. B., *Restriction of Output among Unorganised Workers* (South Illinois Press, Carbondale and Edwardsville 1969).

MCKERSIE, R. B., 'Wage Payments Methods of the Future', *British Journal of Industrial Relations* (June 1963).

MCKITTERICK, T. E. M., and ROBERTS, R. D. V., *Workers and Management: the German Co-determination Experiment* (Fabian Publications, London 1953).

METZGER, B. L., *Profit Sharing in Perspective* (Profit Sharing Research Foundation, Evanston, Illinois, 1964).

MIDLANDS SHOP STEWARDS' STUDY GROUP, *Trade Unions at the Crossroads* (1966).

MILES, RAYMOND E., 'The Affluent Organisation', *Harvard Business Review* (May–June 1966).

MILES, RAYMOND E., 'Human Relations or Human Resources?', *Harvard Business Review* (July–August 1965).

MORSE, N., and REIMER, E., 'Experimental Change of a Major Organisational Variable', *Journal of Abnormal and Social Psychology*, Vol. 52 (1956).

NATIONAL INDUSTRIAL CONFERENCE BOARD, *Problems of Labor and Industry in Great Britain, France and Italy* (N.I.C.B., Boston, Mass., 1919).

PARSONS, TALCOTT, 'Suggestions for a Sociological Approach to the Theory of Organisations', *Administrative Science Quarterly* (1965).

PAUL, W. J., ROBERTSON, K., and HERZBERG, F., 'Job Enrichment Pays Off', *Harvard Business Review* (March/April 1969).

PELZ, D. E., 'Leadership within a hierarchical organisation', *Journal of Social Issues*, Vol. 7.

PERCY, EUSTACE, *The Unknown State* (London 1944).

PETERSON, R. B., *The Swedish Labor Court Views Management Rights* (S.A.F., Stockholm 1968).

PETERSON, R. B., 'The Swedish Experience with Industrial Democracy', *British Journal of Industrial Relations*, Vol. VI, No. 2 (July 1968).

PHILIPS, N. V., *Work Structuring. A summary of experiments at Philips —1963 to 1968* (Philips Gloeilampenfabrieken, Eindhoven, Holland 1969).

POLITICAL AND ECONOMIC PLANNING, 'A Companies Act 1970?', *Planning*, No. 500 (October 1967).

POTTHOFF, E., *et al.*, *Zwischenbilanz der Mitbestimmung* (J. E. B. Mohr (Paul Siebeck), Tübingen 1962).

POWER, DAVID, *On the Responsibilities of Employers* (London 1849).

PUGH, D. S., *et al.*, 'A Conceptual Scheme for Organisational Analysis', *Administrative Science Quarterly*, Vol. 8, No. 3 (December 1963).

RADICE, GILES, 'Workers Directors lose touch with the men', *Financial Times* (24 January 1969).

REFORM COMMITTEE OF THE SOUTH WALES MINERS, *The Miners' Next Step* (1912).

ROBERTS, G., *Demarcation Rules in Shipbuilding and Ship Repairing* (Cambridge University Press, Occasional Papers 14, 1967).

ROBERTS, R. D. V., and SALLIS, H., 'Joint Consultation in the Electricity Supply Industry, 1949–59', *Public Administration*, Vol. 37 (Summer 1959).

ROBERTSON, K., 'Managing People and Jobs', *Personnel Management* (September 1969).

ROSS, N., *The Democratic Firm*, Fabian Tract 242 (Fabian Society, London 1964).

ROSS, N., 'Workers' Participation and Control', *Scientific Business*, Vol. II, No. 8 (February 1965).

SADLER, P. J., *Leadership Style, Confidence in Management and Job Satisfaction* (Ashridge Management College, 1966).

SALLIS, H., 'Joint Consultation and Meetings of Primary Working Groups in Power Stations', *British Journal of Industrial Relations*, Vol. III, No. 3 (November 1965).

SCANLON, H., *The Way Forward for Workers' Control* (Institute for Workers' Control, Pamphlet Series No. 1, Nottingham 1968).

SHEPARD, J. M., 'Functional Specialization, Alienation, and Job Satisfaction', *Industrial and Labor Relations Review*, Vol. 23, No. 2 (January 1970).

SINGLETON, F., and TOPHAM, A., *Workers' Control in Yugoslavia*, Fabian Tract 233 (Fabian Society, London 1963).

SOUTHGATE, J., *The Dependence of the Herzberg Theory of Job Satisfaction upon the Social Context in which it is Tested* (North Western Polytechnic, Research Paper No. 1, London 1969).

STRAUSS, G., 'Human Relations—1968 Style', *Industrial Relations*, Vol. 7, No. 3 (May 1968).

STRAUSS, G., and ROSENSTEIN, E., 'Workers' Participation: A Critical View', *Industrial Relations*, Vol. 9, No. 2 (February 1970).

STRAUSS, G., and SAYLES, L. R., 'The Scanlon Plan: Some Organisational Problems', *Human Relations*, Vol. 16, No. 3 (August 1963).

STURMTHAL, A., *Industrial Democracy in the Affluent Society*, Proceedings of the 17th Annual Meeting, Industrial Relations Research Association (1964).

SYKES, A. J. M., 'Economic Interest and the Hawthorne Researches', *Human Relations*, Vol. 18, 3 (August 1965).

TANNENBAUM, R., and MASSARIK, F., 'Participation by Subordinates in the Managerial Decision-Making Process', *Canadian Journal of Economics and Political Science* (1950).

THOMASON, GEORGE P., *Experiments in Participation*, Institute of Personnel Management (London 1971).

THORNELY, D. H., and VALENTINE, G. A., 'Job Enlargement, Some Implications of Longer Cycle Jobs on Fan Heater Production', *Philips Magazine* (1969).

THORSRUD, E., *Industrial Democracy—Involvement, Commitment, Action, Some Observations during Field Research* (Tavistock Institute of Human Relations, Doc. T.886, October 1966).

THORSRUD, E., 'Socio-technical Approach to Job Design and Organisational Development', *Management International Review*, Vol. 8 (1968).

THORSRUD, E., and EMERY, F., *Industrial Conflict and 'Industrial Democracy'* (Tavistock Institute of Human Relations, Doc. T.358, July 1964).

TOPHAM, A. (ed.), *Workers' Control*—Report of 5th National Conference held at Coventry, June 10, 11, 1967 (Centre for Socialist Education, Hull 1967).

TOPHAM, A., *Productivity Bargaining and Workers' Control* (Institute of Workers' Control, Nottingham 1968).

TRADES UNION CONGRESS, *Interim Report on Post-war Reconstruction* (Trades Union Congress, London 1944).

TRADES UNION CONGRESS, *Trade Unionism* (London 1966).

TRIST, E. L., and BAMFORTH, K. W., 'Some Social and Psychological Consequences of The Longwall Method of Coal-getting', *Human Relations*, Vol. IV, No. 1 (1951).

UNIAPAC, *Participation—La Théorie, La Pratique*, (Brussels 1968).

WALKER, K., *Industrial Democracy: fantasy, fiction or fact?* (*The Times* Management Lecture, 1970).

WALTON, J. S., 'Where Justice is seen to be Done', *Industrial Society* (London, February 1966).

WEBB, S., and B., 'Co-operative Production and Profit Sharing', *New Statesman* (Special Supplements, 1914–15).

WEDDERBURN, K. W., *Company Law Reform*, Fabian Tract 363 (Fabian Society, London 1965).

WEINSHALL, T. D., *Conceptual Schemes of Organisational Behaviour and their Possible Applications*, a paper presented at Ashridge College (September 1968).

WHITE, EIRENE, *Workers' Control?* Fabian Tract 271 (Fabian Society, London 1951).

WINSTONE, H. E., *New Light on Social Problems* (Catholic Truth Society, London 1963).

Index